R and **SOUTHWARK**, with the Additional Buildings to the Year 1777.

The British-Americans

The British-Americans

The Loyalist Exiles in England 1774-1789

Mary Beth Norton

With Illustrations

LITTLE, BROWN AND COMPANY   •   BOSTON   •   TORONTO

FIRST EDITION

T 10/72

THE ENDPAPERS ARE REPRODUCED THROUGH THE COURTESY OF THE
GEOGRAPHY AND MAP DIVISION OF THE LIBRARY OF CONGRESS.

Library of Congress Cataloging in Publication Data

Norton, Mary Beth.
    The British-Americans; the Loyalist exiles in
England, 1774-1789.

    Bibliography: p.
    1. American loyalists--England. I. Title.
E277.N66   973.3'14   72-401
ISBN 0-316-61250-2

Published simultaneously in Canada
by Little, Brown & Company (Canada) Limited

PRINTED IN THE UNITED STATES OF AMERICA

For my Mother and Father

Having devoted his whole Life, to the Age of near Thirty, in preparing himself for future usefulness, Ten useless Years have [closed] the Account: And he now finds himself near his Fortieth year, banished under pain of death, to a distant Country, where he has not the most remote family connection, nor scarcely an Acquaintance, who is not in the same Circumstances — cut off from his profession — from every hope of importance in Life, and in a great Degree from Social enjoyments. And where, unknowing and unknown, he finds, that after having expended the little, he hopes to receive, as above related, that he shall be unable, while he may be said only to wait for death, to procure common Comforts and Conveniences, in a Station much inferior to that of a Menial Servant, without the assistance of Government.

— THOMAS DANFORTH, *memorial to loyalist claims commission, September 8, 1783*

Acknowledgments

In the course of writing this book, I received valuable assistance from a number of persons. My special thanks go to Michael Kammen, Pauline Maier, and the other historians who read all or part of the work at various stages of its development and who offered many helpful suggestions. John Reps, Robert C. Ritchie, and Maris Vinovskis provided essential aid in their respective areas of expertise. Successive drafts of the manuscript were diligently and accurately typed by Karen DiNicola, Leslie Benedict, and Roberta Ludgate. Funds or services supplied by Harvard University, The University of Connecticut Research Foundation, and the Meigs Fund of Cornell University supported in large part the research and writing of this book.

I gratefully acknowledge the kindness and courtesy of the many libraries and archives that extended to me permission to use and quote from their holdings. The reference staffs of these institutions were invariably helpful, but in particular I want to thank Winifred Collins of the Massachusetts Historical Society, Carolyn Sung of the Library of Congress Manuscript Division, William Ewing, formerly of the William L. Clements Library, and the staff of the Long Room in the Public Record Office, London. It should be noted that the William Vassall Letterbook and the Samuel Peters Papers, both of which were consulted on microfilm, are quoted herein with the permission of the owners of the original documents: for the Vassall Letterbook, the City Librarian of the

Sheffield City Libraries, and for the Peters Papers, the Church Historical Society, Austin, Texas.

Finally, I must express my gratitude to Bernard Bailyn, who first suggested to me that a study of the loyalist exiles might prove fruitful, and who thereby acquired the burdensome task of supervising this work as a doctoral dissertation. I owe more than I can say to his unfailingly apt and helpful advice.

M.B.N.

Contents

Illustrations

The British-Americans

Prologue

The American Revolution, seen from the perspective of two hundred years, is an accomplished fact. As everyone knows, independence was won and the republic successfully established. It is difficult, therefore, to recapture the uncertainty of the revolutionary years and to comprehend the process by which well-meaning Americans came to disagree over the question of whether or not to seek independence. Yet that is what must be done before the loyalists or their reasons for seeking shelter in England can be fully understood.

It is customary to begin a discussion of the conflict between loyalists and revolutionaries in 1765, for the Stamp Act crisis serves as a convenient and well-documented line dividing the internally tranquil empire of the early eighteenth century from the imperial turmoil of the 1770's.[1] But such a schema vastly oversimplifies the complex political circumstances of the prerevolutionary period. To the colonists of 1765, independence was not at issue, nor, for that matter, were there many Americans who did not favor some sort of imperial reform. The Stamp Act aroused nearly universal opposition in the colonies — as Jonathan Mayhew said, "Almost every British American . . . considered it as an infraction of their rights, or their dearly purchased privileges"[2] — and they quarreled with each other not so much over *whether* to protest the act as over *how* to protest it. The chief questions in contention were the grounds upon which to base their opposition, the methods they should use to express their displeasure with British policy, and the extent to which they should rely upon extralegal means to make their point. Few colonists ever positively favored the act, though some did argue that it had to be obeyed in spite of its unpopularity. The consensus supporting reform was practically unanimous.

When they were later faced with other revenue acts, most of the colonists continued to function intellectually within the same restricted context. They argued over means, not ends, and they did so within a purely imperial framework.[3] They demanded greater autonomy within the empire while simultaneously recognizing the benefits, even the necessity, of retaining a connection with Great Britain. But by the latter part of the 1760's a major shift in attitudes was occurring among more radical Americans. As recently outlined by Pauline Maier, this change encompassed both the radicals' nascent perception of a ministerial plot aimed at destroying American liberties and their increasing disillusionment with the king himself. Always before they had been willing to concede that the ministers and Parliament had been acting in good faith, though mistakenly; always before they had absolved the king from any participation in his servants' errors. But between 1768 and 1772 — having before them what they thought were numerous examples of ministerial and royal perfidy — the radical colonists discarded their assumptions as to the government's benevolent intentions, replacing them with the contrary assumption that the British authorities were deliberately attempting to enslave the colonies.[4]

Because the radicals' premises had changed, the disruption of Anglo-American relations after the Boston Tea Party in December 1773 proved to be decisive. Instead of continuing the dispute within traditional lines, the radical party, which now included many of the most influential American political leaders, turned to new methods of opposition and protest. And as the novelty of the radicals' approach became progressively more apparent to conservatives and moderates, they began to dissociate themselves from their former allies.

The new direction of the protest movement was publicly revealed for the first time at the First Continental Congress. Although some colonists opposed the very calling of the Congress, most Americans supported the idea in hopes that such an assembly would be the means through which an acceptable settlement with the ministry could be reached. But the Congress, instead of following the moderate course that had been anticipated, took two actions that some colonists believed would widen, rather than conciliate, the differences with Great Britain. The first was its approval of the Suffolk Resolves, an inflammatory statement of American rights drafted by one of Samuel Adams' associates. The second was its acceptance of the Continental Association, a comprehensive nonimportation, nonexportation, and nonconsumption agreement that was to be enforced by local committees established for the purpose. To some Americans, it seemed that congressional actions tended towards "a total independency," because the committees would constitute local governments bearing no relationship to regular imperial structures. If the colonists wanted to protest British policy, these men contended, they should accomplish that end through the mechanism of their properly elected state assemblies. The critics of Congress were therefore not so much opposed to reform *per se* as they were to the means by which reform was being pursued. And their chief objection to the method of protest adopted by the Congress was their belief that it would eventually lead the colonies down the path to independence.[5]

It is important to note that not every future loyalist perceived the issue in this way at this point in time. Indeed, some Americans who would remain faithful to the crown continued to participate in the coalition protesting parliamentary measures even after the armed clashes at Lexington and Concord. As long as American leaders publicly sought no more than reform within the empire, which had been the goal since 1765, colonists who would oppose independence had no difficulty in maintaining their membership in the so-called "revolutionary" movement. On the other hand, once it appeared that the radicals had decided that the connection with Great Britain should be abandoned, the loyalists broke with their fellow countrymen. Many colonists who had vigorously supported the attempts to win imperial reform, who had actively defended the Americans' claim to the rights of Englishmen, were horrified by the idea of independence. Consequently, when they recognized the implications of the course upon which the radicals had embarked, they pulled back, recoiling from the step that seemed so logical to many of their compatriots. The moment of realization did not come simultaneously to all loyalists: some made their decision in 1774, a larger number in 1775, a few not until mid-1776.

The complexities of this dynamic process have often been overlooked by historians of the Revolution. There is no one point — at least not prior to July 4, 1776 — at which the two sides can be completely and irrevocably identified. Before 1774 the political and ideological lines were not at all clearly drawn, as is suggested by the fact that Daniel Dulany, the most widely read pro-American pamphleteer of 1765, was at best a neutral during the war itself; that John Dickinson, the famed author of *Letters from a Pennsylvania Farmer* in 1767–1768, refused to sign the Declaration of Independence;

and that William Smith, a political ally of the radicals in New York in the 1760's, finally chose to side with Britain in 1778 after years of indecision. In short, post-1774 affiliations and opinions cannot be projected backwards upon the pre-revolutionary period. There could be no loyalists until there were rebels, and there were no rebels until after 1773. There could be, and was, conservative criticism directed at the activities of the dominant protest coalition, but that was not loyalism. Not until independence was perceived as the chief point of contention could anything resembling a "loyalist party" emerge.

Moreover, throughout the prerevolutionary years, the radicals retained the initiative. They organized and acted, other Americans merely reacted. It is relatively easy, therefore, to delineate the membership of the revolutionary movement. It is far harder to determine the identity of its opponents. The colonists who can today be identified as loyalists are to a large extent self-selected: they fled to Great Britain or Canada, joined a loyalist regiment, or were singled out by committees or provincial legislatures as enemies to the American cause. As a result any study of "the loyalists" — or, in this case, "the refugees" — is unavoidably limited in its scope to the most extreme representatives of loyalism. There must have been thousands of other Americans who retained their fidelity to the crown but who were neither willing nor able to abandon their homes, speak out against their rebel neighbors, or take up arms to defend their point of view.

This observation suggests another point. Americans did not "become" loyal to the empire: they *remained* loyal to the empire. In 1765, every colonist — including Patrick Henry, Samuel Adams, and Thomas Jefferson — proclaimed his loyalty to Great Britain. Many Americans became revolutionaries in the years that followed, and that was the significant change. It is entirely conceivable that some loyalists adhered to their original allegiance through what might be termed political inertia. The burden of making a break with the past rested with the revolutionaries, not the loyalists — despite radical rhetoric to the contrary.

Because of this pattern of decision-making, there is no reason for historians today to regard some Americans' retention of fidelity to the empire as in any way abnormal. Loyalty was the norm: rebellion was not. But the success of the Revolution has caused historians to reverse the priorities. Instead of asking, What motivated the rebels? we ask, [What motivated the loyalists? And that question is exceptionally difficult to answer, because loyalism can be defined only in a negative sense, only through its relationship to the movement it opposed. Furthermore, a number of the "loyalists" seem to have assumed that guise for reasons unrelated to ideology or independence. They opportunistically chose what they thought would be the winning side, simply continued to oppose old enemies who had become rebels, or acted almost solely out of economic or political self-interest.[6] This is why loyalists were such a diverse group, and why it is practically impossible to delineate any characteristics common to them all, except their adherence to Great Britain.]

By focusing upon the refugees who fled to England during the Revolutionary War, this study attempts to illuminate both the loyalist experience and the Revolution as a whole. Many of the Americans who chose to go to the British Isles had been leaders in the prewar colonies: the exiles included most of the government officials, professional men, wealthy merchants, and large landowners who remained faithful to the crown. And a large number of ordinary loyalists — farmers, artisans, urban laborers, and the like — traveled to Great Britain as well. Consequently, the approximately 7,000

American exiles in England serve as a convenient (if by no means statistically reliable) sample of the total group of perhaps 60,000 to 80,000 loyalists who left the colonies during and after the war. The refugees' frustrating encounters with British bureaucracy, their attempts to re-create America in exile, their opinions on the war constitute a valuable counterpoint to the traditional "patriot" view of the Revolution. An examination of their fate can therefore add significantly to our understanding of the events of the revolutionary era.

I

A Certain Place of Safety

As the Rebellion is general thro' the provinces, the
friends of Governmt have no certain place to fly
to for safety but to Eng.
— HENRY CANER, 1775[1]

THE year 1774 dawned sixteen days after the Boston Tea
Party, and by the time its twelve months ended, the
royal provincial governments were in disarray, the First Continental Congress had convened and adjourned, and the
battles at Lexington and Concord were just three and a half
months in the future. That one year brought the effective
collapse of British authority in America, and it consequently
posed a question that many colonists had previously managed
to avoid or obscure: If it came to a choice, did their primary
allegiance lie with Great Britain, or did it lie instead with the
provinces in which they lived?

This crucial issue did not arise simultaneously throughout
the continent. New Englanders faced it first, because of their
adamant opposition to the laws they called "intolerable," but
it was not until after the outbreak of actual fighting that
other Americans were forced to make an essentially irreversible decision. Whenever the time came, though, the colonists
who chose to side with the crown almost always found themselves in a distinct minority. Outnumbered and unorganized,

the men who remained loyal to the empire were never able to combat effectively the mobs, revolutionary committees, and legislative pronouncements used to silence them. Their only recourse, it seemed, was flight.

[*1*]

On June 1, 1774, Governor Thomas Hutchinson of Massachusetts left his native province for what was to be the last time. Hutchinson, an intelligent and perceptive man, had over the course of his career constructed a network of patronage and influence unrivaled in any other province. He himself served Massachusetts as chief justice, lieutenant governor, and governor, and each time he moved on to a higher post he was replaced by a member of the Oliver family, to which he was related by marriage. No American had been more successful than he in acquiring and retaining political power. Yet Hutchinson had been unable to cope with the problems that arose during his tenure as governor. With the arrival of his successor, General Thomas Gage, he was finally free to sail for the British Isles in the hope of achieving in London what he had failed to accomplish in Massachusetts. Above all, Hutchinson wanted to ensure the preservation of British rule in America. As he left his homeland, accompanied by his daughter and two of his three sons, he was both pleased to escape what he described as "five years constant scene of anxiety" and looking forward to a fruitful visit to the mother country.[2]

The sequence of events that caused Hutchinson's voluntary departure had started, innocently enough, with an act of Parliament giving the East India Company a preferential position in the American tea trade. The law was aimed more at bolstering the company's ailing finances than at affecting colonial commerce, but some Americans interpreted the measure as a British plot to renew a pattern of oppression that had begun with the Stamp Act in 1765. On December 16, 1773, a group of "Indians" publicly protested the new law by dumping more than three hundred chests of the company's tea into Boston harbor.

Britain's response to the vandalism was immediate and enraged. Determined to impose its will on the unruly residents of Massachusetts, Parliament approved the four laws that became known in America as the Intolerable Acts, and neither the legislators nor British officials stationed in America anticipated much resistance to the new program. As Gage later observed, "Nobody here or at home could have conceived, that the Acts made for the Massachusett's Bay, could have created such a Ferment through the Continent, and united the whole in one common Cause."[3]

The four laws that so unexpectedly proved to be the catalyst that ignited the fires of rebellion in the colonies were intended to demonstrate to New Englanders that they could no longer thwart the will of Parliament. The acts took a fragmentary and disjointed approach to the perplexities of governing Massachusetts, one that ranged from the imposition of short-term punishment on Boston to the adoption of some fundamental alterations in the provincial charter. Taken together, the laws succeeded only in creating new difficulties. By punishing loyal and rebellious subjects alike, by denying Gage sufficient discretionary authority, Parliament managed to antagonize a large segment of the population while at the same time it tied the hands of the royal governor. Predictably, the result was chaotic.[4]

The Boston Port Act, which closed the port of Boston until the company had been reimbursed for its tea, was both the first of the four laws to be passed and the first to be proclaimed in America. Its contents presented the citizens of

Boston with a clear-cut choice: either they could loyally acquiesce in a punishment many of them believed was unwarranted, or they could openly resist Parliament's attempt to subdue them. For its part, the town meeting defiantly refused to accede to the conditions Parliament had laid down for the reopening of the port. On the other hand, 124 prominent Bostonians chose a more moderate course. Formally addressing the departing Governor Hutchinson, they assured him that they were willing to pay their share of the cost of the tea, even though they thought the law too harsh. One of their number, the wealthy merchant and distiller Richard Lechmere, explained that despite being "no inconsiderable sufferer" under the act, he would "willingly" submit to it in the expectation that "by suffering" the people would be "brought to their senses."[5]

But Lechmere's hopes, and presumably those of the other Addressors as well, were futile. Rather than convincing their fellow countrymen that the Port Act should be obeyed, the signers of the Address merely set themselves up as targets for radical opprobrium. Ever since 1765 supporters of unpopular British measures had been regarded as "detestable Villains," as "apostate sons of venality . . . wretched hirelings and execrable parricides," and the Addressors were no exception. Vehemently attacked in the newspapers, threatened with political and economic retaliation unless they withdrew their signatures from the petition, many of them were frightened into "Timidity and Backwardness," to use Governor Gage's words.[6]

The colonists' resentment increased when another of the laws, the Massachusetts Government Act, went into effect in August. Its major provisions — a limitation on town meetings and the substitution of an appointed council for the elected one — had long been touted in England as a panacea for the province's reputed governmental ills. But in America the act was taken as a confirmation of Britain's intention to enslave the colonies, because the elected council had for years played a major role in Massachusetts' resistance to Parliament. It now seemed clear to many that the ministry had determined to disregard, even to destroy, those rights of Englishmen that were the colonists' only defense against tyranny.[7]

In the emotional atmosphere engendered by the act, those who dared to suggest that it should be obeyed were condemned as unregenerate villains. And in the forefront of this hapless group were the men who had been unfortunate enough to be appointed to the new mandamus council. In the radicals' eyes, it was bad enough that Parliament was transgressing colonial rights, but it was far worse that the instruments of this heinous deed were to be American collaborators who had been suborned by British gold. Given the circumstances, the newly designated councilors wisely viewed their appointments with more caution than enthusiasm. Several of their number, well aware of the possible consequences of accepting the proffered positions, declined from the outset to serve on the council. Mobs quickly persuaded the few waverers to refuse the posts, and some of the men who initially agreed to take seats on the council were also frightened into recanting.[8]

One typical incident involved Councilor Thomas Oliver, who was lieutenant governor of the colony. On September 2, Oliver's home in Cambridge was surrounded by an angry mob. Although the crowd swore "they would have my blood," Oliver later recounted, he at first "absolutely refused" to resign. But then he considered the "distresses" of his wife and family, and "Nature, ingenious in forming new reasons, suggested to my mind the calamities which would

ensue if I did not comply." Hurriedly he signed the resigna-
tion the mob's leaders thrust at him.[9]

The details varied, but the pattern was everywhere the
same. Throughout the province, men whose names had been
proposed for the mandamus council became the objects of
mob violence. The merest hint that a man was considering
serving on the council was sufficient to attract mobs to his
house or place of business, or to cause crowds to attack him
on the open road. Consequently, many of the councilors
thought it best to flee to Boston, where they could be protected
by royal troops.[10] Before long they were joined in the city by
other fugitives from the countryside, as the campaign of
intimidation was widened to include any man who advocated
obedience to the Intolerable Acts. Just ten days after the
attack on Oliver, Gage informed Lord Dartmouth, the
American secretary, that "People are daily resorting to this
Town for Protection, for there is no Security to any Person
deemed a Friend to Government in any Part of the Country."[11]

The frightened Massachusetts citizens who sought shelter in
Boston in August and September 1774 may properly be
termed the first loyalist refugees of the Revolution. The residents of their province had been the first to confront the
crucial question of where their primary allegiance lay, and
they were the first to suffer the consequences of having supplied the "wrong" answer in the context of the times. Their
response to the Intolerable Acts had been one of grudging
compliance rather than complete acquiescence, but they had
been branded as enemies to America because they had admitted the supremacy of Parliament. Most of them would
never see their homes again.

Like the royal government they supported, they had been
completely unprepared for the sudden explosion of violence

that greeted the Intolerable Acts. As individuals, they could not have hoped to oppose the ubiquitous mobs, and as a group they proved to be too few and too scattered to offer any significant resistance. Isolated and helpless, they watched, frustrated, as their world crumbled around them. From the time they left their homes, they were the prisoners, not the movers, of events. Their fate was to rest not in their own hands, but was rather to be subject to the joint control of the radical colonists they detested and the faraway British ministers who would not listen to them.

[2]

Outside of Massachusetts, the colonists had not yet been forced to choose between their allegiance to the empire and their ties to their particular provinces. The Intolerable Acts, with one exception, applied only to Massachusetts, and in the absence of an immediate threat to their well-being, most Americans remained relatively calm. Thus the other colonies exhibited little of the internecine strife that filled the New England autumn. Instead, in the middle and southern provinces it was still possible to debate openly the issues that had already been decided in the North.[12]

One result of this less highly charged atmosphere was an emboldened public opposition to the radicals. With the notable exception of Daniel Leonard, the young and gifted attorney who wrote his "Massachusettensis" letters in the security of Boston after he had abandoned his Taunton home, the major conservative authors of the period lived outside of New England. In general they were either government officials (like William Allen, chief justice of Pennsylvania) or Anglican clergymen (like Myles Cooper of New York). Both groups readily perceived the threat to the *status quo* posed by the actions of the First Continental Congress, and they exerted themselves to defend the state and the established church from the radicals' attacks.

In New York, the leading conservative writers were the Reverends Samuel Seabury and Thomas Bradbury Chandler, who, along with their fellow Anglican cleric Charles Inglis, deliberately combined to supply "the speediest answers" to such radical publications "as appeared to have a bad tendency."[13] Both Seabury and Chandler were native Americans, graduates of Yale, and missionaries of the Society for the Propagation of the Gospel in Foreign Parts. Chandler, ever the optimist, was an indefatigable worker who bore with fortitude the burden of a painful facial cancer that eventually caused his death in 1790. Seabury, who was to become the first bishop of Connecticut, was both a less penetrating thinker and a more conscious propagandist. He, like Chandler, wrote three pamphlets during the crucial 1774–1775 period.

A less prolific but no less important contributor to conservative literature in the same years was Joseph Galloway, a Pennsylvanian and former political associate of Benjamin Franklin. Galloway, a delegate to the First Continental Congress, presented to that body a conciliation plan that was at first only narrowly defeated but was later expunged from the record. Disheartened by the rejection of his scheme, Galloway published both it and a supportive rationale in 1775, and for years thereafter he submitted and resubmitted modifications of the same plan to the ministry in London. But Galloway was too rigidly legalistic, too concerned with ideological consistency, ever to propose a workable solution to the imperial problems that obsessed him.

The pamphleteers' goal was simply stated: they wanted "to awaken the thoughtless to a sense of their danger" and "to try to reclaim them from their folly, and save them from destruc-

The Reverend Samuel Seabury, from a painting by Thomas Duché

The Reverend Thomas Bradbury Chandler

tion, before it be too late." Each represented himself as having "no interest to serve but what is common to my countrymen," and each was convinced that *"all reasonable Americans"* would "see the necessity of giving up the present system of American politics, as essentially wrong and destructive; and of entering unanimously upon moderate and conciliating measures" once they had been "brought to make use of their own understanding and examine into, and judge for themselves upon, the real grounds of their fears."[14]

Accordingly, the conservative authors set out to persuade their fellow countrymen of three points: that they had no irremediable grievances against Great Britain; that the tyranny of Congress was far worse than that of Parliament; and that nothing could be gained by seeking independence.

Chandler in particular emphasized the first argument. Most of the current difficulty, he declared, had resulted from "misinformation and false alarms." If the tea tax was a grievance, then it was no more than "the weight of an atom on the shoulders of a giant." Boston had deserved its punishment, for its citizens had committed "an act of the highest insolence towards government." Moreover, the residents of the other colonies were "under no obligations to abet the destructive violence of the people in *Boston;* or to endeavour to skreen it from public justice." Far from it: instead of sharing New England's guilt the other provinces "should endeavour to reclaim them, by affectionate admonitions, and especially by a *good example.*" Seabury, by contrast, put his stress on the disadvantages of congressional rule. He attacked the Continental Association at length, arguing that it would not achieve the desired ends and that its sole purpose was to line the merchants' pockets. Even worse, he declared, was the *"oppressive tyranny"* Americans were enduring, "a *tyranny,* not only over the *actions,* but over the *words, thoughts,* and *wills*" of all of them. It was a *"really deplorable"* situation that could be corrected only if his fellow colonists would be willing to stand up to the committeemen and tell them "you are Englishmen, and will maintain your rights and privileges . . . without asking leave of any illegal, tyrannical Congress or Committee on earth."[15]

The pamphleteers became most impassioned when they considered the possible consequences of rebellion. Regardless of whether a revolt was successful or unsuccessful, Chandler predicted, it would "necessarily terminate in ruin and destruction" for the colonies. Could anyone, asked Leonard, be "so deluded" as to think that Great Britain, "who so lately carried her arms with success to every part of the globe," would fail to conquer the weak and disunited American provinces? On the contrary, it was apparent that, "with the British navy in the front, Canadians and savages in the rear, a regular army in the midst," the American landscape would be devastated, "our houses be burnt to ashes, our fair possessions laid waste."[16]

Other writers, taking up the same pessimistic theme, warned that even if independence was unexpectedly won, "we shall inevitably fall under the dominion of some foreign tyrant, or the more intolerable despotism of a few American demagogues." The colonies would become "a theatre of inconceivable misery and horrour," filled with "anarchy and confusion." Galloway painted an especially vivid picture of the dreadful consequences: "Companies of armed, but undisciplined men, headed by men unprincipled, travelling over your estates, entering your houses — your castles — and sacred repositories of safety for all you hold dear and valuable — seizing your property, and carrying havock and devastation wherever they head — ravishing your wives and daughters, and afterwards plunging the dagger into their tender bosoms, while you are obliged to stand the speechless, the helpless spectators."[17]

But despite this perception of an impending cataclysm, the pamphleteers failed to transmit a sense of urgency to many of their fellow Americans. In late 1774 and early 1775, the strategy of the 1760's still seemed viable to many residents of the middle and southern colonies. Believing, as Chandler said, that they had "reason to complain of some late acts, as violations of their constitutional liberty," the Americans thought it likely that the North ministry would surrender in the face of concerted opposition, just as previous administrations had yielded when the colonies had actively resisted in 1765 and 1767. American leaders wanted to avoid an irrevocable confrontation with the ministry, and to that end they publicly advocated reconciliation, expressing dismay at the very idea of independence.[18] Consequently, the vital question that was later to divide loyalist from rebel was not even raised, and in the absence of such a sharply defined issue it was impossible for most Americans to determine with any certainty just what constituted the difference between a loyal opposition to specific parliamentary policies and a treasonable resistance to British authority. The political context was so ambiguous that a conservative colonist who hoped that England and America could peacefully negotiate a mutually acceptable settlement of their dispute did not appear unalterably opposed to his more radical compatriots. Even Galloway admitted as late as August 1775, "However I may differ with many respecting the mode of redress, and the means of accommodating the unhappy Differences between them . . . yet I shall be happy to find in the unfore-seen events of things that I have been mistaken and others in the Right."[19]

The lack of clear ideological divisions in the time of flux between the adjournment of the First Congress and the battles at Lexington and Concord is suggested by three observations that may be made about the functioning of the committees established to enforce the Continental Association. First, they concerned themselves only with overt violators of the Association, with active opponents of Congress, not with men who expressed a more conservative philosophy than theirs. Their role was strictly limited, and their aim was to control certain specified actions, not thought. Their restraint contributed to a second circumstance, the invariable failure of the scattered attempts to form "counterassociations" to oppose them. Only men like the pamphleteers, who were especially sensitive to the committees' challenge to the political and religious establishment, rallied to support the efforts at organized resistance. A third and still more important indication of the underlying consensus was the fact that a number of men who eventually proved to be steadfast loyalists participated actively in the work of the committees and provincial congresses. These colonists saw no contradiction between their fidelity to Great Britain and their desire to readjust the imperial relationship. As long as the issue was not independence but rather reform within the empire, men who were to consider themselves loyalists in the years to come could readily embrace the American cause. There was no inconsistency involved: their ideology remained constant. It was the radicals who changed.[20]

The accuracy of this observation may be illustrated by a closer examination of the ideas of one of the men in question, the Reverend Jacob Duché of Philadelphia. Duché, an Anglican with intellectual pretensions, served as chaplain to both the First and Second Continental Congresses. In July 1775 he preached a sermon entitled "The Duty of Standing Fast in our Spiritual and Temporal Liberties," which was such a strong statement of the American position that another future loyalist, Jonathan Boucher, who was more skeptical of the colonies' claims, felt compelled to respond to it with a learned sermon of his own. But in his presentation Duché carefully declared his "inviolable loyalty" to the king, and, he asked emphatically, "As to any pretensions to, or even desire of independency, have we not openly disavowed them in all our petitions, representations and remonstrances?" More than two years later, in a letter addressed to George Washington, he explained that he had "looked upon independency rather as an Expedient, and a hazardous one indeed, thrown out in terrorem, in order to procure some favourable terms, than [as] a measure, that was seriously to be persisted in at all events."[21] Duché had not altered his opinion one whit in the intervening years. It was Washington and the members of Congress who had abandoned one course of action for another. And the primary event that helped to set them on their new path was the outbreak of war on April 19, 1775.

[3]

The clashes at Lexington and Concord brought to an end much of the uncertainty of the previous months. Although American leaders still denied that they sought independence, ever greater numbers of colonists began to see that independence was indeed the ultimate issue. Furthermore, many participants in the earlier coalition did not believe that Americans should oppose Great Britain with force, regardless of the limited nature of their goals. In the wake of the fighting, such critics of the radical strategy appeared to be potential dangers to the cause of freedom, possible spies and traitors, rather than simply dissenters whose waywardness could be tolerated. The radicals argued that men who opposed the will of the people in this important matter could not expect to participate normally in society. To use the words of the Georgia provincial assembly, they were "inimical to the Liberties of America," and therefore "precluded from the protection of this Congress."[22]

Accordingly, the local committees and provincial congresses set out to expose and neutralize their opponents.[23] Again New England took the lead, and the committees of the area turned their attention to men who had managed to escape the notice of the mobs during the preceding autumn. A typical target was the Reverend John Wiswall, an Anglican missionary stationed at Falmouth, who at first had "determined to espouse neither side, considering himself as a Minister of that kingdom which is not of this world." But Wiswall discovered to his dismay that "even silence is now censured by the people as evidence of what they call tory principles." Like many others, Wiswall was harassed by his local committee soon after the battles at Lexington and Concord. In May he seized the first available opportunity to escape to Boston.[24]

It is important to note that as yet it was only in the North that such silent supporters of British authority came under attack from the committees. In the middle and southern colonies, where the war had not had a direct impact, it was not until September 1775 that the committees' campaign against dissenters shifted into high gear. But from that time on Americans who disagreed with the prevailing revolutionary ideology were confronted with a steadily narrowing range of political choices.

The progression began with a number of provincial laws prescribing penalties for anyone who aided British troops or criticized the Continental Congress. By either formal or informal mechanisms the local committees became responsible for enforcing these laws, and so they started to conduct official investigations of men charged with publicly or privately opposing the war effort.[25] Some especially dedicated committees actively searched out potential troublemakers by circulating defense associations, which were formal agreements to take up arms against Great Britain. Persons who would not sign the associations were immediately exposed as unsympathetic to the American cause. Another tactic that served the same end was an official mustering of the local militia.[26]

The aim of these devices was to identify the disaffected and consequently to make them subject to the committees' control. Once singled out, suspected persons could be "very narrowly watched" (as one was), fined, required to give bond for their good behavior, imprisoned, or forcibly removed from their homes to remote sections of the province or even to other colonies.[27] Moreover, once a man had been declared an "Enemy to the Freedoms and Rights of America," he could be subjected to all sorts of ingenious pressures designed to make him abandon either his beliefs or his property. A Virginia Anglican cleric, for example, had to contend with "officers and armed parties" that "frequently entered his Churches with Drums Guns and Bayonets and with wanton outcrys and profanity disturbed the Sacred Service of Religion," and even "nailed up the Windows and Doors of his Churches and at length placed armed Men to guard them on Sundays." In another telling incident, an unfortunate resident of New Hampshire, afraid to anger the local militiamen by refusing any of their requests, found that the soldiers "in three Nights drank me in the article of Porter, thirty dozen Bottles." It is hardly surprising that both men soon fled to the protection of the nearest British outpost.[28]

Although the committees occasionally utilized more forc-

Virginians being forced to sign the Continental Association in 1775, as seen by a British cartoonist. Note the tar and feathers hanging from the scaffold in the background.

ible coercion, it was likely that the mere threat of direct action would suffice to serve their purposes. Their use of tarring and feathering, for example, has been greatly exaggerated. A few men were tarred and feathered, but more common was the experience of loyalists like George Johnston and Thomas Macknight, of South and North Carolina respectively, who, although mobbed and threatened, were able to leave their homes without being physically molested.[29] And in any case drastic tactics were adopted only as a last resort. A suspected person would usually first be warned to mend his ways. If he persisted in his obstinate refusal to support the rebellion, he would be subjected to harassment short of physical harm, just as a Marylander was "hanged and Burnt in Effigy in different parts of the Province and many threats thrown out daily against both his Person and property." The next step was to present him (as was done with the same man) with the "Alternative of either taking up Arms or Subjecting himself to such Punishment as the Provincial Convention shall think proper to inflict." That, for most loyalists, was no choice at all, and they often selected a third, implicit alternative — flight.[30]

The committees therefore had many ways of achieving the desired end of silencing their critics. The best method of all, perhaps, was to get rid of them altogether. Prominent loyalists who had left their homes could not exercise any influence over their neighbors, whereas if they remained they could sow dissension among their fellow countrymen. Furthermore, once inside the British lines they could do little to harm the American cause. And so, it seems, the committees deliberately created an atmosphere that abetted emigration. As one Virginian accurately observed, the "few friends [of] Government" were "either obliged to go off or subjected to insult and danger."[31]

[*4*]

In 1775, the only haven in America for supporters of royal authority was the town of Boston. British naval vessels anchored in the harbors of New York City, Charleston, and Norfolk could offer temporary shelter to fleeing loyalists, but nowhere else in the thirteen colonies was there a city so securely under royal control. Accordingly, to that sole beacon of safety flocked the New Englanders forced from their homes by committee persecution. By early summer the city was crowded with refugees.

Life in the besieged port was far from pleasant. Most of the civilians, without money or sufficient food supplies, were forced to depend upon military stores for their very existence. The diet was monotonous — one sufferer described it as "salt beef and salt pork one day, and the next . . . salt pork and salt beef" — and the fear that the rebels would eventually break through the British lines to cause "barbarous slaughter and desolation" was all-pervasive. As a result, many of the loyalists soon left for the happier climes of Halifax or London. Jonathan Sewall, judge of the Halifax vice-admiralty court and a leading Boston lawyer, graphically enumerated his reasons for abandoning the city as "Musketry, Bombs, Great Guns, Redoubts, Lines, Batterys, Enfilades, Battles, Sieges, Murder, plague, pestilence, Famine, Rebellion, and the Devil." Many others must have agreed with him and with John Wiswall, who wrote, "The Sufferings and Persecutions I have undergone, together with the Rebellious Spirit of the People has weaned my Affections from my native Country — the further I go from it the better." By mid-July, according to one observer, only one-third of the city's population remained.[32]

But those who stayed clung tenaciously to their little

outpost of the empire. Chief Justice Peter Oliver, a close friend and relative of Hutchinson, retained his confidence in an ultimate British triumph because, he observed characteristically, "the God of Order may punish a community for a time with their own disorders: but it is incompatible with the rectitude of the Divine Nature, to suffer anarchy to prevail." And so Oliver remained in Boston, despite the hardships of the life he described cleverly in November 1775: "We have little else to do now but to take snuff; we snuff in the air for want of food: we take snuff at the rebels for their barbarities: and we enjoy the snuff of candles, when we can get them to burn." Like the other loyalists still resident in the port, Oliver was caught unawares by the "sudden and precipitate" retreat ordered in March 1776. General George Washington's troops had managed to plant cannon on Dorchester Heights, which commanded the entire city, and Sir William Howe consequently directed that the port be evacuated. As Oliver's ship left the coastal waters of Massachusetts, his comments reflected the bitterness he so deeply felt: "Here I took my Leave of that once happy Country, where Peace and Plenty reigned uncontrouled, till that infernal *Hydra, Rebellion,* with its hundred Heads, had devoured its Happiness, spread Devastation over its fertile Fields and ravaged the peacefull Mansions of its Inhabitants. . . . Here I drop the filial Tear into the Urn, of my Country."[33]

With the exception of a single ship that carried dispatches and a few fortunate refugees directly to England, the vessels loaded with civilians and soldiers set sail for Halifax. The ships were crowded, and although the voyage was short, many of the Bostonians arrived in Nova Scotia with "Health and Strength almost exhausted." The circumstances they encountered when once again on dry land did little to improve their condition. As Lieutenant Governor Oliver later reported, the profit-hungry local inhabitants charged the refugees "six fold the usual Rent" for "miserable Lodgings" and double the regular prices of food and clothing. Observing the scene with unusual detachment, Peter Oliver remarked wryly, "Thus Mankind prey upon each other."[34]

The Bostonians quickly discovered that the exorbitant cost of living was not the only drawback to a prolonged residence in Halifax. Many became ill in the "foggy chilling air," and they lamented the lack of the "comforts" of a New England summer. Furthermore, Halifax was simply not a congenial place to live. The town lacked many of the civilized amenities to which the Bostonians had become accustomed, and consequently a number of the evacuees soon made plans to leave. Despite their certainty that the war would be won within a few months, they saw no reason to endure the discomforts of Nova Scotia any longer than was absolutely necessary. As Lieutenant Governor Oliver explained just before his departure from Halifax in May, "To continue in this crouded starved Place without any possibility of being useful to my Sovereign, is a Sacrafice which I am sure his Majesty never will desire his servants to make."[35]

Oliver's intended destination was the British Isles, and London in particular. The city was an irresistible magnet drawing the refugees across the Atlantic: Mandamus councilors, customs officials, merchants, landowners, and civil servants — most of those who could afford to pay their passage — unhesitatingly abandoned Nova Scotia in the summer of 1776 and sailed for England. By the end of the year, more than seventy families, numbering among them many of the political, social, and economic leaders of prewar Massachusetts, had arrived in the British Isles.[36] And these were but the first of a long line of loyalists who would choose to spend at least part of their exile in London. The metropolis attracted American refugees for various reasons, not the least of which were the numerous amusements available to curious visitors with time on their hands. London was, after all, the seat of the empire, the center from which the war was being directed, and it seemed the perfect temporary residence for prominent loyalists who wanted to offer their suggestions on the war to the ministry, or who hoped to better themselves by obtaining royal appointments. By the end of the war, nearly every important American refugee had lived in London for at least a brief period.

But there were some New Englanders who remained in Halifax in the expectation that (as one said) they would be "doing business in Boston before Winter." And when Sir William Howe captured New York City just a few months later, it seemed as if they had correctly anticipated the course of events. But Boston was never to be retaken, and Manhattan of necessity replaced it as the chief haven for refugee loyalists in America. Throughout the rest of the war New York City was the major British stronghold in the colonies. To it regularly came fleeing sufferers, singly or in small groups, and large numbers of refugees arrived en masse following the evacuation of Philadelphia in 1778 and the abandonment of Savannah and Charleston in 1782–1783. The extent of the loyalist migration was reflected in the rising population of the city. It has been estimated that when Howe took possession of New York only 5,000 of its regular inhabitants remained. By February 1777 the civilian population had climbed to 11,000; by 1781 it had become 25,000; and by the time of the final evacuation in 1783 it was at least 33,000, in addition to the 10,000 British soldiers stationed in the port.[37]

The presence of that many civilians caused serious logistical problems for the British military authorities that governed the city throughout the war. Normal difficulties were compounded by the fact that fully one-quarter of the city's dwellings had been accidentally destroyed by fire soon after the British occupation began. As a result, lodgings were both scarce and expensive, and the loyalists had to be satisfied with what remained after the officers and men of the regular regiments had been housed. By December 1778 one refugee was describing conditions in the city as "truly deplorable and almost hopeless." Another recorded his lengthy search for suitable lodgings and complained vividly of the "stinks and ill smells" permeating the port because of poor sanitation and overcrowding. He commented bitterly that the residents of New York exhibited only the most "vicious and unfeeling part of human nature." It was a reflection with which others concurred. In September 1778 Galloway observed, "Everyone here think of nobody but themselves; and friendship is not to be found."[38]

The lot of the loyalists in Manhattan was somewhat improved after Sir Henry Clinton replaced Howe as commander in chief. Clinton appointed two refugees to advise him on the needs of their fellow sufferers, and he directed that military supplies be issued to those in the greatest distress. A number of the Americans were employed by the army in civilian capacities, and others were recruited into loyalist regiments, largely because of Clinton's belief that it was "more satisfactory to themselves and excites less jealousy in others, that they be supposed in real employment, and not receiving a bare elymosynary Subsidy."[39] Clinton's successor, Sir Guy Carleton, continued a solicitous policy toward the refugees, even to the extent of delaying the final evacuation of the city until he was certain that all the loyalists had had the opportunity to leave. As a result, Manhattan was consistently a sympathetic, if not an overly attractive, refuge for loyal Americans fleeing from rebel-held territory.

But not every colonist who remained faithful to the crown found it possible to reach Manhattan. For southern loyalists in particular there were few avenues of escape until Savannah fell to royal forces in late 1778. Before that time the loyal residents of the South were completely at the mercy of the rebel provincial governments. Their one organized attempt to resist — the battle at Moore's Creek Bridge in North Carolina in February 1776 — ended in the rout of the loyal militia, and consequently in uncontested rebel control of the area.[40]

During much of 1775 southern loyalists could still book passage on regular commercial ships crossing the Atlantic, and many took advantage of the opportunity to remove themselves from the scrutiny of the committees. Yet large numbers of British sympathizers remained in America, and they were helpless to resist, or even to escape, as the southern rebels systematically began to isolate and expose them. The revolutionaries' campaign relied mainly upon the use of the loyalty oath statutes that were enacted in most of the states by the end of 1777. These laws required voters, officeholders, and suspected persons to swear allegiance to the state, at the same time abjuring their former loyalty to the king.[41] Especially in the Carolinas the acts were consciously utilized as a means of ferreting out enemies of the rebellion. By the spring of 1778, both states were requiring all free adult males to take oaths of allegiance, under the threat of immediate banishment.[42]

Many southerners were therefore faced squarely with a choice between an expedient submission to the rebel authorities and a public avowal of their principles. In spite of the heavy penalty involved, some steadfast loyalists refused to subscribe to the oaths and were banished to England or the West Indies. Others adopted various subterfuges in order to evade the requirement or, to the same end, attempted to avoid having any contact with the local authorities administering the oaths. But the acts meant, as one South Carolinian later observed, that "Every body who contin[ue]d in the Country was obliged to temporize."[43]

When the British army invaded Georgia in 1778, the time for vacillation ended. For the first time southerners were presented with a viable alternative to the revolutionary state governments, and many of them were emboldened to reassert their fidelity to the crown. The mere presence of royal troops served to crystallize loyalist sentiment, and Americans who had previously acquiesced in rebel rule sought the protection of the redcoats and even enlisted in loyalist regiments. It is difficult to determine how many of these late-declaring southern loyalists were sincere in their reversal of allegiance and how many were simply opportunists seeking the winning side. But there can be no doubt that the chief factor influencing their decision to disavow the Revolution was the comforting accessibility of the British army. Without the assurance offered by the presence of British troops, all but the most fanatically loyal southerners had previously seen little reason to oppose the Revolution openly.

The pattern that developed in the South after 1778 was the familiar one. Loyalists from the region fled to British-occupied Savannah and Charleston, just as their northern counterparts had sought refuge in Boston, Philadelphia, and New York City. And, since conditions in the southern ports were little better than they had been in Halifax or Manhattan, some of the refugees chose after a few months to retreat to England. But at the same time many of those who had managed to escape the South in previous years returned to resume what they thought would be their normal lives in their former homes, once again under British rule. The news of Cornwallis' defeat at Yorktown in October 1781 came as an unwelcome shock to these men, and when in the aftermath of that catastrophe the ministry ordered the evacuation of Savannah and Charleston, one of them remarked that "nothing could exceed the distress to which the Loyalists were then reduced." The refugees had little choice: they could either leave America, abandoning their property forever, or remain behind to risk "the harshest treatment from an enraged enemy."[44] And so, like their predecessors from Boston and Philadelphia, most of them sorrowfully sailed with the troops.

But this time there was a difference. Unlike their forerunners, the evacuees from the South — and later those from Manhattan — knew that they would probably never return to the United States. Consequently, instead of sailing for England and what was only a temporary residence, most of them chose to go to the West Indies or to Canada, where they could begin their lives anew within the remaining British American colonies.[45] The vast influx into the mother country had ended, and many of the loyalists who had originally sought refuge there joined the migration to other parts of the empire. By 1785, the movement of loyalists resulting from the Revolution had largely been completed.

The following table charts the arrival dates in Great Britain for 1,440 heads of loyalist families. This figure represents a minimum calculation of the migration to England, for there is evidence indicating that many loyalist exiles may have disappeared into English life without leaving any trace of their presence. Assuming that each person noted on the chart had three dependents (wives, parents, children, or other relatives), and taking into account the loyalists who

	Pre-1775	1775	1776	1777	1778	1779	1780	1781	1782	1783	1784	Un-known	Total
N.H.	4	3	6	1	4	0	4	2	1	3	0	2	30
Mass.	17	43	74	26	15	15	19	9	5	12	6	22	263
Conn.	2	1	1	3	2	5	1	1	3	6	5	5	35
R.I.	0	1	6	2	1	1	5	3	1	8	6	4	38
N.Y.	7	9	4	6	6	9	16	9	10	46	39	43	204
N.J.	1	5	2	2	4	2	4	0	10	20	20	16	86
Pa.	1	8	6	7	20	11	7	6	7	36	14	36	159
Md.	2	19	4	4	4	5	7	6	5	10	6	10	82
Va.	8	10	15	14	15	5	4	1	9	14	7	21	123
N.C.	2	4	8	4	9	2	3	1	8	20	20	38	119
S.C.	7	15	3	28	21	7	0	8	35	51	19	40	234
Ga.	3	4	10	5	6	0	1	0	5	13	10	10	67
TOTAL	54	122	139	102	107	62	71	46	99	239	152	247	1440

[a] When a loyalist crossed the Atlantic more than once, he has been counted the first time only. Although loyalists continued to arrive in England after 1784, most of them were permanently settled elsewhere and came only for the purpose of submitting claims. Thus they have been excluded from this table, though they are included in the analysis of claims in chapter 7. It should be noted that the figures in the table do not exactly indicate the total number of loyalists in England at any particular time, because there was a good deal of transatlantic travel, especially by southerners who returned to their homes in 1779–1780.

left no records, it seems reasonable to estimate that between seven and eight thousand Americans fled to the British Isles.

In addition to suggesting the total size of the migration to England, the table illustrates statistically several of the observations that have been made in this chapter. The importance of the British army as a determinant of loyalist identification has already been noted in relation to the southern campaign, and the distribution of figures within the table demonstrates that the presence of the army had a similar effect elsewhere at other times during the war. The states that were most seriously affected by the fighting produced far greater numbers of refugees than those left relatively untouched by actual battle. The contrast between neighboring states like Maryland and Pennsylvania, or New Hampshire and Massachusetts, is especially striking, even when population differences are taken into account.

Furthermore, historians have tended to assume that the number of exiles from a particular area or state indicates the relative strength of loyalism in that region. For example, it has been argued that "in most colonies Loyalism was a distinctly urban and seaboard phenomenon," on the basis of figures that show that large percentages of the exiles came from cities like Savannah, Charleston, and Boston, or at least from nearby coastal areas. But when these observations are viewed in the light of the pattern of British military activity, a different deduction emerges. Of the ten cities producing the highest number of loyalist claimants in relation to total population, seven were British garrison towns at some time during the war. Of the states in which major battles occurred, only Pennsylvania had a relatively low percentage of claimants. And the rural areas that supplied the highest numbers of loyalists were the scenes of either significant unrest or large-scale fighting.[46]

A detailed examination of the preceding table reveals the close relationship between the events of the war and the size of the migration from particular states. Most Massachusetts refugees arrived in England in 1775–1776, during and after the siege of Boston; most South Carolinians came in 1777–1778, when the loyalty oaths were introduced, and 1782–1783, following the evacuation of Charleston; and most New Yorkers appeared in 1783–1784, after the abandonment of Manhattan. By contrast, the figures for the states in which few battles were fought show no such fluctuation. The emigrants are rather evenly divided among the war years, indicating an absence of external pressures. The inescapable conclusion is that the number of exiles from any particular area varied directly with the specific circumstances of the war. This does not mean that the size of the migration from a state bore no relationship at all to the size of the loyalist community within that state, but it does imply that the connection is not so close as has previously been imagined. There is no reason to suppose that the Americans who fled their homes were necessarily representative of their fellow loyalists, for though a man rarely became a loyalist by accident, it was through the accidents of war that he became a refugee. It is therefore practically impossible to extrapolate backwards from an analysis of the refugees to obtain an accurate picture of the loyalist community as a whole.

The fact is that unless the British army was nearby to offer him protection, an American had little incentive to declare his loyalty to the crown. Long before the Declaration of Independence was adopted, committees and provincial congresses had taken over the day-to-day government of the colonies. Any man who openly opposed these extralegal bodies could find himself investigated, disarmed, threatened, even jailed. To loyally-minded citizens it must have seemed much more prudent to remain silent until the expected British victory had been achieved, or at least until British forces had triumphed in their respective regions. That many did play this waiting game is demonstrated by the substantial number of Americans who first swore allegiance to the rebel governments and then reversed themselves — honestly or not — when the British army appeared in their vicinity.

The figures in the table also reflect the loyalists' reaction to the progress of the British war effort. Although the loyalists were forced from their homes by committees, battles, and the like at certain specified times, they were not necessarily compelled to go to England at those same times. Even at the evacuations of Philadelphia, Savannah, and Charleston the refugees always had the option of going to another British outpost in America instead of traveling to the mother country. Thus, for example, many of the persons evacuated from Philadelphia in June 1778 did not travel to England immediately. Instead they remained in New York City for months, perhaps years. A number, as shown by the table, left only at the final abandonment of that port.

Because there was this element of choice involved in the timing of a trip to England, the composite arrival figures for each year can indicate the loyalists' assessment of the prospects for a quick British victory. When the refugees believed that the final triumph could be expected within a few months, they were reluctant to make the arduous journey to Great Britain. On the other hand, if the immediate outlook was poor and a British victory seemed years in the future, London was certainly a more comfortable place to pass the intervening time than were the garrison cities of New York, Charleston, or Savannah. With this perspective, the great fluctuation in total arrivals from year to year becomes explicable. In 1775, when the committees were active and Boston was the only refuge for loyalists in the thirteen colonies, Americans flocked to England in large numbers. During 1776 and 1777, years of some military success, the totals fell, if the Boston evacuees and the banished Carolinians, who were not presented with much of an alternative, are excluded. The year 1778 saw a large influx into England, following the serious setbacks of the defeat at Saratoga and the loss of Philadelphia. By contrast, the period 1779–1781, when optimism was at its height because of victories in the South, showed a significant decline in the number of arrivals. Finally, the post-

Yorktown months brought a resurgence of emigration, which continued until East Florida was evacuated in late 1784 under the terms of the Spanish peace treaty.

Whenever they arrived in Great Britain, or for whatever reason, the loyalists all faced the same problem of acclimation. They had always called England "home" even if they had been born in America, but when they arrived in the British Isles they found a culture and even a system of government alien to their experience. Although they had left their property and sometimes their families because of their adherence to the crown, they soon learned that their sacrifices were not appreciated in the mother country. The adjustment to the hard realities of exile was long, painful, and not entirely successful. Ironically, the loyalists realized how American they were only after they had abandoned America.

2

Vain Hopes

Those who bring property here may do well
enough, but for those who expect reimbursement
for losses, or a supply for present support, will
find to their cost the hand of charity very cold;
the latter may be kept from starving, and beyond
that their hopes are vain.

— SAMUEL CURWEN, 1776[1]

THE loyalists who traveled to England during the early
years of the war felt unqualified relief at finally reaching
the safety of the mother country. No prescient glimpse of
their troubled future intruded upon their rapture: Louisa
Wells, the daughter of a loyal South Carolina printer, probably spoke for them all when she recorded in her journal,
"O! how shall I describe what I felt, when I first set my foot
on British ground? I could have kissed the gravel on the salt
Beach! It was my home: the Country which I had so long and
so earnestly wished to see. The Isle of Liberty and Peace."[2]

Before long, though, Louisa and her fellow refugees discovered that England was not in fact their home. They had
expected a warm welcome from the ministry. They had
hoped to influence British policy towards America. They had
looked forward to a brief, pleasant sojourn in London that
would end as soon as the war was won. Instead, they found
their advice ignored, their needs slighted, and their months

of exile stretching into years. It was an intensely disillusioning experience.

[*1*]

The loyalists who fled to England in 1774 and 1775 went to the mother country not only to escape from the colonies but also to achieve a positive goal: effecting a reconciliation between Britain and America. Regarding the incipient dispute as "unnatural," resulting at least in part from the Americans' and Britons' mutual ignorance of each other's true intentions, they wanted to remedy that situation by supplying each side with copious information concerning the other's actions and attitudes. Through such means, they believed, the misconceptions of both the North administration and the colonists could be dispelled, and once that end had been accomplished the few remaining differences between the combatants would readily be resolved. In effect, they attempted to discover in their exile the significance they had lost in America. If they successfully pointed the way to a permanent reconciliation, they could at the same time regain the respect of their fellow countrymen and win favor from the British government.

Accordingly, the loyalists' letters home were intended to convince the colonists that they had incorrectly anticipated the British response to their current tactics. As the exiles well knew, American radicals had argued that strict enforcement of the Association would cause severe economic dislocation in the mother country. The radical leaders had predicted that British merchants, their business destroyed by the boycott, would try to bring the administration to alter its obnoxious policies. Moreover, they had argued that ordinary workingmen unemployed as a result of the boycott would riot or perhaps openly rebel against North's government, thus exerting further pressure on the ministry.[3] The refugees thought it imperative to correct these erroneous notions, and so they repeatedly assured their American correspondents that the Association had not seriously affected British commerce. To the contrary, they asserted, business in the mother country had never been better. "In short my Dear Sir," concluded one New Yorker, "not a single effect which it was thought the Resolutions, Addresses, etc of the Congress would have produced *here,* has happened."[4]

Actually, the loyalists continued, the Americans' violent words and deeds had only "kindled the resentment of the Nation" and had wrought "infinite injury" to their cause. Congressional statements, instead of easing tensions, had succeeded in arousing "the public resentment." Even the merchants were beginning to turn against their former American friends, detesting both their tactics and their "lust of Domination and Empire."[5] With the defection of these traditional allies, "the Nation was never more United" behind the ministry. The Americans had "not the least ground to expect any relief, or any change of measures whatever." The government absolutely insisted on the "Sacred Tenet" of colonial subordination to Parliament, and despite Lord North's willingness to compromise on minor matters, he would never agree to terms that would "imply a surrender of the whole legislative authority of G B."[6]

Thus, the refugees argued, it would be futile for the Americans to persist in their opposition to the ministry, especially because "vigorous measures" would be instituted if they did not soon change their tactics. To the exiles' minds there could be just one answer to the crucial question, "Shou[l]d brave men be lost when what they contend for can be obtained otherwise?" As a New Yorker advised a friend, "In this state of Imperfection, better most assuredly is it, to be contented with a moderate Share of Civil Liberty in enjoyment and well secured, than to be aiming at visionary Schemes of Perfect Freedom."[7]

But it was simply too late for such ideas to carry much weight with many of the refugees' fellow countrymen. Perhaps the radicals might once have been satisfied with "a moderate Share of Civil Liberty," but the difficulty was that they no longer believed they enjoyed that desirable state. It did little good for the exiles to describe the dire consequences of opposition to Great Britain when the radicals believed they were already experiencing the even more dire consequences of ministerial tyranny. Since the loyalists' premises therefore diverged from those adopted by other Americans, the arguments they carefully based on those premises were useless, incapable of persuading anyone who disagreed with the initial assumptions.

The exiles encountered nearly identical difficulties when they tried to present their ideas on America to the North administration. In the first place, loyalists were but rarely consulted on American affairs. Contrary to their expectations, they were neither systematically utilized as sources of factual information about the colonies nor encouraged to propose methods for ending the conflict.[8] And even when refugees were asked for their opinions, their suggestions received short shrift from North and his advisers, who had already decided upon the course of action they would follow. Very few exiles achieved the distinction of having private conversations with members of the administration; indeed, those who did can almost be counted on the fingers of one hand. Foremost among them was Thomas Hutchinson. Then came Thomas Bradbury Chandler and two other Anglican clerics, John Vardill and Jonathan Boucher, both of whom had had previous personal contacts with men who were now on the periphery of political power. Finally, there were George M. Johnston, a South Carolina physician, who in 1775 visited various ministers "frequently," and Thomas Moffat of Rhode Island, whose letter of introduction from Gage enabled him to see North "divers times."[9]

Of these men Hutchinson alone had consistent entrée to administration circles. Within twenty-four hours of his arrival in London in July 1774, Hutchinson spoke with both Dartmouth and the king at length, and, although he never had another private interview with George III, he thought that his reception "exceeded what I had any reason to expect." His "whole time," he told friends late in July, was "taken up in receiving visits and complying with invitations from persons of the first rank."[10] Hutchinson found Dartmouth "friendly to the Province and to me personally beyond conception," and he recorded with pleasure that the minister had assured him "more than once" that he had affected the government's policy on America. Moreover, he noted in September 1774, "the Ministry are always inquisitive after my Intelligence."[11]

But Hutchinson quickly learned that frequent contacts with administration officials did not necessarily indicate that his words were being heeded. In fact, the inability to make any impression on the government's established ideas — an inability that was to haunt Hutchinson for the remaining years of his exile — began at that very first encounter with the king. The governor's version of the meeting was that he had described Boston as thinking the Port Act "extremely alarming" and that his "chief object" had been "to obtain relief for the T[own] of B[oston] on the easiest terms." Yet the king informed Lord North that Hutchinson had called the Port Act "the only wise effectual method that could have been suggested for bringing them to a speedy submission."

George III came away from the meeting convinced that Boston would "soon submit" to the law; Hutchinson, on the other hand, thought he had made it clear that some modification of the act was necessary.[12]

By the fall of 1774 the governor had discerned the reason why he was having such difficulty communicating his ideas to British officials: the ministry simply did not recognize the differences between political circumstances in England and those in America. "The Opposition in the Kingdom is not to the Constitution nor to any particular Law but to the Persons in Administration," he explained. "Opposition in the Colonies is to the Constitution itself and to the Authority of the Kingdom over them." The aim of colonial opposition was not just to advance the interests of a "few particular men"; quite the contrary, "every man is made to believe he is to reap a great personal benefit or to be freed from the danger of a great personal evil the loss of his liberty and he considers himself as contending against his greatest enemies and every advance he makes he is encouraged to go on further." As a result, although in the mother country the fire of opposition might eventually burn itself out, "there is more fewel in proportion in America than there is in England," and the fire "most certainly will continually increase."[13]

But the administration, ignoring Hutchinson's analysis, persisted in regarding the American situation as comparable to the state of affairs in England, and consequently as being susceptible to punitive legislation and to a mere show of force. And so Hutchinson found himself caught between the Americans, who rejected his notion that the supremacy of Parliament was consistent with the protection of their freedom, and the ministry, which refused to believe that extraordinary exertions might be required to preserve that supremacy. Hutchinson, who hoped on the one hand "for every indulgence with respect to taxation, and all other parts of legislation," even for "any concession short of Independency," yet who wanted on the other "to see the Leaders deterred from their pursuits" through the ministry's acting with "more vigour," drew harsh criticism from both sides.[14] "I have been charged in America with false and unfavorable representations of the people there," he observed in 1777. "I am here charged with neglecting to give advice of their intentions to revolt, and representing the body of the people as disposed to live quietly under the authority of Parliament." Only Hutchinson could resolve such a labyrinthine dilemma. "I am charged w[i]th arbitrary principles but I am as far from them as any man in the world and never wished for a greater restraint of natural liberty than is necessary to answer the end of Govt," he wrote in 1775, delineating the position that neither the Americans nor the British ministry ever seemed to fully comprehend.[15]

Within a few months after his arrival Hutchinson had lost what little influence he had ever possessed. He continued to call at the colonial office to talk with Dartmouth or the undersecretaries, but, when the act to restrict New England trade was drafted in early 1775, his opinion was not required. "It was planned very privately and [was] complete as to form before I saw it or was asked any questions about it," he revealed to a friend. A few months later, feeling "perfectly idle and useless," he commented that "there never has been a question asked me about America for a long time past."[16] Yet so long as Dartmouth, his "chief Patron," continued as American secretary, Hutchinson still had some access to the upper echelons of the ministry. When Lord George Germain replaced Dartmouth in November 1775 even that tenuous link was broken. The following February Hutchinson wrote bitterly, "We americans are plenty here and very cheap.

Some of us at first coming are apt to think ourselves of importance but other people do not think so, and few if any of us are much consulted or enquired after."[17]

[2]

Deprived of the political influence they had hoped to wield, the first exiles also found themselves beset with financial worries. Only a few of them had sufficient funds to support themselves indefinitely in England, for they thought (as one Rhode Islander later put it) that "the Provision made by Government was fully competent to subjugate the Colonies in a Campaign or two." Anticipating only a brief stay in the British Isles, they did not bother to make long-term financial arrangements. "When I left Boston I had not the least thought of its continuing so long," wrote one woman in 1778. "I thought I had sufficient to suport me while I was in Briton."[18] But, as the Americans quickly discovered, London was "the most expensive and excessively dear place to live in that is in the whole World." The most frugal practices could not alter the fact that they had finite resources with which to meet infinite demands, and so even those loyalists who had at first believed they could live adequately upon independent incomes sooner or later learned that such a feat would be impossible.[19]

A few refugees attempted to solve their monetary problems by finding employment in London, but that was far from easy to accomplish for a number of reasons. In the first place, London had little need for the services of colonial customs officials, judges, councilors, or landowners. Second, without capital or contacts, artisans, merchants, and small shopkeepers were usually unable to reestablish their businesses successfully in Great Britain. Third, colonial professional men (lawyers and doctors in particular) often lacked the formal training required to practice in England.[20] Finally, the loyalists' chances for obtaining government jobs were almost nonexistent because the ministry shared the refugees' assumption that they were only temporarily resident in England: There simply seemed little reason to employ them.

In any case, the refugees recognized that they could obtain official positions only "by Interest or by Purchase," and they had neither commodity upon which to depend. This applied even to Thomas Hutchinson, who, despite years of effort, failed to find a post for his son William. In 1779 he revealed, "I have never yet met with any person who, when I asked anything for any of my family or friends, would make use of their influence in my behalf, which I attribute to a fear lest it should be considered as a favour which, if granted at their request, would lessen their claims for themselves, or some of their connections."[21]

A close look at the fate of some refugee clergymen shows the types of problems that faced loyalist job hunters. Those clerics who had served as missionaries for the Society for the Propagation of the Gospel in Foreign Parts had a slight advantage over their fellow ministers, for the S.P.G., at the instigation of Thomas Bradbury Chandler, not only continued their salaries during the war but also distributed small amounts of relief ($£50$ or less) to the clergy in the greatest distress.[22] Yet the S.P.G. made no attempt to find livings in England for its missionaries, so they, like other clerics, had to seek such positions on their own initiative, usually with little success.[23] Jonathan Boucher, for example, found the attention of several bishops "sufficiently flattering," but, he noted, "I get only Promises." Much later he admitted that he had "cherish[ed] these hopes for years to no purpose . . . all came to nothing." Eventually Boucher accepted the curacy of a parish in Paddington and was reduced to the necessity of waiting like "a Crow near a Piece of Carrion" for the vicar to die so that he could have sole possession of the living. Ironically, when the moment he had anticipated finally arrived, Boucher learned to his dismay that the post had long been promised to the nephew of a former bishop. His sole triumph was his election as assistant secretary to the S.P.G., which brought him a salary of £100 a year.[24]

Dissenting clergymen encountered the same difficulties, as was discovered by a young New Englander, Isaac Smith, who filled a living at Sidmouth during the war years. Smith's salary was less than he needed for expenses even in a provincial town, and he was obliged to draw supplementary funds from his father's London agent. Smith told his parents in justification, "When I came to this Country, my expectations were not great. I tho't it however easier than I find it to meet with a sufficiency, as a Dissenting Minister, to support myself decently."[25]

The Reverend Henry Caner, who had served as rector of King's Chapel in Boston, described the clerics' experiences most vividly. Upon his arrival in England Caner received "many compassionable expressions" from both the Bishop of London and the Archbishop of Canterbury, but, whenever he mentioned the possibility of being appointed to an English parish, he was told, "We cant think of your residing here, we want such men as you in America." After a number of comparable conversations Caner concluded that the English clergy looked upon the Americans with a "jealous Eye," regarding them "in no better light than as coming to take the Bread out of their mouths." As a result he advised his friends who could remain in the colonies "with safety" to do so, "for as to any provision here, no one yet has, nor is likely to succeed in obtaining anything of that sort."[26] After a few months Caner was offered a curacy in Essex at £50 a year, which he reported that Hutchinson regarded "as an affront, and begg'd I would not so far sink the Dignity of my former Station and character as to accept of it." Caner himself was inclined to take the curacy until he learned that the salary would not even cover the cost of lodgings in the area. In the end, he accepted a sinecure from S.P.G.[27]

The loyalists' difficulty in finding jobs in England, combined with their assumption as to the brevity of their stay, ensured that most of them were never gainfully employed during at least the early years of their exile. Long afterwards a Massachusetts lawyer described his reasoning in this manner: He could probably have qualified to practice law in Britain, he observed, "but I expected every year, to return to America, and well knew, that . . . [this effort] would not have added the smallest weight to my Character in America, and judg'd it to be totally impossible, to make myself known, and obtain business in England."[28]

So, instead of exerting themselves in a futile search for nonexistent jobs, most of the refugees simply looked to the government to supply their financial needs.

[3]

The first requests for aid were submitted to Lord Dartmouth in January and February, 1775, by four New England loyalists who had been forced from their homes by mobs in late 1774. The Lords of the Treasury awarded three of the applicants small sums of money,[29] but, as Hutchinson commented, ·Lord North was "parsimonious beyond example," and so the Treasury's largesse ceased almost as soon as it had begun. Throughout the next year, refugees who asked for financial assistance received only what Hutchinson aptly termed "good words." Even the governor himself was convinced that his salary would not have been continued "if my security had been any thing short of the publick faith."[30]

As the months passed, the number of loyalists in London steadily increased, and the pressures on the ministry rose accordingly. In February 1776 Germain revealed that he had distributed a total of £177 to "Persons who appeared to him to be particular Objects of the Attention of Government," and he persuaded the Treasury to issue him another £200 to continue the practice of "defraying such Contingent Expences of the like Nature as may occasionally occur." But the evacuation of Boston, which took place the following month, brought so many new refugees to London that this small-scale compensation scheme soon proved completely inadequate. In May Germain again went to the Treasury board to request funds to aid the exiles, whom he described as being in a "deplorable situation," and this time the Lords issued £5000 to one of their clerks, Milward Rowe, to be divided among the exiles Germain identified as especially deserving.[31]

Still, though, the ministerial measures fell far short of the loyalists' needs. In July Germain took the further step of recommending that colonial officials' salaries be continued despite their absence from their posts, arguing that "the Honor of Government is pledged to make good [their salaries] to such of them as have adhered to their Allegiance, and stood firm in support of the Constitution." The Treasury agreed with his reasoning, and although Germain's proposal nominally applied only to persons who were paid under the provisions of the Townshend Acts, an identical policy was adopted with respect to admiralty judges, customs officers, and postmasters, whose compensation was drawn from other sources.[32]

But most of the newly arrived loyalists were not fortunate enough to be government officials. What was worse, there were such large numbers of them (said Caner) "that Govmt cannot provide for them all, so think it best to provide for none." The ordinary refugees who were allotted funds still received their payments haphazardly through the colonial office, and by the end of the year Rowe had been issued another £15,000 to be distributed to "sundry persons." The exiles found this arrangement highly unsatisfactory, and they began to press the reluctant ministry to broaden the compensation scheme. In October 1776 twenty-nine Massachusetts loyalists who had not yet received any money petitioned for relief, and two months later the mandamus councilors followed suit.[33] Near the end of the year the New Englanders heard that their memorial was "like to have an answer soon," and in early 1777 the Treasury finally established a formal pension list, allotting annual allowances to approximately one hundred loyalists then resident in London. A majority of the pensioners were New Englanders, since at this point they constituted the majority of Americans in Great Britain, but a number of southerners and exiles from the middle colonies were included on the list as well. The standard stipend was £100 a year, though the mandamus councilors received £200 and other civil officers were awarded up to £500 (salary payments already begun to men like Thomas Oliver were simply transferred to the pension list). Loyalists without pretensions to status or office were generally allotted £40 to £80 annually, and customs officers (whose salaries were being continued under the auspices of the customs commissioners) were given small grants to supplement their other income.[34]

The Treasury Lords, who had shown no great desire to set up the list, added no names to it until midsummer, when in a series of marathon sessions they considered 150 petitions from "American sufferers" and awarded seventy-four new allowances or supplements to current ones. From that time until

December 1781 the Treasury board set aside an average of six days a year, three in summer and three in winter, solely for the discussion of American pension applications. At each session they granted further stipends, and the amount of money allotted for aid to the refugees rose proportionally. In 1777 Rowe was issued more than £58,500, the following year he received an additional £10,000, and although the total fell in 1779, by 1781 the sum supplied him to be paid to loyalists had again climbed to more than £68,000.[35]

As the cost of supporting the refugees increased, so did parliamentary criticism of the pension system. Each year the ministry's request for an appropriation for the loyalists' allowances evoked an acrimonious debate. In 1781, for example, one Member declared that many of the exiles "ought to be rewarded with halters instead of pensions" and charged that "the public money was thus thrown away, not only with profusion and negligence, but to feed a set of vipers, who were gnawing the very entrails of Great Britain, and spilling her best blood." In spite of such repeated challenges, the administration majority held firm on the subject of loyalist stipends throughout the war years. The necessary appropriation was always granted, even after the fall of the North ministry in 1782.[36]

The refugees had their own criticisms of the pension system. If in the minds of certain Members of Parliament the exiles were "drones" living in idleness and luxury, the Americans themselves thought they were not being "suitably rewarded" for their sacrifices on behalf of the crown. In light of the fact that each of them had "forsaken every Thing that was near and Dear" to him in America to serve the king, that each of them had "little expected that my attachment to the authority of this Kingdom, wou'd have reduced myself and family to the Condition in which they are, at this Time," the government's provisions seemed little enough.[37]

Nearly every loyalist, regardless of the amount he received, contended that his pension was insufficient to meet his needs.[38] Yet it appears from scattered evidence that the standard £100 allowance could with some care support a well-to-do single man in London. A family, on the other hand, would probably require more, and the loudest complaints accordingly emanated from refugees with large numbers of dependents.[39] The Treasury indeed seems to have regarded an annual £100 as the necessary minimum income for an American accustomed to a comfortable existence. With that as their starting point, the Lords then either added to or subtracted from that sum depending on their estimate of an applicant's merit and former status. In most cases their awards permitted the recipients to live (as was said of one Marylander) "in a genteel — but strictly œconomical stile."[40]

The chief difficulty with this system was that the loyalists refused to accept it for what it was: a simple, if somewhat cumbersome, charitable operation, intended only to supply them with a minimal temporary support until they could return to their homes. Instead, the refugees insisted on regarding the Treasury pensions as compensation for their sufferings and losses on behalf of Great Britain. Joseph Galloway, who admitted privately that his pension would support him amply (which was all it was meant to do), complained publicly in 1779 that it was "a very small pittance, compared with what I have sacrificed for Government." He elaborated on the thought in a letter addressed to a member of the ministry, probably Germain. "Poverty, my Lord, to persons used to affluence is distressing enough," Galloway asserted, "but if, to that calamity, you add neglect of merit, which in fact amounts to utter contempt, the

Benjamin Thompson, Count Rumford

burthen becomes really insufferable, because it then exceeds the utmost bounds of human patience."[41]

Galloway and others particularly criticized the "inequality" they perceived in the relative size of allowances. A Massachusetts exile observed that "some thro' importunity alone, some by friends and some by a happy manner of telling their own story, and setting forth their own worth and consequence, have been brot into particular notice and handsomely provided for; whilst many of real merit, merely from modesty and reserve, have been wholly neglected."[42] There was some truth to his charge, for the Lords of the Treasury made little attempt to award comparable allotments in comparable cases. Moreover, they were always susceptible to adroitly used influence.[43]

The allowances awarded to friends of Benjamin Thompson, one of the few refugees to achieve success in England, provide a case in point. Thompson, a protégé of Governor John Wentworth of New Hampshire, had fled to Boston in 1774, after his neighbors had correctly suspected him of supplying General Gage with information concerning radical activities in the area.[44] At the evacuation of the city he sailed directly to England, carrying with him his "Miscellaneous Observations upon the State of the Rebel Army." Thompson, with a characteristic flair, insisted on handing the report to Germain in person. Impressed by its contents, the American secretary hired the youthful Thompson as his personal assistant, and during the war Thompson helped to supervise the sending of supplies, equipment, and reinforcements to the colonies. In 1780 he was named undersecretary of state for the northern department.[45]

The loyalists were well aware of Thompson's influence with Germain and regularly sought to make use of it. In 1781 he was described as "uniformly the Patron of our loyal american Brothers," which was something of an exaggeration, but he did at times exert considerable pressure on the ministry on behalf of American acquaintances. Thompson assisted at least six of his friends in their quest for pensions; of one it was said in 1782, "he had originally only 100£ a year but being well acquainted with Mr. Thompson he got him 50£ more." One of the persons he helped, Hannah Winslow, had previously been unable to acquire a pension despite the fact that she had Hutchinson's support for her application.[46]

As Mrs. Winslow's experience implies, it was not always easy to obtain an allowance. Because of the Treasury's policy of considering the loyalists' petitions only once every six months, delays of a year or more were not uncommon if there were initial deficiencies in a memorial. Understandably, the exiles grew bitter as they waited — endlessly, it seemed — to learn whether their applications had been successful. "How thankful ought I to be to that beneficent Congress, which first taught me to live upon air," wrote the Reverend Daniel Batwell of Pennsylvania. "The good Lords of the Treasury seem to think it an wholesome diet, and very much suited to my Constitution." All the applicants would have agreed fully with the disillusioned woman who said of her memorial in 1777: "I had not the smalest thought that it would be attend[e]d with so much trouble, I was told that there was a sume of money voted by Govt for the American Sufferers . . . and I realy thougt . . . that it was a thing of course and that I had as good a right to part as others."[47]

Even when refugees were awarded annual stipends, their troubles were not necessarily ended. As Thomas Hutchinson, Jr., noted, the government transacted business with "the greatest exactness," and the procedures for collecting allowances were exceptionally complex. Loyalists had to call at the Treasury in person each quarter to receive their payments, or, if that was impossible because they lived outside of London, they had to send agents to the Treasury with signed receipts to pick up the money for them. Treasury clerks deducted a fee from each sum paid, and the loyalists were likewise expected to tip the office doorkeeper, so they never received the full amount of their stipends. Furthermore, only Milward Rowe was authorized to make the payments. When he was out of town or simply did not feel like conducting business, no one could collect an allowance. After calling at the Treasury on one such day, a New Englander commented in disgust, "Every expedient is used that craft can devise and power execute to squeeze dependents."[48]

In short, it is not surprising that the Americans found much to criticize in the system that supplied them with their chief means of subsistence. "Inability to provide for one's own support is a mortifying consideration that embitters almost every circumstance of life," wrote one refugee in 1779, and he was echoed two years later by Joseph Galloway's daughter, who declared, "What a humiliating situation are the refugees reduced to from a state of independant affluence, to *rejoice* at the bounty of the public."[49]

And the loyalists had to bear a further burden: that of being treated with what they believed was "Contempt" by the very government for which they had abandoned their homes. As Dr. Peter Oliver, son of the chief justice, put it in 1784: "We are obliged to put up with every insult from this ungrateful people the English, without any redress. . . . What are all the promises of protection and retribution? but to mortify, insult, and disappoint. I have the best authority to say we are well off if our small pittance is not taken from us. Blessed are ye who expecteth nothing, for ye then shall not be disappointed."[50]

In just a few short years the exiles' hopes had turned to

dust. A man like the Reverend Samuel Peters of Connecticut, who had gone to England thinking he could "make himself of much Importance," was reduced within two years to "boast[ing] . . . [of] having learned the Art of not dying upon so small a Pittence" and begging for an increased government pension.[51] Expecting to be lionized in London, the refugees had instead been ignored — an unkind cut indeed for men accustomed to wielding influence in the colonies. Excluded from the kinds of political and social circles in which they had moved in America, the exiles were drawn closer together both by necessity and by choice. They turned to each other for companionship, for if they were not accepted in England they could at least preserve as much as possible of the colonial life they had left behind.

3

America Transplanted to London

I see many faces I have been used to. America
seems to be transplanted to London.
— Samuel Quincy, 1777[1]

THE loyalists who began to gather in London in late
1775 and early 1776 exhibited characteristics common
to any group involuntarily forced into exile. Although no
language barrier divided them from their English hosts, they
largely held themselves aloof from British society. In part
their isolation resulted from the rebuffs they received when
they attempted to enter fully into English political or economic life, but their aloofness can also be attributed to their
own inclinations. They simply preferred the company of
their compatriots — indeed, of the very persons who had been
their closest associates in America. Denied the opportunity to
return to the colonies, the refugees transferred to the British
Isles as much as possible of the familiar pattern of their lives.
Like the Hutchinson family, which continued to live "as
much in the N[ew] Eng[lan]d way as ever we can," the
exiles resisted change in their basic modes of existence. They
tried to obtain American foods, kept themselves informed on
American affairs, and associated almost exclusively with one
another.[2] By such means they preserved for a time the illu-
sion that the war had not permanently altered their lives.

One day soon they would return to their homes in triumph: that prospect they held always before them.

[*1*]

The first task of a refugee newly arrived in London was finding a place to live, and it was not always easy to locate adequate accommodations at a reasonable price. Americans resident in the city tried to help by informing friends of vacant rooms in their neighborhoods, and the exiles in any case understandably preferred to live near acquaintances from the colonies. For these reasons, the loyalists tended to cluster in certain areas of London. On occasion entire streets were practically taken over by refugees, as latecomers were attracted to neighborhoods already replete with their friends.

In 1775, many of the New Englanders arriving from Boston settled in Westminster, rarely going farther north than the Haymarket. The first refugees from the southern colonies, who came about the same time, tended to take up residence on the short streets between the Strand and the Thames. When loyalists began arriving from the middle colonies in large numbers after 1778, they frequently chose to live in Soho or perhaps near Red Lion Square. Only in the neighborhood just north of Oxford Street, sandwiched between Portland Place and the British Museum, did no single provincial group predominate. There, along wide, straight streets, refugees from nearly all the colonies found lodgings in the 1780's.[3]

The pattern of concentration was repeated in suburban areas, for some of the exiles preferred to live in more "retired" sections of the metropolis, ones that were "clean, healthy, and free from Noise." A group of Boston merchants moved to Highgate, near Hampstead Heath; Samuel Peters and other New Englanders settled in Pimlico; some New

Map of a portion of central London showing three of the loyalists' favorite neighborhoods: Soho, the Haymarket, and the Strand. From R. Horwood's map of London, 1799.

Yorkers decided to live in Chelsea; and about twenty Massachusetts refugee families migrated to Brompton Row, Knightsbridge, which one of them described as "country altho only 3/4 of a mile from Hyde Park Corner."[4]

In Brompton and the other neighborhoods the groups of friends constantly exchanged visits. The Boston merchants lodging at Highgate, Hannah Winslow recorded, were "Glad and happy to see me and do every thing in their power to make me Chearful." The New Yorker David Colden chose to reside in Soho because "many more of my American Friends are in this Part of the Town." And, within half an hour after he moved into his rooms on Frith Street, Colden "began to receive visits from the Americans." He later wrote, I "have had a view of many more of my old Friends and Acquaintance, then I Could now have in New York." Colden's experience was not unique. Another New Yorker living in the same area remarked to a neighbor, "Its so much like home," and a third complained that "I never had so little Time to spare. Together with Persons calling upon us, and we in Turn upon them, the whole Day is consumed, and much more of the Night than ought to be dispensed with upon such occasions."[5]

The New Englanders of Westminster engaged in comparable practices. Samuel Quincy, the solicitor general of Massachusetts, spent his days seeing friends, often walking to Brompton to talk with "the whole Circle" there, or else calling upon other acquaintances who lived closer to his lodgings in Parliament Street.[6] The Massachusetts refugees who like Quincy lived near St. James's Park virtually adopted it as their own private preserve. In the spring of 1776 Thomas Hutchinson recorded that "thirteen New Englanders, of which I was one, met by accident to-day in St. James's Park." A year later Edward Oxnard, a young merchant from Falmouth, commented after a walk in the Park that "as usual found it throng'd with Refugees," and Quincy told his wife that it "wears an appearance not unlike the Exchange of Boston."[7] The popularity of the Park as a meeting place continued unabated even after many of the Massachusetts exiles had moved to other parts of the city. In 1778 a New Englander complained that he had been "traversing St James Park till have been quite glad to retire to rest," and the following year Elisha Hutchinson and his father "met a variety of Americans" while walking there.[8]

Although they tended to congregate in certain sections of London, the loyalists often changed their lodgings. If they left town for extended journeys (as many did in the summers), they gave up their rooms and looked for other accommodations when they returned to the city several months later. Furthermore, they were always watchful for less expensive or more conveniently located quarters. Single men changed their residences frequently (perhaps once or twice a year), and even Thomas Hutchinson moved his large family four times between 1774 and 1780.[9]

As a result of this peripatetic existence, many of the refugees used London coffeehouses as their mailing addresses. They therefore had a reason to visit the coffeehouses frequently, not only to pick up letters from and send missives to the colonies, but also to meet friends, read the latest American newspapers, and greet the most recent arrivals from their homeland. Southerners established their headquarters at the Carolina coffeehouse, men from the middle colonies assembled at the New York and Pennsylvania coffeehouses, and northerners frequented the New England coffeehouse. The same geographical divisions that were preserved by the loyalists' choices of places to live were therefore maintained in their usual gathering places. The Massachusetts loyalists seldom called at the Carolina coffeehouse, and the reverse was equally true. Although middle colony refugees did indeed patronize both the Pennsylvania and New York coffeehouses, they did not go so far afield as to call often at either of the establishments that catered to their northern or southern compatriots.[10] In short, there was little sustained intercolonial mingling among the refugees, either in residential neighborhoods or at communal meeting places.

The separation of the provincial groups was heightened by chronological divisions as well. As was pointed out in the first chapter, each section of the thirteen colonies had its own distinct pattern of loyalist emigration, based upon the events of the war, and each exile community in England varied according to a rhythm peculiar to it alone. New Englanders began to gather in London in 1775, and some resided in the city throughout the war, but by 1778, for reasons that will be discussed in chapter 4, many of them had started to disperse through the countryside. At the very time they were abandoning London, refugees from the southern and middle colonies were arriving in large numbers, because of the evacuation of Philadelphia and the strict application of loyalty oath laws in the Carolinas. The size of the Pennsylvania and New York contingents in London swelled steadily for the next six years, but the southerners, on the other hand, returned to their homes in 1779 and 1780, thereby decimating their incipient refugee society. Not until after the evacuation of New York in late 1783 were many loyalists from all areas of the continent resident in the city at exactly the same time. Appropriately, it was only then that the exiles were able to organize themselves into a long-standing, relatively coherent group.

A few exceptions to the general rule of provincial isolation did exist, and they should be noted here. First, some inter-

The Copley Family, by John Singleton Copley. Copley himself stands at rear, his father-in-law Richard Clarke is seated in the foreground. The child with his arm around Mrs. Copley's neck was to become Lord Lyndhurst, Lord Chancellor of England.

colonial contacts came about because of a shared occupation
or a common interest. For example, exiled clergymen from
the various colonies saw each other occasionally, though their
meetings did not usually occur on a regular basis. Similarly,
the professional connection between the artists John Singleton Copley of Massachusetts and Benjamin West of Pennsylvania helped to bring their respective friends into contact
with one another. But in neither case did any lasting relationships form. A Pennsylvanian introduced to the Copley
family at West's thought that Copley's father-in-law's name
was "Hart" (it was Clarke), and even more revealing was the
fact that Thomas B. Chandler, testifying in 1784, stated that
although he had known Jacob Duché well in America before
the war, he "never saw him personally since." At that time,
the two men had been simultaneously resident in London for
six years.[11]

A second exception was those few loyalists who had developed extensive relationships with men from other colonies
before they arrived in England. One such man was Samuel
Shoemaker, a Quaker and former mayor of Philadelphia, who
had served as a civilian administrator of the city during the
British occupation. When Philadelphia was evacuated, Shoemaker removed with the troops to New York, and he remained there until the end of the war. During his stay in
Manhattan, Shoemaker was active in loyalist affairs, and he
came to know many refugees from other provinces who were
then living in the city. When he finally made his way to
London in December 1783, Shoemaker continued to associate with his friends from New York, among them men like
Robert Alexander, a Marylander who had served in the
Second Continental Congress; Daniel Coxe, a New Jersey
councilor; and William Smith, the chief justice of New York.
Even so, however, Shoemaker first encountered another ac-

quaintance from his Manhattan days, Governor Josiah Martin of North Carolina, only after both had been in England for eighteen months.[12]

Another exception was entirely unique: Thomas Hutchinson and his associations. Hutchinson's preeminent position among the loyalists ensured that he would be brought into contact with refugees from throughout the continent, if only because exiles from a number of colonies called at his house seeking advice and assistance. The governor invited those visitors whom he especially liked to return for dinner and conversation, and his non–New England guest list frequently included Thomas Bradbury Chandler and Joseph Galloway. Elisha Hutchinson and his wife Polly grew particularly close to Galloway and his daughter Elizabeth, and the four spent many hours together. But even a man so well known as Hutchinson was on one occasion referred to by a New York refugee as "our friend Govr H——n of Philad[elphi]a."[13]

A fourth and final exception resulted from the occasional physical juxtaposition of the loyalists' lodgings. Although it was not common for exiles from different colonies to live in the same neighborhoods, sometimes they did, and in consequence a few friendly relationships developed across provincial lines. Samuel Quincy became a close associate of the North Carolinian John Burgwin because both lived in the same building. And Arthur Savage of the Boston customs office frequently saw John Savage of Charleston, one of his neighbors at Brompton, especially after they decided they were probably distant cousins. But such contacts were unusual: it appears from copious evidence pertinent to Brompton that the relationship of the Savages had no comparable counterparts.[14]

The various exile circles, then, existed independently of each other. There were a few points of congruence, places where the circles touched or interlocked, but on the whole these connections were both peripheral and accidental. Centered on neighborhoods like Soho or Brompton, reinforced by the insularity of coffeehouse associations and by differentials of time, the little refugee societies were almost totally self-contained. Each revolved around one outstanding figure, usually the man among them who had held the highest political office in their colony before the war. Galloway was the acknowledged leader of the Pennsylvanians; Attorney General John Randolph, of the Virginians; and Lieutenant Governor William Bull, of the South Carolinians. Like Hutchinson (the chief of them all), these men advised other refugees from their home provinces on dealings with the British government, served as hosts at innumerable American dinner parties, and sometimes themselves assisted destitute loyalists. In the strict hierarchy of refugee society, they were usually the called-upon, rarely the callers.[15]

[2]

The Massachusetts community in London is the one most open to analysis both because many of its members arrived in England early in the war and because it is the best documented of the various provincial groups. Thirteen New Englanders kept at least fragmentary journals detailing their daily activities and associations, and the diaries can be supplemented by vast quantities of personal correspondence.[16] A close examination of this evidence can suggest the types of patterns that must have characterized the other refugee societies as well, though they were of course more transitory than that of Massachusetts.

Until his death in 1780 Thomas Hutchinson was the unchallenged leader of the New Englanders in London. His shoes were afterwards filled by the youthful Sir William

Pepperrell, the only native-born American baronet, who had inherited the title and a fortune from his grandfather, the hero of the colonial assault upon Louisbourg in 1745. Neither Hutchinson nor Pepperrell mixed socially with ordinary Massachusetts refugees, instead relating to them as a superior to his inferiors. For instance, recent arrivals from America would pay Hutchinson a courtesy call, and he would graciously return the compliment by inviting them to dinner at his house, but unless the newcomers were of high social status that first invitation was usually also their last.[17] Unsurprisingly, Hutchinson's closest associates (aside from his children and their Oliver in-laws) were the former political and economic leaders of Massachusetts. The most frequent guests at the governor's house were Richard Clarke, Copley's father-in-law and a wealthy Boston merchant; Thomas Flucker, the secretary of the province; Jonathan Sewall; Thomas Oliver; and Charles Paxton, one of the commissioners of American customs. Hutchinson rarely saw either younger or less prosperous refugees, even when the persons in question were friends of his son Elisha.[18]

The New Englanders excluded from an intimate relationship with Hutchinson had their own circles of friends, derived, like his, from their earlier connections in America. Sometimes the social patterns followed town lines, as was the case with a number of former residents of Salem who stayed in touch with each other throughout the war. Other common groupings were based upon age, occupation, or education. So Mrs. John Amory, the wife of a Boston merchant, recorded in her journal her husband's almost constant association with his former business partner Joseph Taylor and with a number of their friends from the Boston commercial community. And the diary of Edward Oxnard reveals that his closest

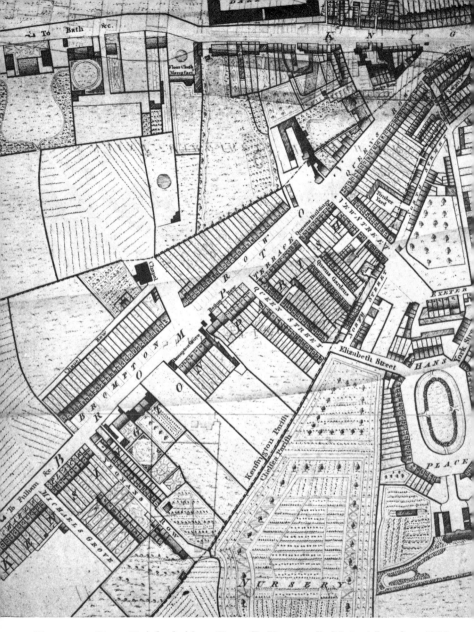

Brompton Row, Knightsbridge. From R. Horwood's Map of London, 1799.

RESIDENTS OF BROMPTON ROW:

No. 1   *Jonathan Sewall*

No. 4   *John Randolph*

No. 7   *Robert Auchmuty*

No. 11   *Thomas Hutchinson Jr.*

No. 14   *John Plenderleath*

No. 17   *Elias Ball*

No. 18   *John Murray (Mass.)*

No. 23   *Samuel Curwen (1777)*

BROMPTON GROVE:

No. 5   *Thomas Flucker*

YEOMAN'S ROW:

No. 1   *Samuel Curwen (1782)*

QUEEN'S ROW:

No. 16   *John R. Grymes (Va.)*

No. 18   *John Graham*

friends in London were, like himself, graduates of Harvard College who were under forty years of age.[19]

The casual relationships among the Massachusetts refugees were formalized to a certain extent by the founding of the New England Club in the late summer of 1775. The organizers of the club were men who had left Boston before the evacuation, a majority of them merchants, lawyers, and civil servants. Although any New Englander could be elected to membership, the exiles who were later added to the organization were almost without exception of similar social status. The club's somewhat elaborate rules provided for weekly dinner meetings to which members could invite guests; among its founders were Taylor, Quincy, Oxnard, Clarke and his son Isaac, Copley, Flucker, and Sewall.[20] After the initial session at the Pauls Head Tavern on August 31, dinners were held at the Queen's Arms, the Crown & Anchor, and the Adelphi. At the latter site in February 1776 Samuel Curwen, a Salem merchant and justice of the peace, attended his first meeting of the club, and he recorded the presence of twenty-one New Englanders, seven of whom had recently joined the group. During the early months of 1776 both Curwen and Oxnard attended club meetings regularly. The highest recorded attendance was twenty-eight, on March 14; the lowest, twelve, on May 17. Sometimes (as on February 15) the club entertained distinguished visitors like Francis Bernard, Hutchinson's predecessor as governor of Massachusetts.[21]

The club, which dissolved during the summer of 1776 while many of its members were vacationing outside of London, reappeared in different form the following September. In his diary Oxnard listed the thirteen members of the "club at Brompton Row." Added to such earlier participants as Curwen, Sewall, the young attorney Sampson Blowers, and

Harrison Gray, Jr., were some recent arrivals from Halifax: the senior Gray; Daniel Leonard; Ward Chipman, a protégé of Judge Sewall's; and Colonel John Chandler, who had been one of the leading citizens of Worcester before the war. All resided at Brompton, and they met to play cards at each other's lodgings approximately every third evening. The sessions continued until the end of March, 1777, when the club once again disbanded for the summer.[22]

This time the hiatus lasted longer than before (because of the dispersal of the Massachusetts refugees), and it was not until July 1782 that Curwen again mentioned attending "an American Thursday dinner club at the New England Coffee-house."[23] But the collapse of their formal organization did not end the general gatherings of the northerners who remained in London. Not only did they organize their own dinner parties at taverns and coffeehouses, but they were also brought together by the social activities of the mercantile firm of Lane Son and Fraser. This company, first organized in 1756 as Lane and Booth, had long been engaged in the New England trade. Many of the Massachusetts exiles had dealt with the firm before 1775, and they continued to rely on its services after they arrived in England. Like other London companies, Lane Son and Fraser shipped goods to America for the exiles, managed their funds, extended credit to them, and sometimes provided them with a mailing address.[24] But, unlike other merchants, the partners — Thomas Lane, his son John, and Thomas Fraser — frequently entertained Massachusetts loyalists at their homes in the city and on their country estates. At one such affair, Oxnard recorded, "drank Madeira, till we were jolly."[25] The cordial relationship of the Lanes, Fraser, and the refugees was founded less on business than on the firm's open sympathy for the loyalists and their cause. The political bias and customary hospitality of the Lanes was in fact so well known that when one New Englander was not invited to John Lane's until after he had been in London for six months, he regarded it as a direct snub and refused the offer.[26]

In all, the Massachusetts exiles may be divided into three separate segments: Hutchinson and his intimates; the many lesser merchants, government employees, and young attorneys who formed the core of the New England Club; and, finally, the poorer refugees who had little or no connection with either of the other groups. Tradesmen, skilled laborers, clerks, and artisans from Massachusetts lived in London throughout the war, but their names never appear in the pages of the diaries of the more well-to-do loyalists.[27] And so, therefore, even the relatively coherent Massachusetts exile community was split along economic and social lines into circles with distinct identities. Despite the proximity of the New Englanders' lodgings, their occasional mutual friends, and their common experience of exile, the social barriers erected in America continued to affect their lives and determine their associations. It is sufficient illustration to quote Curwen's remark upon a chance encounter with Charles Paxton, after both had been living in England for more than five years: "The traces of his countenance have been lost in my memory, and I should have passed him," Curwen observed.[28]

This sort of fragmentation had a noticeably detrimental effect upon the exiles' later attempts to create pressure groups that could advance their interests. Although loyalists from throughout the American continent resided in London during most of the war, each man had few contacts outside his own prewar circle of friends. There was little sense of community among the refugees, each of whom went his own way without much regard for anyone else. Not until 1779 did the exiles attempt to act in concert, and then they achieved only limited (and short-lived) success in building a comprehensive organization.

The lack of cohesion among the refugees also suggests something about the revolutionary movement itself. The loyalists' restricted vision, their provincialism, throws into sharp perspective the successful unification of the Americans under the Continental Congress. What an achievement that unity must have been, if the social patterns exhibited by the refugees in London were at all typical of prerevolutionary America. Not even the overwhelming pressures of exile forced loyalists from different colonies to associate regularly with one another. Yet at the very same time the revolutionaries were in the process of forging a coalition that — however tentative and fragile — successfully defeated the greatest military power in the world. The contrast is both striking and significant.

[*3*]

Obviously, the loyalists did not spend every waking minute seeing each other and sitting in coffeehouses. They were, after all, residents of London, then as now one of the great cities of the world. Supported mainly by government largesse and therefore not required to work to earn their keep, they were able (their limited income notwithstanding) to take advantage of the wide range of attractions available in the metropolis. Although they could not participate in what one of them called "the glitter and refinement" of London society, they could — and did — indulge in many less expensive pleasures.[29]

One of the Americans' "invariable amusements" was walking around the city. Some of the more energetic exiles trekked all the way to Richmond or Hampton Court (a two-day journey), but most confined their excursions to the immediate vicinity of London itself. They wandered about the city streets, sometimes stopping to visit friends, or they strolled in the parks on the outskirts of town. In the winter the Americans watched the skaters on the Serpentine in Hyde Park; in the spring and summer they admired the flowers in Kensington and Kew Gardens. One April Sunday in 1777, Oxnard recorded that Hyde Park was so crowded it seemed "like a Holiday and a Fair." St. James's Park was "equally astonising" that day, being filled with Londoners "from the remotest parts of the City [who had come] to enjoy that pure Air which they are not acostom'd to in the thick settled parts of the Town."[30]

The refugees could also view without charge the city's great public monuments. Westminster Abbey and St. Paul's Cathedral were edifices to be admired in awe, and the Tower of London and the British Museum filled their time in a somewhat less elevated manner. Housed at the Tower were a number of interesting "Curiosities," in particular a zoo that fascinated a number of the exiles. The young Boston physician John Jeffries, who had a taste for adventure and high living, was a master of the trenchant comment: after a visit to the zoo he noted pointedly that the monkeys there seemed "almost human," displaying "more sensibility than a large part of what is called [the] human race." Jeffries and the other Americans were also impressed by the exhibits at the British Museum, which could be seen only by permission of its governing authorities. A Marblehead clergyman especially liked "the Ostrich's egg as big as a quart pot" and "the artificial Crab made out of precious Stones." On the other hand, Chief Justice William Smith was not so pleased with his visit to the museum, for his request "to see the Flesh of an Egyptian Mummy out of the Frames in which they were incased" was refused by a museum employee. Smith, a self-centered man who never hesitated to ask for special treatment, complained in his journal that his guide was "not a Man of Manners, and if a Philosopher readier I believe to acquire than impart Knowledge."[31]

When they had exhausted the public sites, the refugees could visit many privately owned amusements by paying small fees. As Smith and his fellows soon discovered, "your Pocket may be emptied in this great Town by the innumerable Exhibition of Spectacles of one Kind and another in several Streets and Quarters of the City." The exiles viewed scale models of European cities, exhibitions of fine china and stained glass, floral displays, and flower gardens.[32] A Bostonian paid to watch a man eat stones, and Smith spent a shilling to see the "Learned Pigg" tell time, count the number of persons in the room, and answer other questions. In addition, the refugees often attended art exhibits, particularly when works by Copley and West were on display. Copley's *The Death of Pitt* was one of the Americans' favorites, and he presented several of them with "perpetual Ticket[s]" to its showing at a public gallery.[33]

Some of the ways in which the refugees passed the time during the long days in London seem repulsive to modern eyes. Several went to Sunday services at Newgate Prison, in company with debtors, felons in chains, and a number of convicts under sentence of death. On Christmas Day, 1785, the young New Englander Thomas Aston Coffin was there, and in the congregation were fourteen condemned criminals, two under fifteen years of age. "These have a Pew appropriated to them, painted Black, with a Table in the Centre, upon which is Placed a Coffin — all which added to the Clinking of Irons make a most gloomy Impression," he told his mother.[34] The exiles also occasionally attended the public executions at Tyburn. Oxnard appropriately had his pocket picked as he watched the hanging of five criminals in 1775, and Jeffries termed the six executions he saw one day in 1783 "an awfull and solemnly tremendous sight." Yet Jeffries was even more impressed by the death of the French spy Francis Henry LaMotte, which he had seen two years earlier. According to the doctor, the condemned man conducted himself in a "cool and gentlemanlike manner," and Jeffries was no less cool as he calmly set down in his diary a description of the beheading and the drawing and quartering that were ceremoniously inflicted on LaMotte's corpse after his death.[35]

In the evenings, the loyalists often attended acrobatic exhibitions at Sadler's Wells and Astley's Amphitheatre. The tumbling, juggling, and balancing acts that formed the core of the shows amazed the Americans, who had never seen anything quite like it before. "It is almost incredible to conceive the feats of Bodily agility that are perform'd, unless one were an eye witness," wrote Oxnard after a visit to Sadler's in 1775. A year later, though, he had revised his estimate somewhat, observing, "The Tumbling may be justly s[ai]d to be extraordinary the rest of the performance mere Bufoonery." Astley's, which was London's first permanent circus, added "incredible Feats of Horsemanship, a Horse Conjurer, Pantomimes, Air-Balloons, and Fire-Works" to the other acts. Dr. Jeffries especially liked the "imitation of various Singing Birds" and the "Puppet Scenes of Dancing, Duck Shooting, vessell sailing with a Storm and Shipwrack" that he saw there in 1779.[36]

In addition to the acrobatic performances, the loyalists occasionally went to magic shows and lectures, and they sometimes sat in on the discussions at the various workingmen's debating societies, which were open to the public for a small charge. But Oxnard and the other colonists sneered at the "meer mechanicks, who tho't themselves sufficiently able to dispute on the most abstruse and intricate subjects." After listening to a discussion of the question, "Which is the most censurable the Boldness of the Women or the Foppery of the Men of the present Age?" Smith commented that a "great many low laughable Things were said, none stuck to the Point." Of all the loyalists, only Samuel Curwen seemed to enjoy his evenings at the debating associations.[37]

During the theater season, which ran from September to May, many exiles attended performances at Drury Lane and Covent Garden. Both theaters were cavernous by today's standards, but the demand for entrance was so great that the loyalists frequently suffered "thumps, squeezes, and almost suffocation" when they attempted to gain admission. The usual cost of a seat ranged from four shillings sixpence down to one shilling, and most of the refugees chose to sit in the "pit," which was priced between the expensive boxes and the cheaper galleries. The patrons sat on backless benches, and if the play or its cast was especially popular, the spectators were packed together like sardines. A typical evening's performance began with music, then came a five-act play, complete with entr'acte entertainment, followed by some sort of afterpiece, ordinarily a farce or pantomime. The entire affair lasted five or six hours, so it is apparent that the customers received their money's worth.[38]

The refugees were avid theatergoers throughout their years in London and, like other devotees of the stage, they soon developed their favorite plays and actors. Those Americans who arrived in the city in 1775–1776 were fortunate enough to see David Garrick before his retirement, and they were overawed by his great abilities. After watching Garrick perform in *Much Ado About Nothing* in the fall of 1775,

*The Wonderful Pig: one of the attractions viewed by
William Smith in 1785*

Q. to be DEBATD
next Thursday Eve
HOW FAR is it
from the 1 of Aug
to the foot of
WESTMINSTERBRIDGE

The ROBIN HOOD SOCIETY.

Pub. May 25 1783 by W Humphrey. N° 227 Strand.

The Robin Hood Society: a satirical look at one of the London workingmen's debating groups

Oxnard wrote, "He is without exception a compleat actor in all the parts he acts in. He at once enters into the Spirit of it and appears the Character the Author design'd." Jeffries, who arrived too late to see Garrick, quickly became an admirer of Mrs. Siddons. On one occasion he thought a play "unworthy of her" and on another he recorded effusively, "Her sweet upbraidings — and most delicate natural yet extreme Passions in the last scene of Lunacy was above description and [as] charming as the most fertile imagination can conceive."[39]

But the exiles also frequently found fault with the plays they saw. Samuel Curwen, who was the most stringent American critic of the theater, declared in 1780 that "actors fall below my idea of just imitation; to my seeming they overact, underact, or contradict nature." He described himself as "totally devoid of all relish" for the farces and pantomimes that followed the main play, for, he observed, "I consider them as a proof among many others of the depravity of the present day. I would fain call it vulgar." Instead of engaging in the more overt forms of disapproval practiced by dissatisfied London audiences, though, Curwen and the other refugees expressed disdain for the spectators' habits of hissing or throwing apples at performances that did not please them. The loyalists left no room for doubt that they thought the influence of the "Commonality" on the London theater an unqualifiedly detrimental one.[40]

Implicit in the Americans' many comments on the vulgarity of the customers' tastes and the boisterousness of their behavior and, indeed, in their observations on the debating societies was a contempt for the capacities and opinions of the lower-class Londoner. The theatergoing loyalists were educated, relatively well-to-do Americans, and they were not accustomed to the democracy that obtained in the city's

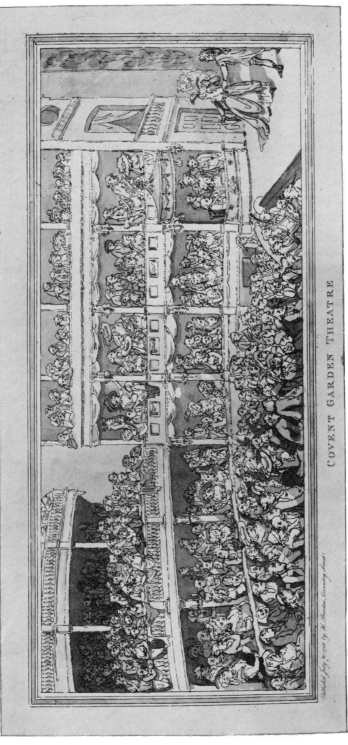

COVENT GARDEN THEATRE

The interior of Covent Garden Theatre, 1786

WINTER AMUSEMENT.

Dublin Printed for Will.ᵐ Allen   Nᵒ 32 Dame Street.

Winter Amusement: skating in Hyde Park

SUMMER AMUSEMENT.

Printed and Sold by Wm Allen.

Nº 32 Dame Street.

Summer Amusement: an afternoon at a pleasure garden

public places. After an evening at the Drury Lane, for example, William Smith concluded that the theater performed a socially useful function because its audiences were "taken from Mischief" elsewhere. "It consists with the Public Peace to amuse the Populace perpetually, if they were [not] drawn together for amusing Instruction they would be worse imployed," he reasoned magisterially.[41]

The refugees expressed much the same attitude about the clientele of Vauxhall and Ranelagh Gardens. The pleasure gardens were open only in the summertime (when the theaters were closed) and they, like the playhouses, drew a cross section of London society. Anyone with the small entrance fee could enter the gardens and stroll along the walks, listening to music supplied by the gardens' orchestras. Food was available for those who wanted and could afford it, but many of the customers simply spent the evening promenading with friends, gazing at the crowds.[42] Vauxhall, in Lambeth, was the livelier of the two attractions, with a more heterogeneous group of patrons. Smith termed Vauxhall "a School of Vice," noting that it only cost one shilling to enter. Although the walks near the orchestra were well lighted, he noted, "there are darker Walks beyond them, very properly called the Lovers Walks, and the Women who come without Men are generally to be suspected." Traditionally, the last night of the season at Vauxhall was particularly boisterous. Oxnard, who attended the final evening in 1776, described the scene vividly. First a pickpocket was arrested, then several ladies were ejected because of their "preposterous Headresses." A barber impersonating an officer was "severly handled," and finally "the Young Bucks behav'd extreamly riotous — broke the Lamps, Kick'd the waiters — Bully'd every[body] — till some were committed into the Hands of the Constable."[43]

Ranelagh, located in Chelsea, was somewhat more fashionable and definitely less rowdy than Vauxhall. Its major attraction was not its gardens but rather the rotunda that stood in the midst of the park. This large building sheltered both the orchestra and the customers and was sometimes used for special events. Oxnard, though he did not care for Ranelagh on his first visit, soon changed his mind. After an evening there in the spring of 1776, he wrote, "This place may be s[ai]d to be the resort of the best Company in London — much pleasd with my Ev[enin]gs Entertainment."[44]

As Smith had indicated, the pleasure gardens (and the city streets as well) were frequented by the many London prostitutes. Of all the refugee Americans, only John Jeffries left a record of his relationships with these "charming alluring Women of the Town." Jeffries fancied himself as something of a playboy after his wife's death in 1780, and he attended a number of masquerade balls and "routs" at which he proved readily receptive to propositions from various ladies of the night. He eventually persuaded a Mrs. Callen "to put herself under my sole protection," but he also formed numerous more casual liaisons. After an appointment with Miss Betsy Spencer, he wrote in self-justification, "Only a compliance to the laws of nature, when no person is interested cannot be criminal — if they be — my Creator forgive me."[45]

Jeffries was unique among the refugees not only because of the frankness of his diary, but also because he participated in one of the most renowned events of the day: the first balloon flight across the English Channel. All the loyalists, in common with the other residents of Europe in 1783, were utterly astonished by the invention of the "air balloon," but few of them saw more than just a passing fad in the ascensions conducted frequently in London after November 1783. William Smith, to cite a prime example, fumed that "these Experiments cost the Nation much in the Detachmt. of the People from their Labour and Trades. . . . The Crowds that flock after these silly Sights dishonor the English Nation."[46] Jeffries, on the other hand, was intrigued by the opportunity for scientific study presented by the flights, and his inquiring mind, coupled with his yen for adventure, led him to make an "aerial voyage" over London in November 1784 with the French balloonist Jean Pierre Blanchard. A few months later, on January 7, 1785, Jeffries and Blanchard ascended from the heights near Dover Castle with the intention of flying to France, and, although they had great difficulty remaining aloft, they eventually landed safely in a forest outside Calais. The two aeronauts were effusively welcomed to France by the Calais officials, and their journey to Paris can only be described as triumphal. In the city itself the greetings were equally unrestrained. The exultant Jeffries met members of the French nobility, was introduced to the royal family, and gloried in the lusty cheers he received from audiences at the Paris Opera and the Comédie Française.[47]

Other loyalists also traveled to France, but they did so by more conventional means. Both before the Franco-American alliance of 1778 and after the signing of the preliminary peace treaty in 1782, the refugees often visited Paris and the French countryside. Thomas A. Coffin thought France "a fine country," flawed only by the fact that its government did not resemble England's closely enough. But he found little to admire in King Louis XVI, "as stupid a looking Gentleman as you wou'd wish to see," or in his queen, Marie Antoinette, whom he described as "bold looking" and "fond of shew and expence, not caring for her Subjects, nor possessing their Affection or Esteem." And Paris too drew its share of criticism from the Americans. Polly (Mrs. Elisha) Hutchinson, though praising the city's public buildings, found the streets "narrow and dirty," permeated with "disagreable smells."

Jeffries and Blanchard cross to the coast of France, January 7, 1785. The print is inaccurate because Jeffries' diary reveals that the wings and other appendages of the basket were jettisoned over the Channel.

Nevertheless, she had to admit that Notre Dame Cathedral was "the most grand and beautiful structure I ever saw." Mrs. John Amory disagreed, terming Notre Dame "much short of my Expectations," but she was in her turn overawed by Versailles, especially its Hall of Mirrors, which she deemed "prehaps [sic] the finest Room in the world."[48]

For the most part, the loyalists who ventured outside of London confined their sight-seeing to the British Isles. Although they complained of the costs of traveling, the exiles thought with Peter Oliver that "the full Purse cannot be lightened in a more agreeable Expence." And so they took as many trips as was possible on their limited budgets. By sharing rooms and coaches, the Americans managed to travel economically through much of Great Britain.[49] Their most frequent destinations were the towns along the southwestern English coast, for the simple reason that the weather there was preferable to that of London. Those refugees who could afford it moved their families to the seashore for the summer months, and those who could not finance a permanent relocation still spent as much time as possible away from the "disagreable" climate of London during the "warm season."[50]

The American vacationers frequented the same resorts that were popular with their English contemporaries: Brighton, Margate, and Bristol Wells in the summer, and during the winter months, Bath, which Thomas Hutchinson called "perhaps the most elegant city in England," and which Oxnard termed "the most noted place in this Kingdom for disepation."[51] One observer accurately noted that although the chief attraction of Bath was supposed to be the beneficial effects of taking its waters, "not one half" those who flocked to the city came "for their health." Instead, the patrons of the Pump Room enjoyed an active social season, and Hutchinson, whose son Billy actually was in Bath to recover his health, felt compelled to caution the young man "against losing in the ballroom in the evening what he gains in the baths in the day." Other loyalist visitors often made no pretense of being ill. A Virginian found the four balls a week "delightfull," and he uninhibitedly joined in the fun at the gaming tables, in addition to attending "routs without number — fine concerts etc. etc." But he soon discovered that "my cash departs very fast much more then what it did in London," and for that reason he was forced to cut his visit short.[52]

In spite of this perennial lack of funds, the exiles had a relatively bearable existence before the winter of 1777. The war presented no immediate threat to their well-being, though they were, like Oxnard, occasionally "much distress'd" by "thot's of America and the situation of my friends." They remained serenely confident that their sojourn in England was temporary, that it would come to a close once the British triumph had been achieved. They seldom, if ever, seriously considered the possibility that the royal forces in the colonies might be defeated. But all this ended when news of the rebel victory at Saratoga reached them in early December 1777. According to Hutchinson, there was "universal dejection," and, he commented, "Everybody in a gloom: most of us expect to lay our bones here."[53] The refugees' self-assurance had been shattered, and with it went the illusionary world they had so carefully constructed during the three preceding years. From that time on, their lives were never the same again.

4

A Distressing Condition

God knows what is for the best, but I fear our
perpetual banishment from America is written in
the book of fate; nothing but the hopes of once
more revisiting my native soil, enjoying my old
friends within my own little domain, has hitherto
supported my drooping courage; but that prop
taken away leaves me in a condition too distressing
to think of.

— SAMUEL CURWEN, 1777[1]

THE refugees in London, who eagerly devoured any news
about the progress of the war, well knew the importance
of the campaign of 1777. They expected it to "crush the
Rebellion, in all Probability," but at the same time they
recognized the "fatal consequences" that would ensue if for
some reason the British army failed to achieve its objectives.
They were therefore surprised when Sir William Howe chose
to attack Philadelphia, which they thought "rather a clog" to
the overall strategy, and were even more astonished when he
decided to transport his troops by sea in a "monstrously
tedious and expensive Voyage."[2] But the exiles nevertheless
believed that General John Burgoyne's "skill, understanding,
and energy" would carry the day, and so when they learned
of Burgoyne's defeat at Saratoga they were "confounded and
staggared" by the news. Jonathan Boucher admitted that he

had been "set up a little, only to have the heavier Fall," and, he confessed, "my Hopes are sunk to the lowest Ebb."[3]

What happened at Saratoga completely altered the refugees' expectations. They still thought they would one day return to America, but they now knew that day would not come in the foreseeable future. The loyalists had been biding their time in London, living from day to day, making few long-term commitments. After Saratoga many of them recognized the necessity of changing their mode of existence. They began to arrange for more adequate and less costly housing for themselves and their families, and larger numbers of them started to look for relatively permanent employment. Moreover, Saratoga affected the ministry's assumptions about the war as well, and government policy towards the exiles changed significantly in 1778 and thereafter.

[*1*]

The refugees' London lodgings had always been expensive and uncomfortably cramped, but they had willingly endured these disadvantages as long as they thought their stay in England would be a brief one. The disaster at Saratoga convinced them that the British victory they awaited would come neither easily nor quickly, and as a direct result many of them left the city for good in the spring of 1778. By May, as William Browne, a Salem mandamus councilor, accurately observed, the Americans who had "hitherto resided in London in hopes of a happy settlement of the national dispute" were "generally dispersing themselves over the Kingdom as inclination or hopes of advantage land them." At the end of the summer Thomas Hutchinson, Jr., told his brother Elisha (who had joined the exodus) that "the very few Americans that are left in and about London wear pretty long faces . . .

it is now become a rare thing to meet a Yankee even in the Park."[4]

The loyalists did not choose their new places of residence without some serious thought. As they were already well aware, "with out sum American Friends lives near you it is very difficult to form any society in this Country," and so just as they had congregated in certain London neighborhoods, they also gathered in a few favored provincial towns. Several former Salemites settled in Shrewsbury, encouraging others of their townsmen to join them. A "great number" of Americans, especially Virginians, went to Glasgow. And a large colony of New Yorkers eventually developed in Chester.[5] As early as August 1778 Hutchinson described one of his lengthy trips through the countryside as an "American Visitation," and by 1786 the loyalists were so scattered throughout Britain that Thomas Coffin reported after a journey that there was "scarce a Town that I passed in which I did not find some American Acquaintance."[6]

One of the first refugees to abandon London was Peter Oliver, who had greatly admired Birmingham when he visited it in 1776, and who decided to move there with his niece Jenny Clarke in the spring of 1778. Although he found Birmingham less interesting than London, Oliver was content with his new life. In a 1779 letter to his granddaughter Polly he jocularly compared the two cities. If in London there were pickpockets, he remarked, in Birmingham there was "no money to pick out of Pockets"; and if London contained people who could drink with their feet and walk on their heads, Birmingham was full of many experts in "Drinking at the Mouth and not being able to walk at all." In time, Polly and her husband Elisha Hutchinson joined Oliver in Birmingham, as did his son Dr. Peter Oliver, his niece and nephew Louisa and Daniel Oliver, his niece Sarah Clarke Startin and her husband Charles, and Benjamin Pickman.[7]

Life in Birmingham was at best unexciting. Pickman's laconic journal recorded his days succinctly: "[May] 10. [1783]. Spent the Evening with Judge Oliver; Mr and Mrs Hutchinson there. 11. Spent the Evening with Jos. Green Esq. Four Russians there. 12. Dind with Mr. Hutchinson and spent Eve with Mr Pemberton." In such an atmosphere, any event that broke the monotony was welcome. The high points of 1782, detailed in Elisha's diary, were the public whipping of a female lawbreaker and the town's celebration of Admiral Rodney's victory over the French fleet in the West Indies.[8] Unsurprisingly, some of the resident Americans were not as satisfied with this kind of life as was the chief justice. His son Peter termed the local theater "poor doings," and Francis Coffin (the younger brother of Thomas), who was assigned to Birmingham in 1786 as an army recruiter, was thankful that he had connections with the Olivers, for, he declared, "without a person has an extensive acquaintance this is the dullest place in England."[9]

On the other hand, according to William Browne, life in Cowbridge, Wales, was even more "sober" than that in Birmingham. But, Browne said, he preferred the "peace and quietness" of Cowbridge to the "turbulence and tumult" he had so recently experienced. Describing Wales as a "plentiful, pleasant Country," having "much the appearance of the best parts of N[ew] E[ngland]," Browne persuaded other Massachusetts exiles to join him in the area. His half brother John Sargent and Colonel John Murray also settled at Cowbridge, and a few miles away in Cardiff William Apthorp found the life so delightful that his enthusiastic letters convinced the initially skeptical Henry Caner to move there as well.[10] Kidwelly, forty miles from Cowbridge, drew

Hutchinson's nephew Samuel Mather and his wife, Jonathan Dowse of Salem, and, for a time, Daniel Oliver. Meanwhile Thomas Flucker and Colonel Richard Saltonstall of Haverhill joined Browne in enjoyment of Cowbridge's "altogether domestick" pleasures, and in November 1780 Browne reluctantly informed another friend, James Putnam, that there were no more empty houses available in the town. Henry Caner liked his life in Wales, though he missed not serving a parish, and Browne probably spoke for his neighbors when he assured a friend, "We should sooner meditate a journey to Heaven than to London."[11]

But even Browne, who so craved quietude, became bored with existence in the little Welsh community. In March 1780 he described his life as "without employment, without entertainment, without Books and without conversation, — banished from every thing that has life and motion," and so he did not hesitate to accept the governorship of Bermuda when it was offered to him a year later. After his departure the original Cardiff-Cowbridge group disintegrated, though at the same time other refugees discovered the advantages of living in the area. The John Ervings of Boston settled at Haverford West, observing "the most severe oeconomy," and a number of southern loyalists likewise chose to live in Wales "for cheapness."[12] They were followed by a large group of interrelated New Yorkers that included the John Plenderleaths (the daughter and son-in-law of William Smith) and Mr. and Mrs. Robert Leake. Leake, like his predecessors, enjoyed living in Cardiff all the more because of the fact that so many of his friends and relatives settled nearby. In early 1788 he described his family as living "in the same Stile" as their plain food, "never dreaming of exceeding at our Tables, except indulging now and then with a Fowl."[13]

In Bristol, across the Severn River from Cardiff, the loyalists gathered in greater numbers than anywhere else outside of London. After a visit to Bristol in 1777 Thomas Hutchinson wrote, "I think, take in all circumstances, and I should prefer living there to any place in England." The other Massachusetts refugees must have agreed with him, for they began to settle in Bristol in 1776, and by October 1777 Curwen could count eighteen New England exiles (some of them visitors) in the town.[14] Initially, Henry Barnes, a Marlborough merchant, complained that the loyalists met with a "Cold reception" from the pro-rebel inhabitants of Bristol, and he later advised a relative not to move to the town because the residents were "so selfish and so united among themselves as to their Interests that a Stranger stands no chance among them." Yet despite this discouraging report the general exodus from London in the spring of 1778 brought many more refugees to the port city in search of "a pleasant place" where the cost of living was reputed to be "a third cheaper" than in the metropolis. A year later Isaac Royall, a mandamus councilor from Medford, complained in London that so many of his friends had gone to Bristol that "I shall be left alone from all my American acquaintances except Mr. Fluc[k]er."[15]

As Royall's comment implied, most of the New Englanders who settled in Bristol were either related to or close associates of each other, and so the Barnes family, for example, found itself "at no loss for agreeable Company." But the little American society could also be too exclusive, as George Inman, a Massachusetts refugee who moved to Bristol in 1780, soon discovered. Although at first he was received warmly by his fellow countrymen, Inman later recalled, he managed to offend a few members of the group, and afterwards his relations with all of them were characterized by "coolness" and more by "form, than friendship."[16]

Life in the Massachusetts community in Bristol was identical in its broad outlines to that led by the loyalists in Birmingham or Wales or London. The refugees called frequently at the American coffeehouse, hoping for news from the colonies; they walked or rode in the countryside, especially to the nearby resort town of Bristol Wells; and they constantly entertained each other and visitors from London at tea or dinner. As late as 1786 Mrs. Barnes reported, "Wee have seventeen American familys in Bristol, very Genteel well bred People, all of one heart, and one mind."[17]

The Massachusetts loyalists were not the only American exiles attracted to Bristol. If Thomas Hutchinson compared the city to Boston, Pennsylvanians thought it "like our dear Philadelphia," and they too settled there in relatively large numbers. Also drawn to Bristol were Carolinians like William Bull and Elias Ball, who recorded in 1785 that the town had been "strongly Recommended" to him as a place of residence.[18] But just as there had been little contact between loyalists from different provinces in London, so too in Bristol the refugee circles remained largely separate. Mrs. Barnes enjoyed the company of the Charles Startins of Philadelphia, but Mrs. Startin was herself a Bostonian, the daughter of Richard Clarke. And when Samuel R. Fisher and Samuel Shoemaker, both exiled Philadelphians, visited Bristol in 1783 and 1784, respectively, they spent their time seeing other refugee Pennsylvanians, never encountering a New Englander — in the same way that journeying Massachusetts loyalists visited only their own fellow provincials living in the city.[19]

[2]

In addition to affecting the loyalists' decisions on places to live, Saratoga altered their approach to seeking employment.

Faced with the certainty of years of exile (though not, as yet, with the notion that the banishment would be permanent and irrevocable), the refugees began to look for more than just temporary positions. Instead of concentrating their job-hunting efforts solely in the British Isles, they started to request posts elsewhere in the empire. In doing this the Americans were taking the first steps towards breaking their ties with the thirteen colonies. Their acceptance of positions in other British provinces indicated a willingness on their part, though of course still a very hesitant one, to abandon their homeland in favor of another, more "British," environment. And they were aided in their renewed search for jobs by a shift in governmental policy. Recognizing that the refugees would not soon be able to return to their former occupations, the ministry began to look more favorably upon loyalists' applications to fill secular or religious positions within the empire.

The new trend first became apparent in 1779, when James Hume, the deputy attorney general of Georgia, was appointed chief justice of East Florida and Samuel Quincy obtained a post in the Antigua customs service.[20] The following year William Browne was named governor of Bermuda, and in 1781 Daniel Leonard became chief justice of the same colony. Both men acquired their jobs through the intercession of Benjamin Thompson, who also arranged to put Browne's salary on a more secure footing than that of his predecessor (while increasing it as well), and who persuaded the Treasury to double Leonard's pension because the position of chief justice was unsalaried. Browne and Leonard remained in their posts for some years after the end of the war, so Thompson's arrangements must have proved satisfactory.[21]

Another indication of the different atmosphere was the fact

that missionaries of the Society for the Propagation of the Gospel in Foreign Parts finally began to obtain reassignments outside the thirteen colonies. The problem was that the clergymen, who were accustomed to a temperate climate and a relatively civilized existence, were often not very pleased with their new posts. In an extreme case, the Reverend James Barker of Maryland exchanged New Providence in the Bahamas, where he suffered from the heat, for Trinity Bay, Newfoundland, where he stayed only two weeks before deciding that he had been better off in the West Indies. Barker was eventually given a Bermuda living by Browne and there he settled, though as a result of his wanderings the S.P.G. dismissed him from its ranks.[22]

Less peripatetic but no less dissatisfied was Joshua W. Weeks of Marblehead, who in 1779 was named missionary to Annapolis Royal, Nova Scotia. On a visit to the settlement he found a church that he considered "unfit for the performance of religious worship," a congregation that treated him "civilly" but seemed to have little inclination to contribute to his support, and a life so rough that he was afraid for his family's safety. After beating a hasty retreat to Halifax, he began trying to persuade the Society that he could not possibly take up permanent residence at his mission.[23] During the next two years, over the vehement objections of the S.P.G., which insisted that he live in Annapolis Royal, Weeks evolved the practice of spending summers at his mission and winters in Halifax, where he not only assisted in the parish but also ran a small school. Although the S.P.G. in consequence replaced him with a more dedicated missionary, Weeks' good standing with the Halifax notables gave him an unbeatable advantage: with their help he officially retained the position of chaplain to the troops garrisoned at Annapolis

Royal, thereby receiving the pay for that appointment while his successor did the work.[24]

The change in the official British attitude towards the loyalists manifested itself not only in a greater willingness to use them to fill existing vacancies, but also in the development of schemes to employ them in relatively large numbers. During the later years of the war the North administration deliberately began to try to provide jobs for the refugees, both by creating a new colony specifically for them and by restoring them to civil positions in the American territories conquered by royal troops. The plans gave new hope to office-seeking exiles, but neither project ever came fully to fruition.

The glimmerings of the idea that was to become a grandiose scheme to found a province called "New Ireland" in what is now Maine began in 1778 when a Massachusetts refugee, John Nutting, proposed to Germain that a fort be built on Penobscot Bay. Stressing the region's strategic importance, Nutting argued that possession of it could prove invaluable in the fight to subdue the rebellious colonists. Other residents of the area later took up the cudgel on behalf of the idea, noting that Penobscot was a major source of masts, timber, and pitch for the British navy. These arguments struck a responsive chord in Lord North, who wanted to develop "some method of permanently providing for the American Sufferers, who will soon be too numerous to be provided for as they have hitherto been. Cannot not [*sic*] a practicable and advantageous plan be devised of settling them in the provinces, which still remain connected with England and of granting them Lands with other encouragements to induce them to settle there?"[25]

Within a month after North expressed his thoughts on the subject, a plan had been formulated that combined the concerns of the Penobscot group with those of the ministry. On

September 3, 1778, Germain disclosed to Clinton that the government was considering settling the loyalists at Penobscot, in order to compensate them, assure a supply of timber to the navy, and protect Nova Scotia all at the same time.[26]

A number of loyalists, including Governor John Wentworth, fell in with the scheme enthusiastically. Thomas Hutchinson, on the other hand, thought the idea "preposterous" because "the American Refugees were in general persons of liberal education, not brought up to labour, and many of them too far advanced in life to begin the world [anew]." Consequently, when Hutchinson was offered the governorship of the new colony in October 1779, he replied dryly that the outcome of the current campaign should be known "before we thought any further on measures for restoring peace to America."[27] Despite Hutchinson's skepticism and delays caused by the fact that Nutting was captured by the Americans on his return voyage to the colonies, planning for the settlements proceeded apace. By August 1780 a formal structure of government for New Ireland drawn up by William Knox had been approved by the king and his advisers. At first a governor and council were to rule the colony, and later a legislature, including an upper house appointed for life, would be added. Land was to be distributed according to merit, and loyalists with large holdings were to be permitted to lease part of them to tenants. (Knox defended this last provision on the grounds that New Ireland would thereby come to resemble New York, which he thought the most loyal of all the colonies.) He explicitly suggested that the system could serve as a model for the proper government to be used throughout a pacified America.[28]

Hutchinson having died two months before the plan won official acceptance, the post of governor was offered to Peter

Oliver, who accepted with alacrity. Daniel Leonard was named chief justice, and Benjamin Thompson exerted considerable pressure to see that the other offices were also filled with his friends.[29] But no further appointments were made before the plan became bogged down in legal technicalities. Since Penobscot had traditionally been regarded as part of Massachusetts, English legal officers raised doubts about the legitimacy of establishing a new colony there. In September 1780 Germain, disgusted by the delay, asked Knox, "Can we not take possession of it as a Conquerd Country and Establish a Government in it . . . and leave the discussion of the rights of the Charter, to the final Settlement of the Colonies, or till we can legally annul it?"[30]

Unaware of the legal difficulties, the loyalists assumed that the plan would soon be put into operation. Daniel Batwell wrote from London that it would be "a very good thing for this Town, as it will rid us of the Swarms of Bostonians — And it will vex the Saints at Boston, which will be another good thing." By early 1781 rumors reported that Sir William Pepperrell would replace Oliver as governor, but Pepperrell told a friend he would not accept the position "if I cou'd possibly avoid it." A number of refugees made plans to settle in the area if the new colony ever materialized, but despite Germain's hope that the scheme "would be in forwardness by midsummer" 1781, nothing was done, and after Yorktown it was too late.[31]

The proposal to compensate loyalists with land and employment in a new settlement therefore failed to attain the desired end. However, at the same time as the plans for Penobscot were being considered, the ministry had another scheme in motion: to return refugees to the positions they had held in provinces that had now been retaken by the king's forces. In January 1779, after the ministry was in-

formed of the success of Clinton's expedition to Georgia,
Anthony Stokes, the colony's chief justice, and John Graham,
its lieutenant governor, were dispatched to the province to
pave the way for the restoration of civil authority there. The
governor of Georgia, Sir James Wright, remained in England
for a few months while attempting to work out the details
prerequisite to his resumption of office. Of the problems he
foresaw, none was more important than to what extent he
should trust repentant rebels. Wright admitted to Germain
that he was afraid such men could not be relied upon even if
they took formal oaths of allegiance to the king, and Germain
found his comment thought-provoking. If Wright was correct, Germain reasoned, "it argues against the settling the
Colony at the Peace of the King, and it must Continue under
Military Government."[32]

Notwithstanding the doubts raised concerning the viability
of a restored provincial government, Wright and the other
civil officials resumed control of Georgia soon after their
arrival in the colony. According to Stokes, the new regime
was "disagreeable" to some of the British officers stationed in
Georgia, but he himself was an enthusiastic supporter of the
plan. So were many other loyalists, who, along with Stokes,
argued loudly and frequently that only by reestablishing civil
government in all the conquered territories could Great
Britain make clear to the Americans the sharp contrast between the rule of the king, "founded in law, and justice," and
the tyranny of the rebels. Particularly insistent on this point
was James Simpson, the attorney general of South Carolina,
who declared that if "some considerable Colony" was restored to its normal state, "the superiour Advantages and
Security, they would then enjoy, above those who lived under
a different Dominion, could not fail, to suggest comparisons
that would daily be productive, of the most important conse-

quences, and an earnest wish, to partake of those Benefits, and Blessings which they saw their Neighbours in the enjoyment of."[33]

Simpson naturally thought that his own province of South Carolina was best suited for such an important experiment, but ironically he was at least partly responsible for the failure to restore civil government there. After the capture of Charleston in mid-1780, Clinton asked Simpson to set up a "temporary Civil Police" to help govern the city, "which must otherwise fall into Anarchy and Confusion." Simpson's creation was so successful that it prevented the very end he desired, for when the other Carolina officials arrived in Charleston from England they found the board of police functioning as "a supreme Court of Law and Equity, and also in some Measure a Board of State Policy." Moreover, Clinton proved to be unremittingly hostile to the idea of reestablishing the civil government.[34] Dismayed by the general's attitude, the civil officers appealed to England in hopes of persuading the ministry to overrule him. William Bull, who had been named governor of the colony in 1779, informed Germain that "nothing can more effectually restore and establish the public Tranquility on a lasting Foundation" than reinstituting civil government, and Simpson continued to argue eloquently for the same goal.[35] Loyalists from other provinces entered the fray as well: Joseph Galloway and William Smith, to name just two, declared that the perpetuation of martial law would "disgust the minds of the People and make them very restless Subjects," for Americans, like all Englishmen, "will never be quiet, because unhappy, under any Form of Governmt, but the good old Constitution delivered down to us by our Ancestors."[36]

It must be admitted, though, that the Carolinians' opposition to the continuation of military rule in their province was not entirely based on principle. Indeed, one of their major objections was founded on pure self-interest. As Thomas Irving, the receiver general, explained in 1782, when the Treasury ordered the Carolina civil officers to return to their posts, it cut off their allowances and left them without any income until they were formally restored "to the Emoluments of our respective Employments." As a result, Irving complained, "at the same time, that We are in some Measure under the necessity of supporting (at least) the appearance of the Rank We formerly held in the Country, We are not only deprived of the Profits of our Employments but also of our private Fortunes, whilst We find every Necessary of Life raised to a Price barely credible." And even though many of the officials in question were serving on the board of police, Bull declared, the salary for that job was "not sufficient to support any person in this Country in the Character and appearance of a Gentleman."[37]

The ministerial proposals to provide employment for groups of loyalists can most accurately be described as almost total failures. The Penobscot colony never went beyond the planning stage, and only in Georgia was civil government ever fully restored. In each case military considerations played a major role in sabotaging the original idea. Because some strategists (colonial and English alike) thought a fort on the Penobscot River could be of military use, that was the site chosen for a new province, despite its unsuitability for large-scale, immediate settlement. And as a consequence of Clinton's assessment of military necessity, civil government was never reinstituted in South Carolina, nor, for that matter, in New York City.

The plain fact was that the war influenced every aspect of the loyalists' search for employment. Their original expectation that the rebellion could not last more than a few months made them reluctant to apply for positions in the first place. When that reluctance was overcome in the later years of the war, they still tended to prefer jobs that could be readily abandoned once the final victory was achieved. Furthermore, the ministry, operating under the same assumptions as the refugees, was inhospitable to their requests for jobs until their sheer numbers became so large that there was little alternative. And even then the provisions the government tried to make for them proved completely inadequate.

[*3*]

The loyalists may have found it easier to obtain jobs after 1778, but on the other hand they found it much more difficult to acquire sizable pensions. Like every other aspect of the refugees' lives, their allowances were affected by Saratoga, though somewhat belatedly. Not until 1779 did the Lords of the Treasury show signs of realizing that they were now going to have to support increasing numbers of Americans for an indefinite period. But, once they had faced this unappetizing prospect, the Lords started to economize wherever possible.

Beginning in 1779, they came to rely upon two simple devices for easing the government's financial burden: first, they doled out smaller allowances than before, and second, they replaced some pensions with single grants that carried the proviso, "in full of all claims as an American sufferer." By these means the Lords drastically cut the number of pensions over £100 and slowed the rate at which the total number of allowances had been climbing. They also began frequently to deny requests altogether, on the grounds that the petitioners did "not seem to be within the Rules for Relief, as . . . American Sufferer[s]." And the Lords sought ways to compensate memorialists outside of the pension system; a Virginia refugee, for example, was permitted to collect his father's customs salary in lieu of receiving an allowance.[38]

Another new policy that yielded fruitful results, even to the extent of lowering the total amount disbursed to refugees, was the Treasury's determination to take advantage of every opportunity to reduce or stop current allowances. The death or departure of a recipient became an automatic excuse for ceasing or lessening the support allotted to his family, and once a name had been removed from the list it was practically impossible to persuade the Lords to restore it.[39] The Treasury furthermore stopped the stipends of persons ordered to return to their homes in America as a result of British victories in the South. In March 1779, July 1780, and July 1781 pensioners from Georgia, South Carolina, and Virginia respectively were struck from the rolls and directed to take passage for America. They were granted travel allowances and were specifically told that they would not "receive any further Relief on staying here." In addition, southern loyalists whose applications for allotments had not yet been considered were given varying amounts of assistance and ordered to return to the colonies.[40]

These tactics lowered the number of pensioners, but by early 1782 the sum distributed for loyalist allowances still amounted to more than £38,000. When Lord Rockingham and his coalition government took control of the administration from Lord North in the spring of 1782, they were faced with a sizable annual outlay, an ever-increasing pile of petitions, and, in the wake of Yorktown, with the knowledge that the Americans' stipends might well have to become permanent. The new Lords of the Treasury therefore decided to review the entire pension list in the hope of reducing it still further.

As a first step, the Treasury agreed to continue existing

allowances but refused to "grant Relief to any fresh Claimants till the Pretensions of the former ones are all considered." Next the Lords ordered an end to salary payments to former American officials. This directive, as the outraged admiralty judge Robert Auchmuty noted, "converted my rightfull claim on government into a mere favour." Auchmuty and the rest of the refugees understood the implications of the new policy, and they protested mightily, but to no avail.[41] By this device the Lords successfully ensured that all the American allowances would be open to revision, that none were any longer in the category of fixed, immutable payments. They had begun to effect a transition from a system in which at least some pensioners had been entitled by right to a certain amount of support, to one in which all pensioners would be equally dependent upon the good will of the government for their subsistence.

The practical results of the Lords' changed attitude toward salary claims may be illustrated by the case of William Smith, who had been appointed chief justice of New York in 1779. Since the province was ruled by martial law throughout the war, he had never actually fulfilled the duties of his office. Nevertheless Smith, under previous practice, would have been entitled to receive the full salary authorized for the position. By the time he first applied for the arrears owed him, though, the new policy was in effect, and Smith made the additional mistake of requesting payment in the amount of three times his nominal salary, on the grounds that the cost of living in New York had trebled during the war. The combination of Smith's exorbitant claim and the Treasury's insistence that all payments to loyalists were now by favor rather than by right sealed the fate of his application. For more than two years he fought to have it accepted, bombarding the ministry with petition after petition, haunting the offices of the Treasury and the secretary of state. Nothing worked. Finally in July 1786 Smith surrendered. Recognizing at last that whatever he received "must be the Effect of Interest . . . and not on the Justice of the Case," he submitted a pension memorial. Within a month he was granted an allowance of £400 a year, retroactive to January 1784. In his diary Smith recorded his disgusted comment: "What a Lesson does my Example teach to all that have Demands upon Governmt. or Business with Ministers!"[42]

The same policy that so incensed Smith was put into effect with respect to the pension list as well. Refugees attempting to collect their allowances in June 1782 were told that the rolls were being examined and that payments would be temporarily suspended. But it was not until August that the Treasury board asked Lord Shelburne, who had become prime minister on Rockingham's death, to appoint some qualified persons "to enquire generally and minutely into the Cases of all the American Sufferers." Shelburne selected for the task two Members of Parliament, John Wilmot and Daniel Parker Coke, both of whom had opposed the American war. In order to avoid "the imputation of a ministerial job, or undue influence in their parliamentary conduct," they decided to serve without pay.[43]

The list turned over to Wilmot and Coke contained 315 names and represented a yearly disbursement of £40,280. The investigators' major assignment was to examine each case, in order to ensure that no loyalist was receiving more (or less) than he deserved. They began their work in October 1782, and they meticulously insisted that pensioners appear before them in person to present evidence to prove their loyalty and losses. According to the woman who cleaned their rooms, the two men "seldom left the office before 12 o'clock at night" while they were pursuing the inquiry.[44]

Wilmot and Coke decided to consider the cases both collectively, "with a view to the general Disposition of them," and individually, "with a reference to each particular Case and the Allowance we think should be made to each till they can be otherwise provided for." From the first standpoint, they divided the pensioners into three general classes: (1) landowners, merchants, and tradesmen, who should be encouraged to settle in the remaining British provinces in America through the allotting of assistance "proportioned to their several Ranks, and Situations in Life"; (2) civil officers, professional men, and customs officials, many of whom could not so readily relocate and who should receive financial aid and new positions, if possible; and (3) widows, minors, and aged and infirm persons, who could neither return to America nor be profitably employed and who were as a result "more particularly objects of the Bounty of the Government."[45]

After reviewing the cases carefully, Wilmot and Coke recommended that 134 allowances be continued at the current rate; 90 be reduced; 25 be stopped because the recipients either did not need the money or were not properly "American sufferers"; 10 be increased because of "extraordinary Merit or Losses"; and 56 be suspended because the recipients had not appeared to testify on their cases. The total amount disbursed for pensions was reduced by approximately one-fourth, from the £34,695 received by the 259 persons whose claims had been checked to £26,400.[46]

The investigators' final report to the Lords of the Treasury revealed the general bases for their decisions. Their chief tenet was that the allotments "were not intended as Compensation or Satisfaction for the Losses of those Persons to whom they have been paid, but as *temporary Provisions for their Support* till the Close of the War, and till the final Issue of the Contest with the American Colonies could be known." As a result the amounts Wilmot and Coke awarded were not strictly tied to the size of a man's losses, but instead bore a vague relationship to three separate and independently determined considerations: loyalty and service to the crown, loss of property or income in very general terms, and present need and circumstances.[47] An examination of the investigators' comments in individual cases shows how they weighed each of these elements before reaching their final decisions.

First it must be emphasized that, since the primary purpose of the inquiry was to reduce the pension list, Wilmot and Coke continually sought ways to do just that. Whenever a loyalist could claim only a small property loss, they thought it an "advantageous bargin" to exchange his allowance for a single sum. Or, if they were confronted by what they believed to be false testimony, they did not hesitate to stop a stipend altogether. And, if a recipient did not need government assistance, his allotment was usually halted.[48]

Above all, the pensioners had to prove their loyalty to the crown. When their allegiance was "at least Problematical" (as Wilmot and Coke commented in one case) or when applicants had not particularly exerted themselves in the British cause, their allowances were more often than not reduced. If, on the other hand, a pensioner had served the king well, the investigators were inclined to overlook the fact that he had little property or even that he was reputed to be of bad character in order to award him an allowance somewhat out of proportion to his actual losses. As Coke explained to the House of Commons some months later, "Whenever they found, on enquiry, that a Loyalist had borne arms, and been in active service in the cause of Great Britain, they had always considered that as a great merit, and acted accordingly."[49]

Loyalty alone was not sufficient to win a claimant a substantial allowance: wealth and status were also of importance. Men who had had little property often had their stipends reduced, as did the refugees unable to supply adequate proof of their former holdings. These deductions derived specifically from Wilmot and Coke's belief that the status of the pension recipients had not been "sufficiently attended to" previously. By this they did not mean that certain wealthy loyalists should have received more; rather, they were concerned lest an exile of low social origin be rewarded with an allotment so high as to put him "in a much better Situation than he was ever in [in] America." In accordance with this policy, the investigators frequently lowered pensions that seemed to them out of proportion to a loyalist's "Rank in Life, Originally."[50]

The third element considered by Wilmot and Coke in determining awards was that of need. Since the Lords of the Treasury had not particularly concerned themselves with the actual needs of applicants, the addition of this consideration to the list of relevant criteria for assistance constituted a major innovation. Time and again in recommending allowances Wilmot and Coke showed that they believed need to be perhaps the most significant factor in their decisions. If a claimant was in poor health, was elderly, or had a large family to support, the investigators would disregard both deficiencies in evidence and a low social status in order to allot pensions that "we should think . . . otherwise rather too much."[51] The decisions in such cases were unwelcome portents of the future for the loyalists, because they indicated that the pension system was steadily becoming nothing more than a charitable operation. As greater emphasis was placed on need, claims of merit received increasingly less attention from the government.

Two further considerations influenced the investigators. Unlike the Lords of the Treasury, they took into account the relative size of allowances, and on several occasions they ordered stipends reduced because they were "too much compared with those made to others in similar circumstances." But, on the other hand, Wilmot and Coke made no substantial changes in the basic structure of the system itself. Feeling themselves bound by the former decisions of the Treasury, they merely reviewed the cases and refused to make new determinations on the merits of claimants. Their remarks concerning a Pennsylvania farmer illuminate their attitude. "If it had been a New Case perhaps we should not have thought ourselves justified in recommending any thing to be given to him," they wrote. However, since "a Case ought to be very strong and the impropriety very great" before a stipend should be stopped, they merely suggested a reduction in the size of his pension.[52]

The most complex problem Wilmot and Coke encountered in their efforts to revise the pension list involved the salaries of customs officials. In December 1776 the Lords of the Treasury, at the recommendation of the American board of customs commissioners, had authorized Charles Steuart, the cashier of American customs, to use receipts from American ports to pay salaries to refugee officers. By June 1779 the fund from which the salaries were drawn had nearly been exhausted, and the commissioners asked the Lords to continue customs payments from general revenues.[53] Instead of complying with the request, the Treasury directed Andrew Elliot, superintendent of exports and imports at New York, to collect duties on prize vessels brought into the harbor there and to remit the proceeds to Steuart, to enable him to meet the customs payroll. For several years Elliot tried to collect the duties, but then in August 1781 an English legal officer ruled that the prize ships could not legally be taxed.[54] By that time some customs officials had not been paid for almost two years, and the Lords of the Treasury at last agreed to supply the lesser officers with some "present relief" and to pay the commissioners' salary arrears. But further than that they would not go.[55]

At this point the matter was referred to Wilmot and Coke. They recommended that other customs officers be paid in full to the same date (October 1782) as the commissioners had been and that all salaries be stopped from that time. As a substitute, they proposed to increase the pensions of the customs officers by approximately one-half, and they suggested that henceforth the revenue officials should be treated like other refugee loyalists. Although the Lords of the Treasury nominally accepted Wilmot and Coke's recommendation, in response to petitions from various customs officers they modified the decision several times, ordering additional payments to those officers not receiving government stipends and eventually awarding the commissioners special allowances in the amount of one-half their former salaries.[56]

Wilmot and Coke submitted their final report to the Treasury on January 29, 1783, expressing the hope that Parliament would be convinced "that some Pains have been taken to see their Bounty is not distributed to unworthy Objects, and that the American Sufferers on their part will be satisfied, there is a desire at least in Government to do them all the Justice in their Power." Wilmot and Coke's first wish was indeed fulfilled, but, as one might imagine, the second was not. The numerous reductions in allowances sparked countless appeals from loyalists for reconsideration of their cases. All the appeals, however, were rejected by the Lords on the grounds that they had accepted the commissioners' report in its entirety and would not depart from it. At least they were consistent: if Thomas Swan, a Boston storekeeper, was not successful in his appeal, neither was John Randolph.[57]

The most frequent complaint offered against the new allowances was that they constituted deliberate insults. Andrew Allen, the former attorney general of Pennsylvania, insisted that Wilmot and Coke must have had some "Misapprehension" of his case when they decided to lower his annual allowance from £400 to £300. "What affects me beyond all other Considerations," he wrote, "is the Insinimuation [*sic*] which this new Regulation must necessarily convey of some Demerit in point of Pretensions or Conduct, which I am by no means conscious of." Peter Oliver, whose £400 pension was also reduced to £300, exhibited an identical reaction. "If to be uniformly confirmed in Loyalty to the most amiable of Sovereigns and to the british Constitution is to be deemed criminal," Oliver declared in a letter protesting the cuts, "I do acknowledge myself to be immerged in the deepest Criminality."[58]

The loyalists' anguished comments reveal the source of the difficulty. Not understanding that Wilmot and Coke had based the new awards partly on their assessment of applicants' need and relative merits, the refugees assumed that any reduction meant that their devotion to Great Britain was being questioned. Nor, given their interpretation of the pension system, was any other conclusion possible. Since they believed that the size of their allotment was directly related to the ministry's judgment of their loyalty and services, a lessening of that amount was more than just a financial disaster for the exiles — it was an emotional catastrophe as well, for it indicated, at least in their eyes, the contempt with which they were regarded by the government they had faithfully supported.

There was still another unpleasant implication inherent in the new system. The Treasury's adherence to Wilmot and Coke's formula irretrievably altered the basis on which pension decisions were made. Before the Rockingham coalition took over the ministry in early 1782, a loyalist could successfully petition the Treasury for compensation as a matter of right. After Wilmot and Coke's report substituted the clearly defined criteria of need, loyalty, and loss for the somewhat vague determination of status and sufferings that had previously been the Treasury's grounds for awarding allowances, a claim of right became both meaningless and worthless. As William Smith had discovered, it got one nowhere. Yet the refugees, led by Joseph Galloway, resisted to the end the inevitable conclusion that they were thereby to become totally dependent on government charity. The loyalists, said Galloway, "will not yet so far degrade themselves as to consider their claims on goverment [sic] wholly founded on compassion." On the contrary, he continued, they had a "just right of claim on goverment [sic] for past services . . . [and for] the meritorious and matchless sacrifices they have made in support of it."[59]

Galloway's arguments won the plaudits of other exiles, but they had little impact on the ministry. For both financial and political reasons the government simply could not afford to admit the validity of Galloway's position, and as the years passed the trend towards turning the allowances into nothing more than benevolent handouts continued unabated. After 1783 pensions were awarded only as "temporary support" in conjunction with the investigation of claims for property loss during the war. These procedures and the final disposition of the allowance system will be discussed in a later chapter.

[*4*]

The related and practically simultaneous developments resulting from the defeat at Saratoga combined with the effects of that loss itself to produce readily identifiable changes in the loyalists' mental attitude. Knowing that they would not be able to return to America for some time, many of the refugees surrendered themselves to despondency. The boredom of life in provincial towns did nothing to offset their gloom, and the new pension policies adopted by the government only contributed to it. Even before 1778 their lives in London had been characterized by an everlasting sameness, an unremitting tedium. Walks in the parks, afternoons at coffeehouses, and occasional visits to the theater had filled their time pleasantly for weeks, perhaps for months, but certainly not for years. As Samuel Curwen said in 1776, once the "harmless amusements" had "lost their novelty," they could "delight no more."[60] This discontent doubled and redoubled after Saratoga, because now the refugees could see no end to their misery, no conclusion to their rootless, meaningless existence. And so they increasingly described their lives as "dull, heavy and insipid," or characterized themselves as being in "that torpid inanimate state which deprives a man of the hopes of anything better and rids him of the fear of any thing worse to come."[61]

The exiles' pessimistic mood contributed to their already endemic homesickness. The routine emptiness of their daily lives, their belief that Britain did not fully appreciate their sacrifices, and what would today be called "cultural shock" brought home to them the sharp contrast between their former lives in the colonies and their current existence in England. They grew ever more critical of Britain and, concomitantly, they became ever more inclined to look upon

St. James's Park, a favorite refugee meeting place, in 1783

America with a "filial fondness."[62] In exile, after all, they no longer had to face the opprobrium of the rebels. They were safe from the ravages of the war, their lives were not in danger. They read or talked about the distresses of America, but they did not themselves undergo wartime hardships. As the weeks and months passed, their memories of persecution faded, and, instead of dwelling upon the difficulties of the immediate past, they began to recall their happiness in the years before the rebellion. So Thomas Hutchinson wrote, with perhaps greater perception than he realized, "I find my attachment to my native Country increased by my distance from it."[63]

Yet nostalgia alone would not have been sufficient to produce the pattern of thought that led Sir William Pepperrell to exclaim in 1778, "I earnestly wish to spend the remainder of my Days in America, I love the Country, I love the People." Contributing a major share to such expressions of patriotism was something quite different: the loyalists' theory of the causes of the war. Their analysis will be discussed at length in the next chapter; at this point it is enough to say that the exiles believed that the Revolution had been brought on by a small group of malcontents who had deluded the naïve, well-meaning colonials into thinking that they were being oppressed. Or, to use Jonathan Sewall's words, "the Artifices of a few Demagogues have insensibly led a once happy innocent People to the Summit of Madness and Rebellion, and involved them in Distress, Poverty and ruin."[64]

This theory absolved the majority of the American colonists of guilt for the sufferings caused by "the ambition and Envy of the *few*," and as a result Sewall could retain his "predilection" for his native land at the same time as he continued to "curse and swear, most devoutly, without ceasing, at the folly and views of my Countrymen." Moreover, the refugees' analysis of the war had a further advantage: it enabled them to believe that one day the correctness of their position would be recognized by their erring fellow Americans. "The people of the Town of Milton will not persist in what they know to be wrong," said Thomas Hutchinson in 1779. "If the present generation is not convinced of its error the next will be and truth will finally prevail and our lost reputations be restored."[65]

In the interim, though, while waiting for the revolutionaries to recant, the loyalists found their lot "damnable Hard." Pepperrell spoke for all of them when he observed in 1778, "How hard it is to be exiled from one's Country, for trying to save it from ruin." Joshua Weeks revealed the following year that "every object around me fills me with melancholy. Even the beams of the Sun do not shine with their wonted cheerfullness, places of amusement seem to wear a dismal gloom, and even the house of God does not afford me that pleasure it used to." In short, remarked Sewall, "the situation of American loyalists, I confess, is enough to have provoked Job's wife, if not Job himself."[66]

The exiles' experience in England was so unsatisfactory that some of them, most notably Samuel Curwen, even began to have second thoughts about having left America. Curwen decided in 1777 that he might have been better off had he remained in the colonies to endure "the comparative trifling conditions of insults, reproaches, and perhaps a dress of tar and feathers," which he thought preferable to "the distresses of mind I am daily suffering." Two years later Hannah Winslow wrote regretfully, "Sincerely wish I had never left Boston, but," she added, "its now t[oo late] and my unhappy fate is fix'd."[67] Most of the loyalists would have agreed with her that there was little to be gained from recriminations. Instead of lamenting their mistakes (and of course most did not view their departure from America as an error, despite their love for the colonies), the refugees rather had to develop some means of rationalizing their current difficulties and of dealing with the afflictions thrust upon them by the rebellion.

Some found their answer in a pessimistic interpretation of man and his past. "The History of Mankind, from Adam, through all the succeeding Generations . . . is little else than an History of War, Tumult and Bloodshed," asserted Benjamin Pickman in 1781. Browne concurred. "The balance of happiness is and ever has been against all the sons of Adam," he observed; "that the evils of this life should preponderate the enjoyments appears to me to be the established constitution of Nature."[68] Yet there was much that could be gained from adversity. Pickman saw the possibility that he might discover "Virtues which lie concealed in the Sunshine of Prosperity," and John Randolph outlined those virtues in some detail. Difficulty, he commented, "offers a season for Reflection, calls forth the Powers of the Understanding[,] fixes its Principles, and inspires a Fortitude, which shews the true Dignity of Man."[69]

Other exiles, especially clergymen, turned to religion for solace in their time of trial. "As your troubles increase, so let your faith also increase," Henry Caner advised his elderly friend Silvester Gardiner, "and rest assured that your confidence in the hand that guides the Universe, will not finally be frustrated." Caner's words evidently had the desired effect, for some months later Gardiner told a friend, "What comforts me in my distress is that God governs the world, Sees and Suffers these things, no doubt for Some good and wise ends." With a similar acquiescence in his fate, the Reverend Harry Munro of New York wrote, "God's will be done. — All is for the best; — whatever is, is right; — and we are assured from the best authority . . . that all things shall work together for Good to Them that love God."[70] The clerics too thought that much could be learned from undergoing hardships. Isaac Smith prayed that his afflictions might increase his "reliance on, and submission to the all-disposing hand of the wise and righteous Governor of the universe," and Mrs. Jacob Duché declared, "I have found the distresses I have suffered Heaven's best gifts to me," precisely because they had led her "immediately to God."[71]

The ultimate consolation of religion was that expressed by the Reverend Samuel Peters of Connecticut in 1783. Religion, he asserted, "conquers Death Kings and congress." So-called "Liberty" might "cast down the greatest Patriots" or "change Rebellions into Revolutions," but, he warned, "time with all her fickle vanities can never change Eternity." And so, he concluded, "We have Jacobs Ladder to climb to Heaven on — at its Top we shall meet and find Tranquility durable as Eternity. . . . Viewing this happy Prospect I am content in Hope, and in my Fortune."[72]

The refugees had still another source from which they could draw the strength necessary to endure adversity, and this was the absolute certainty that they had acted correctly. To a man they relied upon this knowledge in an attempt to compensate for the many trials they had undergone. Harrison Gray made his thinking explicit in a 1789 letter to John Hancock: "The cool reflections on the conscientious part I early acted in the late unhappy dispute between Great Britain and her Colonies affords me the most exalted pleasure and is a source of consolation to me under the loss of my property of which I have been unjustly deprived, A pleasure which I could not part with for all the honors which your *State* could bestow."[73]

Although few of the exiles expressed themselves so openly,

they all found solace for the destruction of their former lives in an unswerving confidence that they had done their duty and that they had been motivated by (in Pickman's words) "the purest Principles of Loyalty." "My Conduct, in America, was not influenced by Events; but by Duty to his Majesty — an attachment to my native Country — and a Sense of mine own Honor," wrote Anthony Stokes; "nothing therefore can annihilate my Attachment to my King and Country." "I repent not of what I have done," declared the New Yorker Peter Van Schaack; "my Heart condemns me not for any Part of my political Conduct."[74] "[I] have been the true Patriot," wrote Pepperrell; "My Heart tells me — that I have done my Duty," Duché asserted; "I enjoy the intire Approbation of my own Mind, and I am therewith perfectly content," concurred Isaac Low, who had been a member of the First Continental Congress.[75]

Emerging from these statements was an attitude cogently outlined by Robert Auchmuty in 1779: "Though I am deemed an enemy to that country, I know the contrary. In fact I am not, nor ever was." His only crime, Auchmuty observed, was that he "differed in opinion with many touching political matters." And that disagreement made him no less a patriot, for his judgment was just as "honestly," as "rationally" framed as were the ideas of the rebels. Other loyalists agreed that they too had been influenced only by "the most sincere affection" for America, by a "warm attachment" to the colonists' welfare.[76] Van Schaack put it best: "My attachment to her [Great Britain] (great indeed as it was) was founded in the relation she stood in to America, and the happiness I conceived America derived from it."[77]

This set of priorities was, of course, the reason why the refugees found their experience in exile so frustrating and perplexing. *They* knew that they had had the best interests of their country at heart. *They* knew that they had acted out of love for America, out of a sincere concern for her future. But their fellow Americans not only did not recognize that fact, they also impugned the loyalists' motives, accusing them of betraying the colonies. The exiles saw no treason in their actions: they considered themselves British-Americans, and while in the colonies, they had not been able to separate the two facets of that identity. After living in England for a time, they realized that those halves of their existence were in fact separable, and that it was their identity as Americans, their allegiance to the colonies, that was primary. This recognition did not make them change their minds about independence — the vast majority still opposed it — but it did mean that they were never completely at ease in the British Isles. They conceived of themselves as persons "upon an excursion from home,"[78] not as emigrants seeking a permanent place to resettle. And, as the years passed, they thought ever more longingly about the land they had left behind.

5

The Seeds of Sedition

I saw the small seed of sedition, when it was im-
planted; it was, as a grain of mustard. I have
watched the plant until it has become a great tree;
the vilest reptiles that crawl upon the earth, are
concealed at the root; the foulest birds of the air
rest upon its branches.

— DANIEL LEONARD, 1775[1]

PERHAPS the most important facet of the refugees' psy-
chological state after Saratoga was their suddenly acquired
compulsion to discuss and explain the origins of the Revolution. In the pamphlet wars of 1774, a few writers like
Leonard and Seabury had ventured tentatively into the field
of historical analysis, but always within the context of the
immediate political dispute. In 1779 and 1780, quite a different phenomenon emerged: for the first time, the loyalists
began to produce formal, comprehensive histories of the
colonies and of the rebellion itself. The destruction of their
initial assumptions about the war forced them at last to find a
way of coming to terms with the reality of the revolt. This
they did in books that superficially differed from one another
but that concurred on essential points. Although these loyalist authors had disagreed among themselves during the 1760's
and early 1770's, their retrospective analyses of colonial history were strikingly alike. The common experience of exile

(and of post-Saratoga depression) served to erase the very real ideological lines that had once divided them.

[*1*]

The loyalist historians who took up their pens after Saratoga were a variegated lot. There was Joseph Galloway, the perennial proposer of conciliation plans; Peter Oliver, the acerbic chief justice; Alexander Hewatt, a Scottish Presbyterian clergyman who had settled in Charleston in 1763; George Chalmers, another Scot who came to America in 1763 and who thereafter had practiced law in Annapolis and Baltimore; Samuel Peters, an arrogant, opinionated Anglican cleric from Connecticut; and Anthony Stokes, the able lawyer who had served as chief justice of Georgia from 1769 to 1775. These men and the other refugees who commented less formally on the history of the revolt discerned one overriding pattern in the materials they studied. Within that pattern their emphases varied: Anglican historians, for example, tended to stress the religious side of the conflict, while colonial officials put their emphasis on legal, political, and constitutional issues. But the general outline was in most cases the same.

The historians began with the assumption that prerevolutionary America was idyllic, a *"Golden Age"* when the colonists were prosperous, happy, and living in "harmony, concord, mutual love, and reciprocal affection." This vision of the past was an important component of the undisguised nostalgia with which, from the vantage point of exile, they viewed their homeland. For them, it was axiomatic that the Americans had been "seated in the bosom of peace and never-failing plenty, — enjoying the benefit of mild and equitable Laws, — secured . . . against every Suspicion of danger from Foreign Invaders, and contributing far less than their Propor-

tion towards defraying the general expences of Government."
Before the war, they declared, "the bounty of the mother
country was extensive as her dominions, and, like the sun,
cherished and invigorated every object on which it shone."[2]
The flourishing state of the colonial economy was "owing almost solely to the protection and patronage of the Parent
State": the colonies had been "nourished in their infancy, and
supported in their more adult age, with all the attention of a
most affectionate parent." Britain had been ever solicitous of
the Americans' interests, and the result was that the colonists
in the 1760's had been "in full possession and enjoyment of
all the peace and all the security which the best government
in the world can give." In short, concluded Silvester Gardiner, "I don't believe there ever was a people in any age or
part of the World that enjoyed so much liberty as the people
of America did under the mild indulgent Government (God
bless it) of England."[3]

Such an idealized assessment of life in the prewar colonies,
although providing the exiles with a convenient vision of the
Utopia they sought to regain, contained a major theoretical
drawback: it made the rebellion inexplicable by traditional
standards. The refugees admitted that most recorded revolutions had been motivated by "extreme injustice and oppression by the rulers." But their halcyon description of prerevolutionary America obviously prevented them from applying
this interpretation to the colonies, and so they argued that
there was "no such concurrence of adequate causes" for the
Americans' revolt.[4] The denial of parallels between the
present and the past solved one of the loyalists' problems,
allowing them to maintain their roseate view of prewar
colonial life. But at the same time it created another, even
more pressing dilemma. In the words of Myles Cooper, presi-
dent of King's College in New York, "How then (it will

Chief Justice Peter Oliver,
a miniature by J. S. Copley

COURTESY OF ANDREW OLIVER AND
THE FRICK ART REFERENCE LIBRARY

George Chalmers,
by Andrew Geddes

COURTESY OF SCOTTISH
NATIONAL PORTRAIT GALLERY

naturally be asked) could a people, thus happily situated, be persuaded to sacrifice these advantages, and to hazard their Fortunes, their Lives, and their Souls, in such a Rebellion?"[5]

Some refugee authors did not even attempt to supply an answer to this crucial question. Instead of engaging in a systematic analysis of the causes of the Revolution, loyalist historians often contented themselves with narrative summaries of facts, broken infrequently by comments that the colonists had been "infected with pride and ambition" (Hewatt) or that they had acted "from an excess of liberty and affluence" (Stokes). The extent of the exiles' difficulties in reconciling the reality of the rebellion with their insistence that all had been well in America prior to the war is amply illustrated by Peter Oliver's lame conclusion (to which he was inexorably driven by premises he dared not deny) that the colonists had in the end "run Mad with too much Happiness."[6]

But in spite of the obvious analytical problems involved in assuming an absence of "adequate cause" for the Revolution, the loyalists refused to concede that it might have been justified. "The Colonists were not in a state of Oppression," asserted Cooper; their so-called "grievances" were either "evidently no grievances at all" or else were "much more than counterbalanced by peculiar Advantages." "Had the rebellion originated from real grievances," argued Charles Inglis in 1779, "a redress of those grievances, repeatedly offered on the part of government, had long since composed our troubles." Moreover, declared Daniel Leonard, once the Americans' complaints and assumptions were carefully examined, "the terrible fabric of grievances vanishes, like castles raised by enchantment, and leaves the wondering spectator amazed and confounded at the deception."[7]

The responsibility of conducting a detailed examination of

the Americans' grievances was shouldered by Joseph Galloway in 1780. The Americans claimed that Grenville's 1765
plan to tax the colonies had been oppressive, Galloway noted,
but that assertion was utterly false. It was only reasonable for
Grenville, as prime minister, to expect the colonies to contribute to the costs of imperial defense, and, as for the Stamp
Act itself, "no law within the compass of human wisdom
could be found more just and adequate to its purpose." The
tea tax instituted at the behest of Charles Townshend two
years later was also justifiable, Galloway argued, and the
repeal of the objectionable Townshend duties on glass,
paper, and dyes proved the ministry's responsiveness to colonial complaints. The East India Act of 1773, examined
dispassionately, actually benefited the colonies by making
cheaper tea available, and the "Intolerable" Acts had punished Massachusetts only as that province deserved. This was
no program intended to enslave the colonies, concluded
Galloway; to the contrary, were the British ministers "tamely
to permit the supreme authority of the State to be insolently
trampled on by its ungrateful subjects, without supporting
it?"[8]

Reasoning like Galloway's led many loyalists to decide that
their fellow countrymen had rebelled "more from other
causes, than those which were openly avowed." After all, said
Chalmers, "a contest with regard to abstract propositions of
law . . . could never have produced universal disaffection"
without additional contributing factors. And so Galloway,
Chalmers, and a number of other exiles resolved to expose
the truth about the rebellion, and to "endeavour to demonstrate by what *progressive* means, and fatal succession of
events, the original spark has been produced, and nourished
up to its present flame."[9]

With the exception of eccentrics who attributed the Revolution to causes like the "insidious" influence of France or the lack of adequate educational institutions in America,[10] the loyalists generally agreed that the seeds of revolt had been "co-oeval with the Colonies themselves" and that the rebellion had "necessarily flowed from causes interwoven with their very existence." The chief flaw they perceived in the early colonies was that the provincial governments had originally been "laid out more by accident than by plan." The American constitutions were "discordant[,] contradictory, ungovernable — forming on incidental convenience and temporary expedients a motley system, which wore the Face of Dominion without its Energy and power." In fact, declared Galloway, the colonial polities were based upon principles so "erroneous" and so "totally different" from those of the British government that by their very existence they "tended to break in time the uniformity of the State."[11]

The refugees found particular fault with the distribution of power inside the respective governments. Jonathan Boucher, who asserted that the executives had never had sufficient "Pith and Energy," was echoed by Stokes, who bewailed the governors' lack of an unlimited power of appointment.[12] What made matters worse was the fact that in America "too much weight was . . . thrown into the popular scale," and the strength of the assemblies was such that the governments appeared to be on the "Verge" of republicanism. Furthermore, the colonies lacked the independent aristocracy "necessary to check the illegal attempts of an arbitrary governor, or the ambitious and licentious designs of a popular assembly." All in all, Galloway concluded, the American governments failed to exhibit "those Principles of Policy that alone ever have or can bind the Members of a free Society together."[13]

Aggravating the original problem was the "irresolution

and unsteadiness" of British colonial administration. Britain's "supineness" in not correcting her early errors had allowed "mismanagements" to become rebellion, Boucher charged angrily, and Chalmers observed with regret that British ministers had generally applied "palliatives . . . to disorders which required effectual remedies," substituting "temporary expedient for uniformity of system."[14] In addition, the "Timidity" of recent administrations had resulted in "great, and indeed too much, condescension on the part of the State towards its subjects," in a "lenity of disposition" that had perhaps encouraged the Americans in their recalcitrance.[15] The whole theory was very neatly summed up by George Chalmers in one sentence: "The original defects of the provincial constitutions, the genuine source of successive usurpations, were permitted to exhibit standing monuments of continual complaint, of general neglect, of the imbecility of man, till they ended, by a natural progress, in the worst evils that can afflict a people, revolt and civil war."[16]

Comprehensive as it sounded, there were two major reasons why this formulation could not supply the final, definitive explanation for which the loyalists were searching. First, an overemphasis on British mistakes would bring the refugees perilously close to a denial of their initial proposition that the prewar colonies had been unqualifiedly happy, prosperous, and well governed. Second, and more important, such a long-range interpretation could not account for the exact timing of the Revolution. It was all very well for Chalmers to write of a "natural progress" toward rebellion, but that statement was insufficient to explain why the conflict had surfaced after 1763 and had broken into open warfare in 1775. So, in order to supply this deficiency, the loyalists were forced to examine recent events as well as the distant past.

[2]

The refugees began their investigation into the immediate causes of the revolt with some general observations on the inherent characteristics of mankind. Chalmers wrote of the "active principle" motivating men to attempt "to throw off present evil or to grasp at future good," and Boucher thought it axiomatic that "those who are governed are always ready to set themselves against those who govern." Coupled with this tendency to restlessness, to perpetual dissatisfaction, was the disquieting fact that "the Common People seldom, if ever, think or judge for themselves in Matters which concern the whole." Indeed, declared Oliver, "the Mobility of all Countries" could best be described as "perfect Machines, wound up by any Hand who might first take the Winch," and many hands were more than willing to try to control the machinery.[17] "In every society," Boucher commented, "there always have been, and too probably there always will be, men of restless and ambitious minds; who are never long satisfied with any system of government, or with any administration." Such men, asserted Chalmers, used "riots and tumults" and played upon men's "malice, revenge, bigotry, envy, pride, and avarice" in order to cause "anarchy and confusion." They usually met with little difficulty in deceiving the "low and vulgar," because, James Simpson noted, "it is more easy to delude the Populace, by specious pretences, than to Govern them by arguments deduced from sound reason, and calm reflection." And, even though the wiser men of the community might try to thwart the plot, they most often would find themselves powerless to combat it, for, as Chalmers warned, the people, "freed from all restraints," would "with a ravishing degree of pleasure, feel their mad strength."[18]

To support this assessment of man's natural tendencies, the loyalists cited the lessons of history. A brief glance at the recorded past, Leonard asserted, would show that "the same game, and with the same success, has been played in all ages, and all countries." The history of England provided especially relevant examples. Boucher referred to the lengthy conflict between the houses of York and Lancaster to demonstrate that political commotions "originated, first, in the ill-governed passions of some popular leader or leaders; and, next, in the misled reason of the people." Even more pertinent was the English Civil War, because the common folk had been incited into rebellion by demagogues who, once they had attained their objective, had themselves turned into tyrants. The message was undeniable: "The generality of the people, who are thus made the dupes of artifice, and the mere stilts of ambition, are sure to be losers in the end."[19]

Unfortunately for the stability of colonial government, it seemed to the loyalists that Americans were "peculiarly fitted" for the role of the deluded multitude in this oft-performed historical scenario. Their "early Prejudices," wrote Boucher, "fostered by Education, and confirmed by Religion" combined to make them particularly vulnerable to demagogic appeals. Since in the colonies "literally and truly, all Power flows from the People," the populace could readily be persuaded to oppose anyone wielding authority, regardless of whether or not that authority was actually oppressive. One small spark, one smoldering coal, could set America aflame.[20]

And that, said the refugees, was exactly what had happened. The Americans had been lured into rebellion by "the lies and misrepresentations, of artful, wicked, and desperate men." Certain colonists had pursued a "determined design . . . to promote an Independency" and had "gradually trained" many "better meaning but less cunning Men than themselves" to view "their governors as despots, and even laws as mere arbitrary decrees."[21] The people had been "insidiously induced to believe" that Britain was "rapacious, cruel, and vindictive" when in fact nothing could have been further from the truth. Accordingly, "the Wheel of Enthusiasm was set on going, and its constant Rotation set the Peoples Brains on Whirling; and by a certain centrifugal Force, all the Understanding which the People had was whirled away."[22]

It was now very easy to resolve the paradox that had at first seemed so perplexing: how happy, prosperous, contented people had come to engage in a needless rebellion against the very source of their prosperity. Oliver's formulation was succinct: "Why is the sudden Transition made, from Obedience to Rebellion, but to gratifye the Pride, Ambition and Resentment, of a few abandoned Demagogues, who were lost to all Sense of Shame and of Humanity?"[23]

There remained but the task of describing the types of men who had fomented the revolt, and, although the loyalists' emphases differed somewhat, they agreed with respect to the chief characteristics of the rebel leaders. The plotters were, in the first place, looking out for their own "private Interest." "Ambitious and needy Adventurers," seeking "plunder," they had recognized that in order to advance their own careers they would have to destroy British authority in the colonies. The rebellious coalition was therefore led by men "whose *importance* and *political salvation*" depended upon keeping America "in a continual flame."[24] These "pretended patriots" had been joined in their endeavors by "smugglers, debtors, and men of desperate fortunes," a set of "worthless Fellows" who were "mostly bankrupts, and mean People."[25]

The resulting combination of crafty leaders and ruthless

followers was formidable, but even so it could never have succeeded in its objective had it not been for "the loose principles of the times." The pervasive influence of these principles had been the *"one great cause"* of the Revolution, asserted Boucher, and he was seconded by Inglis and Galloway, among others. Foremost among the dangerous notions circulating in America was a "deep rooted republicanism, democratic, levelling principles, ever unfriendly to monarchy." And, because the Anglican clerics believed that "Church and State mutually support, and are supported by, each other," they in particular saw republicanism as a threat to both secular and religious authority. "A republican spirit can never rest," explained Henry Caner; "the same levelling principles which induce them to withdraw from the wholesome est[a]blishment of the Ch[urc]h operate with equal force in throwing off the restraints of civil Govmt."[26] Inglis argued that "one of the principal springs" of the rebels' conduct was their desire to destroy the Anglican church in America. "The independent mode of religion," wrote Samuel Seabury, "is, from its very nature, incompatible with monarchical government," and Caner likewise warned that "they who disapprove of the established religion will ever be laboring as far as their Influence extends to undermine and destroy that power by which it is protected."[27]

With this stress on the Revolution as an attack upon church and state alike, the loyalists' chief villains had to be both dissenters and (in their estimation) republicans. And so when they set out to discover the exact identities of the conspirators responsible for inciting the rebellion, they fixed upon two groups of men who fit both descriptions. Refugees from the middle colonies sometimes named the New York "Triumvirate" as the prime movers of the American revolt, but more commonly the loyalists placed the blame for all the

troubles in the colonies on the New England Congrega-
tionalists.

Among the authors who ascribed the major role in the
rebellion to the Triumvirate was Thomas Jones, a former
judge of the New York Supreme Court. William Livingston,
John Morin Scott, and William Smith had been "presby-
terians by profession, and republicans in principle," Jones
charged. They had early determined "to pull down Church
and State, to raise their own Government and religion upon
its ruins, or to throw the whole province into anarchy and
confusion." Their main instrument in this endeavor had
been the Whig Club, which they had founded in Manhattan
in 1752, and whose members had been "the promoters, the
advisers and counselors" of the revolutionary effort from its
very beginnings. In their publications, both pamphlets and
newspapers, they had attacked government "with a rancor, a
malevolence, and an acrimony" unparalleled elsewhere in
America, and as a result New York "in a short time, from a
state of happiness, became a scene of confusion, of uproar,
and disorder, thanks to the triumvirate Livingston, Scott, and
Smith, and to them only."[28]

Although a few other loyalists agreed with Jones at least in
part, most focused their attention upon the New Englanders
when they sought scapegoats for the rebellion. Massachusetts, wrote Peter Oliver, was "the *Volcano* from whence
issued all the Smoak, Flame and Lava which hath since
enveloped the whole British american Continent." And the
reason why the province had played such an important role
in bringing on the revolt was deeply embedded in its history.
"Many of the first settlers imported with them an aversion to
the *regal* part of our Constitution, and were thorough-paced
Republicans," declared Thomas Bradbury Chandler. Such
men, charged Boucher, had not had "the courage to defend

their principles in England" and had "transplanted them into a more genial soil; and thus preserved them from that humiliating reverse of fortune which was experienced by their brethren in the Mother Country." The dangerous ideas that had been eradicated in England were "handed down by an uninterrupted succession, from father to son, and from generation to generation, to the present day." Chandler warned that the New Englanders were therefore prepared, "whenever the word is given, to declare and exert themselves to all hazards for an *independent* government of their own modelling."[29]

Because of the loyalists' belief that Massachusetts "acquired habits in her infancy, which though checked in her youth, were strengthened as she grew up, and became inveterate during her age," they devoted many pages of their accounts of the war to explicating the early history of the factious province. Both Oliver and Galloway began their discussions of the American Revolution with lengthy accounts of the effects of the Reformation upon religious belief and practice. They then proceeded to describe the ideas of Separatists and Puritans in some detail, noting that "their principles of ecclesiastical polity were as directly repugnant to those of the established Church, as their ideas of civil government were to those of a mixed monarchy." As a result, declared Galloway, the charter of Massachusetts Bay "was manifestly calculated to efface all the laws, habits, manners, and opinions which it ought to support," and more specifically "to level all the orders, arrangements, checks, and balances, wisely graduated and tempered, of a mixed monarchy, to the lowest and most imperfect of all political systems, a tumultuous, seditious, and inert democracy."[30]

The consequence of this imperfect form of government was, as might well be imagined, continuous anarchy. In

Massachusetts, Chalmers wrote, "a perpetual fever rushed through every vein of the body politic." Under such circumstances, observed Galloway, it was only reasonable "to expect that a faction would be formed, ever watchful to seize the first opportunity of throwing off the small remains of subordination to the State." So it was without surprise that Chandler commented in 1775 that "a set of people . . . at Boston, have for many years been aiming at, and preparing the way for, a government of their own modelling, independent of Great Britain."[31]

The "hereditary disaffection" and conspiratorial tendencies of New England still did not explain "what were the inducements and the causes which led others not so circumstanced into rebellion." Boucher, who raised the point explicitly, argued that the other colonies were drawn into the Revolution because of defects in their charters, the ineffectiveness of their governors, the failure of their clergymen to uphold government properly, and their citizens' desire to escape the debts they owed British merchants.[32] Other loyalists were more inclined to ascribe the general participation in the rebellion to New England's successful exportation of her "peculiar principles," and they discerned several methods by which this had been accomplished. First, there was the fact that "republican tenets" were "taught in their colleges, and disseminated through the provinces by dissenting teachers." Second, emigrants from New England to other areas of the colonies had "carried their own tenets and customs with them, and were zealous in propagating them." Finally, the northern dissenting churchmen had encouraged their southern counterparts to join together in a synod, and "a dangerous combination of men, whose principles of religion and polity were equally averse to those of the established Church and Government," was formed with "the secret and real motive" of promoting American independence.[33]

In spite of the New Englanders' machinations, it was obvious to the loyalists that the attempts to foment trouble in America "most certainly would have expired in contempt, had not such been cherished, applauded, and kept alive in Great Britain, by the minority." As a result the refugees saved some of their bitterest invective for English opposition leaders. They despised the rebels' English supporters, men who should have known better than to encourage the Americans in their delusion, men who, Galloway charged, had "intentionally laid the foundation of future insurrections and resistance . . . to that very authority which they were *bound by oath to preserve.*"[34]

The American rebels and the British opposition had the same goals, Chalmers explained. "They both wanted the direction of each country — envied their superiors — coveted their neighbours property, and wished an entire change of men and measures." Unsurprisingly, they had coalesced into "a Cabalinarian Combination" directed at the constitution. After 1765 they had acted in concert, the Americans depending upon their English patrons for protection from the wrath of the ministry, the Britons receiving support from the colonists for their efforts to unseat the majority government. Much of the responsibility for the Revolution therefore rested with the opposition party, which had convinced the Americans that the colonies' position was widely supported in England, that the merchants would actively aid them in their struggle, and that the ministry was incompetent and would be unable to quash their resistance movement. Chalmers concluded, "Had there been no such intercourse, but instead of it only an unanimous frown of parliament, on the then conduct of the Americans, no rebellion, in that country, would have taken place."[35]

This, then, was the loyalist historians' interpretation of the Revolution. The dispute between England and her colonies had been deliberately fomented by a small group of designing New England republicans, who were supported by ambitious American politicians, debtors, smugglers, and members of the British opposition party. Each element of this coalition had its own reasons for joining the movement: some participated because they were ideologically dissatisfied with the British government and the established church, others because they saw an opportunity for personal advancement in the hoped-for disruption of regular government. In either case the desired goal was from the beginning the complete independence of the American colonies.

[3]

When the refugees set out to analyze the period preceding the Revolution, they applied this theory to its major events. Yet in a larger sense they rejected the notion that the specific occurrences of the years 1763 through 1775 had intrinsic significance. In rejecting the rebels' contention that the revolt had been caused by a series of oppressive acts, they denied that those acts were important *per se*. Rather, it was the activities of the rebel conspirators that were of primary significance. Since the rebellion had resulted from a deliberate plot, the details of this or that act were irrelevant. After all, the laws and ministerial policies complained of had not caused the trouble. They had merely provided the conspirators with the excuses they needed in order to incite the colonists to revolt. Thus, as Thomas Hutchinson wrote in 1776, "if no Taxes or Duties had been laid upon the Colonies, other pretences would have been found for exception to the authority of Parliament."[36]

Essential to this interpretation of the 1763–1775 period was the loyalists' assumption that their fellow countrymen (or at least some of them) had knowingly sought independence long before any of the supposedly oppressive acts had been passed. They saw the events of the prewar years as the culmination of the rebels' plots, as the working out of what Galloway called "their long meditated and so often disappointed" plan for independence. The refugees absolutely refused to accept as valid the Americans' continual protestations of loyalty to Great Britain before 1776, and by the same token they were for the most part blind to the changes in the Americans' ideology and tactics that took place during these critical years. For them, looking back, the period was all of one piece, a uniform sequence revealing throughout the pervasive and wicked influence of the conspirators. To cite Hutchinson again: "There were men in each of the principal Colonies, who had Independence in view, before any of those Taxes were laid, or proposed. . . . Those men have conducted the Rebellion in the several stages of it, until they have removed the constitutional powers of Government in each Colony, and have assumed to themselves, with others, a supreme authority over the whole."[37]

Ironically, the exiles began, it was the complete victory of Great Britain in the French and Indian War that had provided the plotters with the opportunity "to execute their dark and insidious design of revolting from the parent state." After the French withdrawal from Canada, wrote Oliver, "the Buds of the present Rebellion began to swell." The Americans were now able to oppose the mother country, to put their plan into operation, because they no longer had to worry about the presence of a "formidable Enemy" on their frontiers. Consequently they began to cast about for "real or imaginary" grievances that could serve their purposes, and they started to make preparations for embarking upon a titanic struggle with Great Britain.[38]

In 1765 came the first major opportunity for the Americans to advance their plan. Beset with financial problems, Parliament passed the Stamp Act to raise revenue from the colonies. The "distrust, jealousy and ferment" caused by the act, reported Leonard, "afforded scope for action" by the conspirators. The subject of taxation was, as Hutchinson noted, "most alarming to the people, every man perceiving immediately that he is personally affected by it," and so the Americans were nearly unanimous in opposing the act. "All parties, all denominations, and all ranks of people" joined in protesting the measure, Thomas Jones later recalled, and that indeed gave the plotters their chance.[39] They quickly began to organize opposition to the law, pretending "that they were driven to such measures by necessity; but in reality [asserted Hewatt] they had nothing less in view than their favourite plan of independence." The New Englanders "vomited out Curses against *Great Britain,* and the Press rung its changes upon Slavery": they "hung out the Flag of Defiance." In all of this the Americans "adopted the arguments of the minority in parliament, and took encouragement from them to resist the authority of the supreme legislature."[40] The leaders of the plot then managed to incite "abandoned men" in each of the American seaport towns to form mobs to destroy the hated stamps, and "these flames, kindled in New England, soon spread through all the capital towns along the coast."[41]

The ministry's response to the uproar only played into the conspirators' hands. Instead of exerting force to require obedience to the law, Parliament repealed it, thereby giving (in Hewatt's words) "such importance to the licentious party in

America, and such superiority over the good and loyal subjects as had a manifest tendency to throw the colonies into a
state of anarchy and confusion." Even worse, Hewatt continued, the repeal "served to promote a doctrine . . . that
the obedience of subjects was no longer due to the laws of the
supreme legislature, than they in their private judgments
might think them agreeable to their interest, or the particular notions which they may have framed of a free constitution."[42] And the Declaratory Act had done little to offset this
false impression because, Oliver noted, a "Law without
Penalties" was "useless," except to induce "Contempt."
Galloway therefore concluded that although the repeal of the
one act and the passage of the other "cannot be said to have
been the original cause of the rebellion, yet . . . so much
timidity and weakness in the councils of this country tended
to encourage and nourish the seeds of American sedition,
long before planted, and now growing fast to a dangerous
maturity."[43]

During the Stamp Act crisis, the plotters gained the
people's confidence and became the spokesmen for what
appeared to be the public good. All they had to do to achieve
their goal was to maintain this position. As a result, said
Leonard, "sensible that there was no oppression that could be
either seen or felt," they decided "to work upon the imagination, and to inflame the passions." By their "perpetual incan-
tation" they managed to keep the colonists in a state of
"continual alarm," and when their next opportunity — the
Townshend Acts — appeared, "the whole system of American
opposition was again put in motion."[44]

This time the leaders of the opposition to Britain were
merchants (that is, smugglers) who, Oliver declared, "dis-
guised their Private Views by mouthing it for Liberty." The
word liberty was so "Magick" that "the deluded Vulgar were

charmed with it" and were thereby thrown "into the harpy
Claws" of the conspirators. It was at this time (1768), Oliver
later asserted, that *"Adams* and his Junto" made their final
plans for independence. Playing an especially large role in the
plot was what Oliver termed "the black regiment" — the
dissenting clergy of New England, who were "strongly tinc-
tured with Republicanism" and who "distinguished their-
selves in encouraging Seditions and Riots." Indeed, Leonard
wrote, "what effect must it have had upon the audience to
hear the same sentiments and principles, which they had
before read in a newspaper, delivered on Sundays from the
sacred desk, with a religious awe, and the most solemn
appeals to heaven, from lips which they had been taught, from
their cradles, to believe could utter nothing but eternal
truths."[45]

The conspirators kept up the pressure even after they had
intimidated Parliament into repealing all the duties except
that placed on tea. The climax to their efforts to involve the
people in their schemes came in 1770 with the Boston
Massacre, which they had "previously planned," and which
they used deliberately to collect the sparks of rebellion "into
a Focus" and to cause them to "burst into Flame." After the
Massacre the royal government of Massachusetts was, Oliver
said, "pretty thoroughly dissolved," and there was nothing
loyal subjects of the king could do to oppose "the Torrent,"
for they were without protection once the royal troops had
been removed from Boston. "Some indeed dared to say that
their Souls were their own," Oliver observed, "but no
one could call his Body his own; for that was at the mercy of
the Mob."[46]

When the New Englanders had at last acquired control of
their home province, they moved with "premeditated design"
to bring their fellow countrymen into the movement for

independence, choosing the arrival of the East India Company tea in Boston to see "how far the other colonies could, by art, and management, be induced to take part with them." They executed "their rash purpose," the destruction of the tea, and waited to see what would happen elsewhere in America. To their great joy, recorded Seabury, the "more furious and fiery zealots" in the other colonies supported them fully, and they themselves became even more "turpulent and unruly."[47] But their action had an unexpected consequence as well: Parliament altered the Massachusetts charter. Through this one "fatal stroke" to their plans "all their fancied greatness vanished, like the baseless fabric of a vision." Therefore the "disappointed, ambitious, and envious men" had to oppose what was actually a measure calculated to improve government. They successfully convinced the people that the changes were oppressive, and, Leonard recounted, "a match was put to the train, and the mine, that had been long forming, sprung, and threw the whole province into confusion and anarchy. . . . Every barrier that civil government had erected for the security of property, liberty and life, was broken down, and law, constitution and government trampled under foot by the rudest invaders."[48]

The New Englanders' next step, revealed Seabury, was to call for a continental congress. This move was supported by many moderates in the colonies as well as by the "wrongheaded, blustering people," and the Congress itself contained "many men of the first abilities and independent fortunes, who knew the sense and wishes of the people." But the New Englanders continued to conduct themselves "in such a manner, as should have the greatest tendency to inflame the minds of the congress," and the result was that the republicans managed to control the entire proceeding.[49] The conspiratorial group at the Congress was composed of "congregational

or presbyterian republicans, or men of bankrupt fortunes,"
and, according to Galloway, who was present as a delegate,
they used "every fiction, falsehood and fraud" to carry the
day. In the months that followed, the conspirators continued
on the same deceitful path, inventing one "monstrous lie"
after another, concealing their "real designs and perfidy,"
until, at last, fighting broke out at Lexington and Concord,
occasioning the "general Uproar" that had been their objective since 1763.[50] The long-sought victory had been won.

[4]

This account of the coming of the war is, of necessity, a
composite, because individual loyalist historians differed in
their assessment of the relative importance of the various
causes they perceived for the Revolution. Some stressed the
rebels' hope for personal gain, others emphasized the Americans' ideological disaffection from the British constitution.
Some saw the New Englanders primarily as republicans,
others viewed the northerners' acts mainly in the light of
their dissent from the established church. And the loyalists
on occasion interpreted particular events of the prewar
period in disparate ways. But the differences were no more
than variations on the single theme that the revolt had been
fomented by a small coterie of determined agitators. The
loyalists did not uniformly agree on the composition or the
motivation of this group, but they all postulated — indeed,
assumed — its existence. Their belief that the rebellion had
been caused by a minority, in fact by an almost infinitesimal
minority, of Americans inescapably affected all their writings
about the war and blinded them to many of the realities they
might otherwise have recognized.

In the first place, if only a small number of Americans
supported the Revolution wholeheartedly, it was illegitimate

in terms of traditional theory. Many of the loyalists were willing to admit that perhaps, under certain conditions, resistance to an established government could be justified. But, according to John Locke and his successors, a legitimate revolution (as opposed to a rebellion, which was specifically defined as illegitimate) had to have the support of most of the people of the nation. More than a simple majority was required: the decision to revolt had to be made by an overwhelming percentage of the populace. Obviously, given their assumptions, the loyalists could never conclude that the American rebellion was an acceptable and justifiable one. Since it had been incited by a small group, it did not have the support of most Americans, and so it had no claim whatsoever to legitimacy.[51] The refugees' absolute insistence on this point — to the extent that they always referred to the dispute as the American Rebellion, not Revolution — meant that they were incapable of perceiving the widespread colonial involvement in the independence movement.

Second, when the loyalists' interpretation of the rebellion is examined in depth, it is revealed as circular, as leading nowhere but back upon itself. Once the circle was entered (at whatever point) there was no logical exit. Acceptance of any one of the assumptions necessitated acceptance of the other assumptions as well. Their train of thought can be outlined in the following manner: Since (as the loyalists insisted) the Americans had no legitimate, irreconcilable grievances against Great Britain, the Revolution itself could not be legitimate. Since the Revolution was not legitimate, it was not supported by a majority of the people. Therefore only a minority of the colonists agreed with its aims, which indicated that most Americans felt little dissatisfaction with British rule and had no real grievances.

Or the chain of reasoning could just as easily be reversed:

In the absence of well-founded complaints about British government in the colonies, most Americans remained loyal to the crown. If most colonists were still loyal, the revolt had been caused by a minority. If such was the case, it could not be legitimate and as a result could not involve legitimate grievances.

The circle was complete, self-contained, and totally misleading.

The importance of the loyalists' circular interpretation of the Revolution lies in the fact that this was the viewpoint they repeatedly impressed upon the British administration during the war. Convinced that most Americans were, like themselves, faithful to their old allegiance, and that the Revolution had been incited by a small, conspiratorial minority, they successfully persuaded the ministry to accept this same formulation. After Saratoga the British government decided to act upon the loyalists' theories, and the consequences were exactly the opposite of what the refugees would have wished.

6

Strange and Unaccountable Conduct

> The whole conduct of the war has been hitherto strange and unaccountable.
> — SILVESTER GARDINER, [1779][1]

AFTER the defeat at Saratoga, both the refugees and the ministry began searching for a new strategy that would bring victory in America. The loyalists, who since 1776 had more or less acquiesced in the administration's military plans, started to produce detailed tactical proposals of their own. And the ministry, which in 1774–1775 had given short shrift to the exiles' suggestions, finally began to pay them some heed. Lord North and his advisers eventually came to accept the refugees' interpretation of the Revolution, partly because it happened to coincide with their own views, and the result of the combination of these disparate interests was a military strategy that was to have disastrous consequences.

[*1*]

The Saratoga defeat was not the only shock the refugees experienced during the waning days of 1777 and the first months of 1778. In February came the announcement of the Franco-American alliance (at which the loyalists were "struck dumb," according to Hutchinson) and the revelation of North's conciliation plan, which offered far greater concessions to the revolutionaries than the exiles believed warranted. "So strange a measure is not to be paralleled in history," Hutchinson commented in his diary, and Thomas Bradbury Chandler termed the proposals both "entirely unexpected and altogether unaccountable."[2] The refugees were pushed still further into the depths of despair. In the spring of 1778 Henry Barnes reported himself "very much in the Dumps," Edward Oxnard recorded that he was "very low in spirits," and Henry Caner decided that America was "irretrivably lost."[3]

But just a few months later the exiles' mood began to change. The crucial event that lifted their spirits was, intriguingly enough, the total failure of North's peace mission. The unsuccessful attempt at reconciliation, wrote one loyalist, would "answer the good purposes of rousing and uniting the Nation, silencing opposition, and giving vigour to our Councils and future plans." In addition, the refugees hailed the appointment of Sir Henry Clinton as commander in chief, because they thought him "a very different Man from his unworthy predecessor," Sir William Howe. After a year of depression they had started the long climb up from the melancholy into which they had been thrown by the Saratoga catastrophe. They were convinced that all that was needed to bring the Americans "to absolute submission in the course of one Campaign" was a "well regulated plan under able and spirited Officers," for they had concluded that "it is not owing to the Prowess of the Rebels that the rebellion has not been reduced; much less to the want of Spirit or Numbers in the Kings Army, but to the repeated Errors and Mistakes of those who have had the conduct of it."[4]

The difficulty was that the exiles themselves disagreed over just what constituted the best possible "well regulated plan." Each would-be loyalist tactician regarded his home province as the logical focal point for British military action, arguing that possession of it and it alone would prove to be the key for the royal conquest of America. James Simpson asserted that Charleston's capture was essential for victory; Sir James Wright called for the reduction of Georgia; several Marylanders advocated an expedition to the peninsula between Delaware and Chesapeake bays; and Silvester Gardiner urged an attack on New England.[5] Since the proponents of each plan cited the same arguments on behalf of their schemes, it is hardly surprising that British authorities at first paid little attention to the details of any one proposal. When the ministers were told that closing the port of Boston (Charleston, Baltimore) would stop most American shipping, that possession of the Delmarva peninsula (Connecticut, the Hudson Valley) would cut the major rebel lines of communication, or that the local rebels (anywhere at all) were a particularly vile lot, deserving to be punished more than those in other regions, the administration quite rightly termed the loyalists' notions "most Extraordinary."[6]

In spite of the variation in their proposals, the refugees agreed on one point: "Good Policy" dictated that the loyal American population should be "favoured and encouraged" by British forces in the colonies. Jonathan Boucher and the other exiles recognized that "there is infinitely less Difficulty in gaining a Victory, than in turning it to any good Account, when gain'd," and so they argued that royal commanders should be careful to discriminate between loyal and disloyal Americans, that they should deliberately try to attract men to the British cause, and that they should both arm and protect local loyalists. With the assistance of such men, the refugees declared, the British army would have little difficulty in securing the colonies for the king.[7]

It was to the generals' failure to follow this scheme that the exiles ascribed previous British defeats. Although they disagreed on tactical details, the refugees believed that a successful strategy would have to rely heavily on indigenous loyalists, and they assured the North ministry repeatedly that such a strategy would inevitably bring victory. Until December 1778, their ideas were expressed individually and in somewhat inchoate form. But in that month Joseph Galloway arrived in London from New York, and under his leadership the exiles' proposals took on new strength and importance.

[2]

Unlike Hutchinson, who timidly confined his criticisms of British policy to his diary, Galloway did not hesitate to condemn publicly "all past measures" for their lack of "system." Within a short time after his arrival he embarked upon a vigorous campaign against the Howe brothers, Sir William and Admiral Richard, asserting that they bore the sole responsibility for the ineffectiveness of prior attempts to subdue the rebellion. He played a pivotal role in the parliamentary investigation into the conduct of the war, which was pursued sporadically during May and June of 1779, and as a result, by July he and his daughter were "scarce on speaking terms with any of the *Howe party.*"[8]

In his testimony before Parliament Galloway emphasized two major points: that "more than four-fifths of the Americans would prefer a union with Great Britain to independence," and that the Howe brothers' egregious mistakes were the reason why the colonies had not yet been conquered.[9] At first glance these premises seem quite distinct, but Galloway's peculiar loyalist logic linked them together through a chain of reasoning most readily apparent in his pamphlet, *Letters to a Nobleman, on the Conduct of the War in the Middle Colonies*. Galloway based his argument upon the assertion that most Americans were still faithful to the crown, and he explicitly derived this conclusion from a study of the history of the revolt. Everyone agreed that the colonists were perfectly loyal during the French and Indian War, Galloway observed. He then characterized the subsequent difficulties between the colonies and England as so minor and trivial that most Americans simply could not have become completely disaffected from their former allegiance. It was, he contended, absolutely impossible for a loyal populace to be weaned so rapidly from a mother country it had always loved and respected. Why then did some persons falsely assert that a majority of the colonists favored independence and that a victory over the Americans was therefore impracticable? Obviously, their intention was "to conceal from the public eye the shameful misconduct of the American war."[10]

Aware that the colonists were truly loyal, Galloway could see where the blame for the American fiascoes should be placed: squarely on the shoulders of Sir William Howe. He had "veteran troops" with which to oppose "new raised and undisciplined" militia, yet he allowed his enemies "to escape without pursuit" after defeating them on Long Island. He did not move across the Delaware River in late 1776, though to have done so would have brought victory, for "all the Middle Colonies were ready to submit." Even worse, Howe committed "blunder upon blunder" during the 1777 campaign, the greatest of which was his decision to travel to Philadelphia by sea via Chesapeake Bay. His errors were "so gross — so contrary to the least degrees of military knowledge, that their possibility almost exceeds the utmost extent of our belief."[11]

When Howe in an answering pamphlet specifically denied Galloway's assumption that a majority of Americans still adhered to the crown,[12] Galloway's response was immediate and intemperate. With his most important premise under attack, he escalated the dispute and ascribed Howe's actions to a "dark and heinous conspiracy of the Faction." Howe had served as the "arch-agent" of the English opposition party, "taking every step to procrastinate the war; to plunge the nation yet farther in debt, and a more general despondency; and to render Administration more odious to the people." In particular, the general deliberately "depressed the spirit of loyalty," refused to accept loyalists' offers of aid, and, "with an unaccountable versatility, adopted one plan after another, always choosing that which was most *expensive to the nation,* and *ruinous to the success of his own operations.*"[13]

The other refugees applauded Galloway's efforts to expose Howe's "shameful and scandalous" conduct.[14] Like Galloway, all of them had to find a reason other than rebel strength to account for British military misfortunes. If they once admitted that the American army could legitimately defeat royal troops, the exiles placed themselves in an impossible quandary, since such an admission would contradict their basic assumption that the colonial forces were weak, divided, and without significant support in the American countryside. A decisive rebel victory that could not be explained away could mean only one thing: that the rebels were *not* a small, unrepresentative minority, that most Americans were *not* in fact loyal to the crown. And that of course the refugees could not afford to admit, because the contrary proposition constituted the very foundation of their philosophy and their self-image. So, since they continued to insist that the royal army was the most powerful in the world, they had no choice but to conclude that previous British defeats had stemmed from inadequate, perhaps even treasonable, leadership.

For the loyalists, then, the widespread English revulsion against the Howes after 1777 proved to be a godsend. The exiles' explanation of British failure in the war was the same as everyone else's: the Howes became the universal scapegoats because they provided superficially logical and accessible targets. It was far easier to blame them for the army's difficulties than to look for other possible sources of trouble. Even more significantly, the ministry had especially compelling reasons for acquiescing in the loyalists' interpretation. North and Germain had no little stake in proclaiming the Howes' culpability, for by placing the responsibility for the American disasters on the generals in the field, they removed it from themselves. The refugees' analysis of the reasons for Britain's military losses therefore meshed nicely with the ministry's own self-interest, and so North relied heavily on the loyalists — especially Galloway — for evidence to impugn the Howes' actions. When Benjamin Thompson at one point told Galloway that "we should scarcely know what to do without you," he did not stretch the truth.[15]

The loyalists and the administration thus formed a community of interest on the question of the Howes' guilt. And since the refugees tied this issue to their fundamental assumption that most Americans continued in their traditional fidelity to the crown, it is not surprising that the exiles undertook a concerted attempt to persuade the ministry to accept that point as well. Nor, under the circumstances, is it surprising that the ministry, after ignoring the refugees for years, began to prove receptive to their arguments.

The immediate impetus for the loyalists' drive came from the testimony of one of Sir William Howe's witnesses in the parliamentary investigation. General Charles Grey declared in early May 1779 that the rebel forces were so strong they could not be beaten, that most Americans supported the goal of independence, and that even the allegiance of the refugees themselves was questionable. His statements, said one Rhode Islander, seemed "to fix a sigma upon all the Americans," and the exiles accordingly determined "to wipe it off."[16]

The means they chose to answer Grey's allegations was to organize themselves into a Loyalist Association and to present a formal memorial to the king, "setting forth their original Political Principles, their continuing Loyalty and attachment to the cause of Government etc. etc." On May 21, 1779, a number of Americans gathered at the Spring Garden Coffee House under the leadership of Sir William Pepperrell. Those present at this preliminary meeting scheduled a general convocation of American exiles for May 26 at the Crown & Anchor tavern in the Strand, "to consider of measures proper to be taken for their Interest and reputation in the present Conjuncture."[17]

When the refugees' second meeting convened as planned, approximately ninety persons were in attendance. They formally chose Pepperrell as their chairman and named George Chalmers to serve as secretary. In addition, a committee of twelve was directed to decide upon "the proper measures to be pursued . . . and to prepare every thing relative thereto, and make Report at the next meeting."[18] Galloway, John Patterson of New York, and Daniel Leonard, who were appointed to the committee, then proceeded to prepare a draft of an address to the king, which they presented in early July to an informal gathering attended by Elisha Hutchinson, Chandler, and Boucher, among others. "After 3 or 4 Hours debating and several amendments proposed most of them rejected the Address was voted," Hutchinson recorded. On July 6, at a full meeting of the Loyalist Association, the final version was approved and signed.[19]

The purpose of the address was stated in its first paragraphs: The refugees wanted to correct the erroneous impression that British failures on the battlefield had been caused by the disloyalty of the colonists. To the contrary, the exiles could "assure your Majesty, that the greater Number of your Subjects in the confederated Colonies, notwithstanding every Art to seduce, every Device to intimidate, and a Variety of Oppressions to compel them to abjure their Sovereign, entertain the firmest Attachment and Allegiance to your Majesty's sacred Person and Government." As evidence for this contention, the refugees cited the "counter Resolves" against Congress adopted in various sections of the country, the formation of loyal militia units to combat rebel troops, the many colonists who had fled their homes or enlisted in the British army, and the numerous petitions presented to English generals asking for protection from the rebels. The loyalists surrounded this basic argument with effusive protestations of their "unfeigned Thanks" for the king's "unparallelled [*sic*] Exertions" on behalf of his loyal subjects, and they concluded with a prayer that "the supreme Disposer of Events" would "crown your Majesty's Endeavors with a Success proportioned to the Righteousness of your Cause."[20]

In Elisha Hutchinson's opinion, this address contained "such strong assurances of greater number of the Inhab[itan]ts in America retaining the firmest attachment and allegiance to the King as will I imagine prevent the majority of Americans in England from signing." Hutchinson himself refused to approve the petition for that very reason, but George Rome, a Rhode Island merchant who also had his doubts about its contents, was eventually persuaded to sign it.[21] There is simply no way to determine how many other refugees knew of the address but did not agree with its assessment of the colonists' loyalties. By mid-1779 many of the

Americans in the British Isles were living far from London and were probably unaware of the Association and its goals. One hundred and five exiles did sign the petition, most of them merchants, farmers, and tradesmen, their distribution by colony roughly reflecting the proportions of the exile population then in Great Britain. Massachusetts led the list with twenty-nine signers; then came Virginia with thirteen and South Carolina and Pennsylvania, each with twelve. Only New Hampshire was not represented, but New Jersey had just one signer and Rhode Island only two. Among the prominent names missing from the petition were those of Thomas B. Chandler, Thomas Hutchinson, Peter Oliver, and Martin Howard, who had nominally been a member of the drafting committee.[22]

Elisha Hutchinson's comments, coupled with the fact that some well-known signatures were noticeably absent from the petition, indicate that there was some disagreement among the refugees over the theory set forth in the address. But, like Elisha, dissenters evidently kept their thoughts to themselves, noting them privately in diaries and letters but not expressing them publicly. Perhaps some, like Rome, were prevailed upon to give nominal assent to a position they did not truly support. In any case, the fact remains that there were few refugee voices raised openly against the argument presented in the address. To all intents and purposes, the exiles were unanimous in their insistence that the Americans' continuing allegiance to the crown could not be questioned.

The refugees' confidence in this assertion was further demonstrated by the subsequent activities of the Loyalist Association. At the same time as the Association approved the address, its members established a permanent standing committee to "manage all such public matters as shall appear for the honor and interest of the Loyal in the Colonies, or who have taken Refuge from America in this country." The new group was formed by adding Sir Egerton Leigh of South Carolina and James Ingram of Virginia to such veterans of the drafting committee as Galloway, Patterson, Chalmers, and Leonard.[23]

In August the committee embarked upon two ambitious projects. The first, which seemingly never came to fruition, was to collect "Documents, Facts, and Informations" pertaining to "the Rise, Progress, and present State of the Rebellion in America." In connection with this inquiry each committee member was to answer a series of twenty-nine questions about the Revolution in his particular province: these included such queries as "At what Time and on what Pretence, did a formal Opposition to Government commence, and in what manner was it formed and conducted?" and "What measures were taken, and Arts used by Congress to reconcile the Minds of the People to Independency before they dared openly to declare it?" If the committee members ever supplied the material requested, it has apparently been lost, but the very wording of the questions is sufficient to suggest what the answers would have been.[24]

The second endeavor, by contrast, met with substantial success. The committee decided to inform the refugees in New York of the organization of the Loyalist Association and to request their "Co-operation and Correspondence." The committee's letter emphasized "the important Advantages of a Coalition of the Loyalists on both Sides the Atlantic," and it elicited an immediate response from the New Yorkers. One of them revealed to Chalmers that they too had been "roused" by Grey's testimony and that they had also sought "some Method to oppose the Arts of their Enemies and of course those of Great Britain and America." Following the London pattern, the New York refugees held a general meeting, appointed a board "to watch over their mutual Interests," and decided to address the king. That petition, like the one earlier presented by the Loyalist Association, asserted that most Americans retained their affection for Great Britain and would eagerly join in the battle against the rebels whenever "proper measures" were adopted to encourage them.[25]

It was not only through such group efforts that the loyalists pressed their analysis of the war on the ministry. In private letters as well they told Germain and North that the Americans "ardently wish to see a respectable Army of the King's Forces sent into their Country, and say they would far rather see the whole Country laid waste, though their property would be destroyed with others, rather than live under such Tyranny as they are compell'd to at present." The colonists, the ministers were told, "suffer so much from the Cruelty of their present Rulers, that there is scarce anything they would not do to get rid of their oppression." Even though many colonists had been forced to swear allegiance to the new state governments, the British officials were assured, "their Principles are the same as before."[26] With comparable statements emanating from almost every loyalist of note, it is not surprising that the administration finally began to listen to the refugees' suggestions. For once the Americans were telling the British government what it wanted to hear: that there was a panacea that would end all its battlefield difficulties. That the losses in the colonies were not irreversible. That the Americans had not inexplicably abandoned their ties to the mother country. And, most of all, that the solution to Britain's problems would not require any extra effort on her part, but that the colonists could be depended upon to carry a major share of the burden.

Small wonder that the ministry, especially Germain, found

much merit in the loyalists' arguments. A number of historians have since pointed out that the major mistake of the British ministers during the later years of the Revolution was their assumption that most Americans opposed the rebellion and could easily be mobilized to fight alongside the royal army.[27] This misconception unquestionably received vital support from the loyalists. Their interpretation of the conflict, vigorously promulgated by Galloway and others, convinced the ministry that the war after Saratoga should be pursued in the supposedly loyal South rather than in the reportedly more disaffected northern colonies.[28] In the end, the refugees' refusal to face the reality that the Revolution had wide support helped to entice the British army to Yorktown.

[*3*]

Early in 1779 came the "Glorious News" that Savannah had fallen to the king's forces, an event confirming the loyalists in their belief that the strategy they were recommending to the ministry was correct. During the following year their spirits continued to rise as new victories were reported, and in May 1780 a refugee in New York declared confidently, "The Rebellion declines daily, and is near its last Gasp." Just a month later the announcement of the capture of Charleston added to the loyalists' elation. "Can anything prevent the southern provinces from returning immediately to their allegiance?" William Browne asked his half brother rhetorically. "Their force being annihilated, their resistance must cease of course."[29]

In the autumn of 1780 the exiles received new evidence that the revolutionary effort was crumbling. Benedict Arnold, one of the best-known American generals, defected to the British, and the reason he cited for his desertion of the rebel cause coincided exactly with the loyalists' view of affairs in the colonies. Arnold declared that he had never favored independence, desiring only "a redress of grievances," and he reported the "Distress and Discontents" of the Americans in lurid detail, concluding that "the Eyes of the People are in general opened, they Feel their Error and look back with Remorse to their once happy Condition, and most ardently wish for a reconciliation on Terms safe and honorable to both countries." The refugees jubilantly took Arnold's treason as "proof that the fabric of congressional Tyranny is mouldering and tottering to it's downfall," and Germain noted approvingly that Arnold's testimony showed "the Congress Resources to be nearly exhausted, and their Cause universally sinking."[30]

Adding to the impact of the defection were countless letters the refugees received from friends in New York, all of which described the Americans as "heartily tired of the war, and groan[ing] under the yoke of tyranny, and the heavy taxes that are imposed on them." The loyalists still in the colonies reported that "the Tyrannical Congress are Quarreling amongst themselves"; that "their Money is depreciated, in every part of the Continent"; that the rebel army was in a "miserable State"; and that the Americans "should sooner or later suffer more from Wars within themselves, than they had done from the British forces."[31]

Understandably, the exiles did not keep this authoritative information to themselves; they systematically passed it on to members of the administration or published it in order to demonstrate that "there is an almost certain prospect of annihilating the rebellion in America, in one year."[32] Not that the point seemed to need much proving. The ministry and the loyalists agreed that the Revolution was on its last legs.

The refugees' confidence in their interpretation was such that they discounted any evidence contrary to it. In August 1780, for example, an American ship sailing under a flag of truce from Boston brought several Massachusetts loyalists to England, among them Robert Temple, who had been interned in Cambridge since 1775. Robert Hallowell, the former comptroller of the Boston customs house, thought Temple talked about America "in a very strange manner" because he insisted that the rebels would be satisfied with nothing less than independence. "Was you to hear Mr. T," Hallowell told his father-in-law Silvester Gardiner, "you would suppose they never could be subdued." Temple and the other passengers had to be putting the "Best face" on American affairs, Hallowell concluded. "I do not think full credit is to be given to what some of them have related — for they [the rebels] are certainly in a most distresed situation — and I do not suppose they got the men for their Army with that facility they would make us beleive [*sic*]."[33]

By early 1781 some of the more sanguine exiles were discussing possible peace missions, compensation by the government for their sufferings, and returning to America.[34] But in the minds of a few a lingering doubt remained. "I have learned to expect little to prevent disappointments which we have heretofore suffered," wrote Thomas Hutchinson, Jr., and Samuel Curwen concurred, telling a friend, "One swallow makes no summer." "I can only say, I am not hopeless," commented Boucher after reporting the aura of confidence that surrounded most of the refugees. And Peter Oliver observed that although the news from America was hopeful, he had seen "such repeated Misconduct after great Advantages" that he was not yet ready to celebrate a British victory.[35]

There was indeed, in the minds of some loyalists, ample

reason for pessimism. Sir Henry Clinton, whom they had expected to "reverse the policy and conduct of his predecessor," had failed to do so. Like Howe he sat "sleeping in New York" with his troops "while Ld Cornwallis calls in vain for Succours to the Southward." One disgruntled refugee poet put it this way, writing as if he were Clinton:

> If growlers complain
> I inactive remain
> *Will do nothing, nor let any others;*
> 'Tis sure no new thing,
> *To serve thus our King;*
> Witness B——e* and two famous brothers.[36]

The most active refugee critic of the conduct of the war was still Joseph Galloway. By early 1781 he was charging that Clinton was "utterly incompetent" and that he had done everything "which ought not to have been done" while he "shamefully neglected" everything "which ought to have been done."[37] By contrast, Galloway at first unabashedly admired Lord Cornwallis, whom he called "our second *Caesar,*" or perhaps *"Alexander."* "By his exertions," declared Galloway, Cornwallis proved "with a handfull of men what may be done in that Country." He concluded in July 1781, "Such a general as this . . . is the one I have ever said was necessary to the conquest of that or any other Country." Yet just a month later Galloway accused Cornwallis of going the "old wretched way" by failing to protect the loyal population of the territory he had taken. Cornwallis' victories, Galloway told Elisha Hutchinson, had "but little fruits attending them. Like a Bird he passes through the Country but conquers no part of it." Wrote Galloway in frustration, "When I see a General enter a province — give the people

* Burgoyne

assurances that he does not mean to desert them — cordially invite the Loyalists to take up arms and to seize upon and bring in the disaffected then and not till then will I presage an end to the rebellion."[38]

With all his pessimism, though, Galloway was no better prepared than the other loyalists for the report that Cornwallis had surrendered to the combined American and French forces at Yorktown, Virginia. "The unhappy American news has quite stunned us all," observed Thomas Hutchinson, Jr., and William Franklin, the last royal governor of New Jersey (who was the son of Benjamin), took the defeat as irrefutable evidence of the "Blunders and Mistakes" committed during the war.[39] But the "great national Calamity" was itself less important to the refugees than the specific terms of surrender, for the articles of capitulation did not protect the loyalists who had served with Cornwallis from rebel retaliation. To Franklin's mind the terms put the loyalists "in no better Light than as Runaway Slaves restored to their former Masters," and the refugees in New York expressed "great uneasiness and apprehensions" when they learned the details of the surrender agreement. Indeed, said one, "if Great Britain thus permits her friends to be sacrificed, she may bid adieu to America; for no government can expect subjection without protection."[40]

In London Galloway was reported "busily employed in counteracting this Misfortune," and the exiles continued to hope — rather desperately, it must be admitted — for "new measures, new men, and new reinforcements" that would "retrieve every thing but *the lives of our martyrs.*" Even after what Galloway termed the "wretched votes" in the House of Commons that halted offensive operations in America and caused the downfall of the North administration, the refugees clung to the notion that all was not yet lost. Grasping at feeble straws, Chandler decided that the new ministry knew

"in their consciences" that the war should be continued
(despite the fact that members of it had for years termed the
war "unjust and impracticable"), and he took heart from the
fact that Lord Shelburne, now one of the secretaries of state
under Lord Rockingham, had always opposed independence.[41]

It was with a renewed urgency that the refugees once again
flooded the government with plans to win the war, each
guaranteed to bring victory in return for little effort. Galloway contributed another pamphlet reiterating his position;
Gardiner proposed an attack on Boston harbor; another New
Englander advocated a march from Quebec to Ticonderoga;
Benedict Arnold offered to organize a compact mobile
marine force to harass major American ports; Lord Dunmore, the exiled governor of Virginia, thought the loyalists
should be allowed to conduct the war by whatever means
they chose; and a southerner asked for authorization to raise
ten thousand black troops from among the slave population
of the South.[42]

Moreover, the refugees continued their efforts to convince
the ministry that the war should not be abandoned, efforts
that were redoubled after they learned in August 1782 that
Britain was prepared to concede independence to the colonies. In London the exiles publicized accounts of the rebels'
"horrid cruelties" to loyalists and printed a series of letters
describing the state governments as being on the verge of
collapse. According to Thomas Hutchinson, Jr., the letters
"occasioned much talk and many opinions," but they seemingly persuaded no one. The refugees in New York, for their
part, prepared a new address to the king, urging him not to
grant independence to America, and they quickly dispatched
it to England in the care of William Franklin.[43] But by the
time Franklin arrived in the mother country it was already

too late. On November 29, the provisional peace treaty was signed in Paris, and its terms were far worse than the loyalists had anticipated even in their most pessimistic moods.

[4]

The movement towards a peace settlement began in April 1782, when the ministry sent Richard Oswald, an elderly merchant, to Paris to hold exploratory talks with his friend Benjamin Franklin, the American representative in France. Although serious negotiations were not undertaken until after Oswald's official instructions were issued on July 31, it was apparent from the very first that the fate of the loyalists would constitute the major topic of discussion at the peace table. There was disagreement over the boundaries of the new nation, the extent of American fishing rights in the Newfoundland banks, and the future political and economic relationship between the two countries, but in the positions of both sides on these questions there was ample room for compromise. The issue of the loyalists was quite a different matter.[44]

Oswald's instructions were explicit: he had to protect the loyalists. In particular, he was directed to press for the release of any persons still imprisoned in America because of their loyalty, to request "a Restoration of all [property] Rights as they stood before the Commencement of Hostilities," and to propose "a general Amnesty of all offences committed or supposed to be committed in the Course of them."[45] In stark contrast, the American negotiators had been specifically ordered by Robert R. Livingston, the secretary of foreign affairs, to resist any British efforts to win treaty stipulations in favor of the loyalists. In a lengthy letter Livingston outlined for Franklin an impressive list of arguments that could be used to exclude such provisions. "Every society may rightfully banish from among them those who aim at its subversion," Livingston declared, and so the loyalists' property was thereby "justly forfeited." Moreover, to allow the refugees to return would not only cause "general dissatisfaction and tumults" but also inject into American society a group of "dangerous partizans" of Great Britain who would "neglect no means to injure and subvert our constitution and government." Finally, in any case, it would be "equally unjust and impossible" to restore to the loyalists land that had already been confiscated and sold to others.[46]

The lines were therefore clearly drawn, and when Oswald first raised the question of the loyalists' fate with the Americans, they uncompromisingly rebuffed his overtures. Indeed, reported Oswald, Franklin refused even to discuss the matter, on the grounds that the negotiators had no power to reach agreement on the question, "as it was exclusively retained under the Jurisdiction of the respective States upon whom the several Claimants had any demands." In response to this obstinacy, the ministry (now headed by Shelburne) retreated from the strong stand taken in the original instructions. On September 1, Secretary of State Thomas Townshend told Oswald that the king "for the salutory purposes of precluding all future delay" was willing to waive the requirement that the loyalists be compensated by the treaty. Consequently, the first draft treaty proposed by Franklin and his colleague John Jay and forwarded to London by Oswald in October did not even mention the refugees. Its four articles set the boundaries of an independent United States, provided for the evacuation of British-held ports and the immediate release of all prisoners of war, allowed the Americans fishing rights in the Newfoundland banks, and established a reciprocal commercial agreement between the two nations.[47]

Even though the terms of the draft were the direct result of the changes in Oswald's instructions, the ministers quickly rejected the overly generous concessions that their negotiator had made. Henry Strachey, Townshend's secretary, was dispatched to Paris to strengthen Britain's hand, and Shelburne warned Oswald meaningfully that "many of the most weighty advocates for Independence [in Parliament] are strenuous for the Subject of Boundaries, and of a Provision for the Refugees."[48]

After Strachey's arrival, the tone of the discussions changed radically. Oswald had compliantly agreed to almost anything the Americans proposed, but Strachey, by contrast, was described by John Adams (who joined the American delegation in mid-October) as "the most eager, earnest, pointed Spirit," a man who was "artfull and insinuating," who "pushes and presses every Point as far as it can possibly go."[49] And so in early November the serious bargaining on the loyalist clauses began.

The first point carried by Strachey was that of debt repayment. Franklin had been as adamant on this issue as he was on the question of the loyalists, insisting that only the individual states had the power to decide policy on debts. But Adams did not concur: "The Question of paying Debts, and that of compensating the Tories were Two," he told Franklin, and assured Strachey that he had "no Notion of cheating any Body." On November 4, after a long session, agreement was reached on a clause (roughly approximating article 4 of the final treaty) providing that "no lawfull Impediment" could be placed in the way of the collection of debts contracted on either side of the Atlantic before 1775. Adams' motive for conceding this important point was far from altruistic. He correctly foresaw that the clause would divide the British merchants from the loyalists by silencing creditors' criticisms of the peace, thus preventing them "from making common Cause with the Refugees." He also astutely recognized that for this reason the ministry would welcome the proposal.[50]

At the same series of talks Strachey for the first time won a specific provision for the loyalists. The Americans agreed to a general amnesty applicable to any loyalist not attainted before the final British evacuation, and they also accepted a proviso that loyalists and British subjects would have six months after the evacuation to sell or remove their property and to emigrate freely into British territory. This, Strachey told Townshend, was "all that could be obtained," but before he left Paris to carry the draft of the new articles to London, he nevertheless addressed a formal appeal on the subject of the loyalists to the American negotiators, warning them ominously that their "Gratification of Resentment against Individuals" was threatening "every favorite object of America." Their refusal to indemnify the loyalists, he emphasized, was "the great obstacle" to reaching agreement. But Franklin, Adams, and Jay remained adamant even in the face of this strong statement of the British position. They replied once again that they had no authority to discuss the question, that even if they did, the return of confiscated property would be impracticable, and that they could not even think of compensating the loyalists because of the damage such men had inflicted on the United States.[51]

The negotiations therefore appeared to be deadlocked. It was obvious that the concessions in the new draft would be insufficient to satisfy the ministry, though some progress had indeed been made, and it seemed equally as certain that the Americans would not soften their position further. But on November 6, after Strachey's departure, came the conversation that was eventually to lead to a breakthrough.

On that morning Oswald called upon Jay to discuss the

loyalists once more. Of the three American negotiators, Jay was the least vindictive on the subject; he believed that some loyalists (including his close friend Peter Van Schaack) had acted from principle, and consequently he advocated that some men — all the loyalists "except the perifidious and cruel" — should be pardoned by the United States.[52] And that was what he told Oswald, revealing his personal opinion to the British negotiator for the first time. Although some loyalists could never be forgiven, Jay said, the "less obnoxious" would be treated by the states "with as much lenity as their case would admit of." Since most of these were "of low rank," they could easily resume their normal lives, and the British government would not have to reimburse them. As to the few loyalists who had been attainted, Great Britain could compensate them with property in Canada, or even with cash, and the cost "would be a small matter in comparison of the Expence of going on with the War another Year."[53]

A week later Oswald, acting upon the conversation with Jay, suggested that the loyalist clause of the treaty should be a "Recommendation to the Congress in their favour in general, leaving them to discriminate, according to circumstances." At this point the Americans were notably unenthusiastic about Oswald's idea, but it was eventually to become the basis for the crucial fifth article of the treaty.[54]

In the middle of the month Strachey returned from London with the ministry's draft of a stipulation for the loyalists, the government having unsurprisingly rejected the previous version. Like Oswald's proposal of a few days before, the ministerial draft was obviously based upon Jay's hints that the Americans would be amenable to differentiating among different classes of loyalists. The ministry proposed, as the ideal article, that any person whose property had been confiscated would be able to recover that property by refunding to its current owner the "Bona fide" price he had paid for it. But if this version could not be obtained, Townshend told Strachey, a number of alternatives were acceptable to the ministry. Each successive modification further restricted the types of persons to whom the clause would apply. The government was also willing to agree to a secret attainder article that would list by name those refugees not included in the terms of the treaty. Townshend was confident the Americans would agree to at least one of the suggested clauses, for, he declared, "it is impossible to suppose them so blind to their real Interests, as wantonly to proscribe so large a number of their fellow Citizens, whose repossession of their Property and re-union to their Country, is as essential to the prosperity of America, as to the honor of Great Britain."[55]

With the ministry's draft as the basis for discussion, the negotiations entered the final phase. After "a vast deal of Conversation" and "endless" sessions on the loyalists, agreement was finally reached on November 29. The debt and amnesty articles were little altered from the previous draft, but the loyalist clause differed from all the ministry's modifications, resembling instead Oswald's tentative proposal of two weeks earlier. In its final form, the fifth article provided that Congress would "earnestly recommend" to the states the restoration of the property of "real British subjects" and of persons who had not borne arms for the king and who were then residing in areas under British control. All other persons (that is, refugees and those who had fought for the crown) were granted twelve months in which to attempt to recover their property, and Congress was to "earnestly recommend" that persons of this description be restored to their property if they paid a purchaser his "bona fide" price. Strachey, for one, thought this version "much more advantageous" than any of the ministry's alternatives, especially because it avoided the "humiliating" secret article, and, he declared, "if this is not as good a Peace as was expected, I am confident it is the best that could have been made."[56]

The wording of the loyalist clause can only be described as ambiguous. But, as the American negotiators later explained to Livingston, "it is not to be wondered at, when it is considered how exceedingly averse Britain was to expressions which explicitly wounded the tories, and how disinclined we were to use any that should amount to absolute stipulations in their favor." Indeed, the "middle line" taken in the fifth article was truly ingenious.[57] The only definite provision for the loyalists was the year's period of grace granted some of them, yet Congress was committed by treaty to take affirmative action on their behalf. By the same token, the article — in line with Jay's suggestions — discriminated among different types of loyalists, giving preferential treatment to British nationals and to loyal native Americans who had not played an active role in trying to thwart the Revolution. The most reprehensible loyalists, in American eyes, had the least provision made for them: nothing more than a year in which to try to regain their property, and even if successful they were then required to reimburse its present owner.

Because the phrasing of the fifth article was so convoluted, and because so much of its effective force depended upon the discretion of the Americans, it is useful to ask how each of the parties involved in the treaty-making process interpreted its meaning. The American negotiators, for their part, thought they had perhaps purchased the desired boundaries and fishing rights by "a little too much 'reciprocity' to the tories." They believed they had "exceeded their instructions" — as indeed they had — by conceding even a congressional recommendation on the loyalists' behalf. Yet once they had agreed to the fifth article, they thought it should be enforced. They expressed a wish that Congress would make the recommendation called for, that the states would act upon it, and that "the legislatures may not involve all the tories in banishment and ruin, but that such discrimination may be made as to entitle the decisions to the approbation of disinterested men and dispassionate posterity." For example, Jay thought that complete forgiveness should "indeed extend to very few, but even if it applied to the case of one only, that one ought, in my opinion, to be saved."[58]

Congress, by contrast, had quite a different understanding of the clause. Livingston found it "a very slender provision," one which seemed "rather to have been inserted to appease the clamor of these poor wretches than to satisfy their wants." He informed the negotiators that the clause "will operate nothing in their favor in any State in the Union" and added significantly, *"but as you made no secret of this to the British commissioners, they will have nothing to charge you with."* The Americans, of course, had done nothing of the sort. In fact, if Strachey is to be believed, they had told him exactly the opposite: "The American Commissioners continued to assert . . . *that the Recommendation of the Congress would have all the Effect we proposed,"* he informed Townshend when explaining why he and Oswald had accepted the specific language of the fifth article.[59] Despite this obvious contradiction, though, Franklin, Adams, and Jay were not necessarily guilty of deliberately misleading their British counterparts. All three men had been absent from the United States for several years, and they probably were not aware of the depth of American hatred for the loyalists, nor could they have foreseen the disregard for the treaty that was to result from that hatred.

But if the American negotiators were not fully cognizant of their countrymen's attitudes, the refugees certainly were.

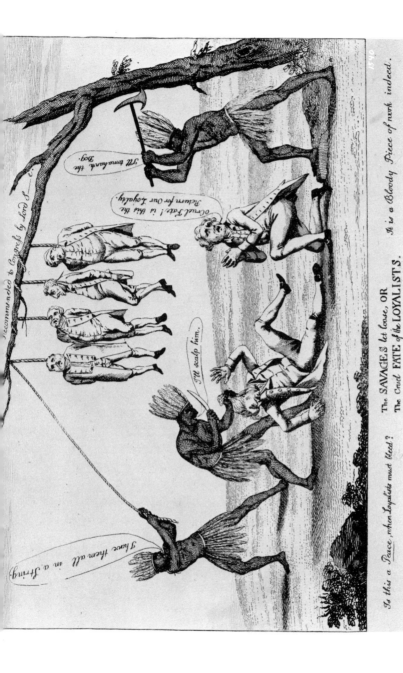

A British cartoon criticizing the peace terms. Americans were commonly portrayed as Indians in works of this kind.

Like Livingston, they knew immediately that the recommendation to Congress was the same as "casting them off altogether." Wrote John Watts, an exiled New York merchant and councilor, "It might reasonably have been expected the Treaty wou'd take care of those who had been quiet and inoffensive, far from it, we who were proscribed and our Estates confiscated remain just as we did, with only this difference, to be *mercifully* recommended by Congress to the several States, to be treated as seemeth good in their own Eyes, a comfortable Situation, to be sure."[60] A discouraged Galloway declared, "America is given up — Rebellion has triumphed and Britain is rapidly on the high Road to Ruin." All his efforts "to set the Nation right" had failed; "the Government know the whole and more and yet will do nothing and the people are too dissipated to think of any thing but their private Interest." What was the use of his continuing to fight? "It might be the subject of a day's conversation and no more."[61]

The British negotiators, on the other hand, were optimistic in their interpretation of the fifth article. In fact, Strachey told Oswald, "My idea was, and is, that the Resolution of Congress to the different States concerning the Restitution of Property will be equivalent to a Message from the King to Parliament, and that it is not probable any refusal will be given, except to a very few, who are particularly obnoxious." This view was widely accepted in Britain in the months following the signing of the preliminary treaty. As a North Carolinian informed a friend, "A generous performance of the Articles of the provisional Treaty is fully expected on their parts."[62] There was no better indication of this expectation than the content of the parliamentary debates on the subject of the peace treaty, for Shelburne, in defending the terms negotiated under his direction, insisted that there was good reason to believe that Congress would fulfill the terms of the fifth article. And, he argued, if the Americans reneged on their word, "is England so lost to gratitude, and all the feelings of humanity, as not to afford them an asylum?" With less than twenty percent of the cost of one year's campaign, the loyalists could be given "happiness and easiness . . . in as ample a manner as these blessings were ever in their enjoyment."[63]

Later in the debate Shelburne's words were echoed by John Wilmot, who had just completed the revision of the pension list. Although he disagreed politically with the loyalists, Wilmot declared, he thought them "with some exceptions, persons of the greatest merit, and entitled to every consideration from this country." Yet even so he did not find it reasonable to expect Americans to "give up their estates and possessions again to those with whom they had been contending." Consequently, the government planned to make "some solid provision" for refugees unable to obtain compensation under the fifth article. But Wilmot emphasized his belief that this group would comprise only a small proportion of the larger loyalist community. Furthermore, anyone "recompensed with sterling money, instead of a ruined estate, or American paper currency," would have little cause to complain. In conclusion Wilmot assured his fellow Members of Parliament "that everything has been done in their favour that could be reasonably expected, though not every thing that could be wished; . . . that the treaty does provide effectually and completely for by much the greatest part of the American Loyalists, that the interests of the remainder are attended to; that the number of those, who will derive no benefit from the treaty, are few in comparison of the rest, and that they will be provided for, as is most just, at a much more moderate expence than is generally imagined."[64]

Clearly, there were almost as many interpretations of the fifth article as there were groups involved with the treaty. The American rebels and the loyalists both agreed that the clauses were meaningless; the American negotiators thought them partially enforceable; and the British ministry expected them to prove almost completely effective. In order to cut its losses and escape from the war as quickly as possible, the Shelburne administration elected to shoulder the responsibility for compensating what it thought would be the few loyalists too obnoxious to receive consideration from the Americans. But the treaty it accepted on those grounds not only brought down the government but also involved Great Britain in the affairs of the loyalists for years to come. For, because of American hostility towards the loyalists, what the ministry had originally envisioned as a brief inquiry into a limited number of claims from refugees not compensated by the United States turned into a comprehensive, detailed, and exceptionally complex investigation into the cases of more than three thousand loyalist exiles.

7

A Debt of the Highest and Most Inviolable Nature

It is . . . a debt of the highest and most inviolable nature, from which Parliament can never honourably and justly discharge itself, but by making adequate compensation; nor can the moral obligation to do it be by any means suspended, for a moment, but by national inability and insolvency.
— JOSEPH GALLOWAY, 1788[1]

CONVINCED that the Americans would not enforce the ambiguous terms of the peace treaty, the refugees decided that the only way they could obtain compensation for their American property was to persuade the British government to make good their losses. The ministry had indeed promised them restitution, but a key question was left unanswered during the parliamentary debates on the treaty. It was not clear whether the administration would act quickly, or whether it would wait for years before taking positive steps to reimburse the exiles. A prolonged delay would obviously cause hardships for the loyalists, who were eager to make permanent plans for their future. And so, as a result of their desire for immediate compensation, the refugees for the first time since 1779 organized themselves into a coherent pressure group.

[*1*]

On January 28, 1783, the Massachusetts loyalists living in London gathered at Sir William Pepperrell's house on Wimpole Street to discuss the possibility of petitioning Parliament for rapid and complete restitution. Since some of their number questioned the utility of a formal memorial, the New Englanders instructed Pepperrell to ask for Lord North's opinion on the subject before they reached a final decision on the strategy they would pursue. North not only heartily approved of the project (perhaps because he knew it would embarrass Lord Shelburne's government), but also advised "all the colonies to unite together." The loyalists quickly adopted the strategy he proposed, and on February 4 refugees from throughout the continent met in London to consider "proper measures for obtaining redress in the article of the provisional treaty." The exiles concluded that "delegates should be selected to represent the several provinces that felt themselves particularly aggrieved," and they directed a committee composed of Pepperrell, William Franklin, Galloway, William Bull, and Lord Dunmore "to adopt such measures they might think proper." The next day the Massachusetts refugees convened again to empower Pepperrell "to consult and act in all cases in conjunction with the agents from the other provinces, giving his private word not to take any important step without consulting his constituents."[2]

But other loyalists were not convinced that a unified organization would serve any useful purpose. Samuel Peters, for example, was so opposed to the plan that he managed to persuade his fellow Connecticut refugees not to participate in the new group. Peters explained, "Upon the whole I think our Strength is in setting still, since we must stir up Enemies

against us, and by our striving we cannot make any Friends."[3]
Yet despite this strain of hostility, and notwithstanding the
mutual mistrust reflected in the New Englanders' suspicion
that Galloway had "sinister designs," the board of loyalist
agents was soon a functioning body. All the provinces except
Connecticut eventually chose representatives to sit on the
board; its first members were, in addition to the men just
mentioned, Thomas Boone (coagent with Bull for South
Carolina), John Wentworth of New Hampshire, Sir Robert
Eden of Maryland, Thomas Macknight of North Carolina,
and Sir James Wright, who was elected chairman.[4]

As its first official act, the board dispatched Wright, Franklin, Wentworth, and Eden to Lord Shelburne with the draft
of the proposed petition to Parliament. Shelburne's administration was at that very moment under attack for having
agreed to a treaty that did not sufficiently protect the loyalists, so he understandably refused to lend his support to the
refugees' memorial, which asserted exactly the same point.[5]
The constituent exile groups thereupon voted to submit the
petition to Parliament over Shelburne's objections, and the
agents revised it to meet some of his arguments. The refugees
informed the House of Commons that "upon a serious consideration of the Treaty with the United States" they could
"entertain no expectation of relief" in America — that they
had to rely solely upon the justice and magnanimity of Parliament to repay them for their "sufferings, losses, and distresses" in the service of the crown. The agents contended
that it would be an "unprecedented hardship" if the loyalists
were required to bear the entire financial burden of the peace.
Rather, the costs of this "national Benefit" should be
"equally distributed among and borne by the whole Society."
In other words, Parliament should tax other British subjects

in order to reimburse the refugees, so that the price of peace could be spread evenly across the nation.[6]

The agents did not stop with the presentation of this memorial to Parliament. Before the month was out they published the first of many pamphlets, *The Case and Claim of the American Loyalists Impartially Stated and Considered,* in which they asserted that the refugees had "an incontestible right" to restitution. Basing their contention both on the specific circumstances of the war and on a peculiar interpretation of the principle of eminent domain, the agents argued that because Great Britain had surrendered the loyalists' property in order to achieve the common good, the nation was thereby obligated to compensate them for their possessions. If adequate restitution was not forthcoming, Britain would stand revealed before the world as an "unjust, dishonest, and oppressive" state. Therefore, the board concluded, "the Nation is bound, as well by the fundamental laws of the Society, as by the invariable and eternal principles of natural justice, to make them a compensation." Being practical men, the agents did not rest their case wholly upon these theoretical considerations. A collateral publication, *Collections with regard to the Case of the American Loyalists,* recited at some length the various official proclamations that had promised protection to loyalists and also listed a number of precedents for the reimbursement of persons injured in the service of the king.[7]

The exiles' intensive campaign for compensation, which was predicated upon the inadequacies of the treaty, may well have contributed to the toppling of the Shelburne administration late in the month. On February 21, Lord John Cavendish, a Rockingham Whig who had refused a position under Shelburne, introduced in the House of Commons a series of resolutions censuring the peace terms. The first four motions passed with the support of a coalition that included both Lord North and his longtime opponent Charles James Fox, and Cavendish then withdrew the fifth, which vaguely promised compensation to the refugees. In spite of their failure to win specific assurances of restitution from Parliament, the agents had at least helped to bring about the downfall of the ministry that had betrayed their interests at Paris.[8]

In the next few months, with the government in disarray because of the changeover in administrations, several of the state exile organizations initiated projects intended to make Parliament more receptive to the refugees' demands for reimbursement. Acting at the suggestion of the board of agents, some state groups attempted to estimate the "Aggregate Loss" of their constituents, in order to discover the approximate amount of relief that should be requested from Great Britain.[9] The Virginians and South Carolinians appointed committees to examine in detail the financial statements of refugees from their states. The goal of this inquiry, Dunmore noted, was to reduce "the Claims as much as possible from a hope that the smaller the demand was the more likelihood there was that parl[iamen]t wo[ul]d make them compensation." The South Carolina committee had already begun meeting by mid-February, and the Virginians were busily investigating claims in June. Both groups deliberately undertook the task of passing judgment on the cases they considered.[10]

The report of the seven-man South Carolina committee is of special interest because it revealed for the first time the types of problems that were later to plague the official claims commission. Although they worked "with all possible diligence," the committee members explained, their progress was "considerably retarded by the different, as well as the deffective, manner in which several of the claims are stated." The South Carolinians commented that a large number of the items on the loss schedules "were estimated above their real value," and even though they had tried to make compensatory deductions, they believed that "many of the Demands will probably be further and very Considerably reduced upon a more perfect investigation." In particular, the committeemen recorded their failure to place accurate valuations on claims involving extensive debts, regardless of whether those debts were owed to or by the claimants.[11]

While its constituent organizations were engaged in their studies of the refugees' losses, the board of agents devoted itself to propaganda activities. On numerous occasions during the spring London newspapers and magazines printed news items designed to show "what the Loyalists have to trust to from the mercy of the Americans." British readers were informed of the town meeting in Worcester, Massachusetts, that decided on May 19 that it would be "extremely dangerous" to allow refugees to return; of the April 9 Boston meeting that reached the same conclusion; of the opinion of some residents of Morristown, New Jersey, that "those despicable wretches" should be hanged; and, above all, of the likelihood that a congressional recommendation in accordance with the fifth article of the treaty would have no effect whatsoever on the recalcitrant states.[12]

In late June the board finally saw its efforts achieve success. On the twentieth Cavendish, who had become chancellor of the exchequer in the new North-Fox administration, presented a second formal petition from the loyalists to the House of Commons. Four days later he asked permission to submit a bill to extend the authority of John Wilmot and Daniel P. Coke, who were then hearing pension cases, "to render them competent to discover and ascertain, with some tolerable degree of precision, who were and who were not persons distressed in consequence of the civil war, and persons entitled to the protection and relief of parliament." Cavendish explicitly stressed the preliminary nature of the inquiry he proposed. By the time Wilmot and Coke reported their findings, he argued, Parliament would be better informed as to America's intentions with regard to the treaty, and, through the cooperation of both countries, "effectual relief would be administered to those who had been distressed in consequence of the late unfortunate civil war."[13]

The limited scope of Cavendish's plan dismayed the refugees. In an attempt to convince the ministry that a more comprehensive scheme was called for, the agents presented Fox with a "General State of the Circumstances of the Property belonging to the American Loyalists, which has been confiscated by Laws of the American States." While the compensation proposal was before Parliament, the board met every day, and it hurriedly published a pamphlet drafted by Galloway that criticized Cavendish's plan. *Observations on the Fifth Article of the Treaty with America* contended that Great Britain should under no circumstances postpone making definite provisions for reimbursing the loyalists. Galloway pointed out that some of the property of "real British subjects" had already been sold by the states. As a result, such persons would be unable to recover their possessions even if the terms of the treaty were enforced. Moreover, he noted, the Americans probably would not restore property to any loyalists who had borne arms against them, regardless of the fact that soldiers nominally had a year in which to try to obtain compensation. He urged Parliament to authorize a "judicial enquiry" into these classes of claims at least, even if it was decided to delay consideration of the cases of other types of refugees.[14]

Perhaps the agents' arguments had some effect, for the compensation act passed by Parliament in July 1783 was far more comprehensive than Cavendish's original proposal. The law established a five-member commission with the authority to investigate the loyalists' claims in detail, rather than simply to survey them in general terms. Furthermore, the commission was empowered to consider the cases of refugees of all descriptions, not just the cases of those particularly penalized by the treaty. It was expected that the commissioners would complete their task within two years, and March 25, 1784, was established as the deadline for submitting claims. Wilmot and Coke, already experts at considering loyalist pension requests, were logical choices for the commission; also appointed were Robert Kingston and Thomas Dundas, two army officers who had served in America, and John Marsh, an experienced civil servant. Together the men were directed to inquire into the "Losses and Services of those who had suffered in their Rights, Properties, and Professions, in consequence of their *Loyalty* to his Majesty and Attachment to the British Government." On August 30 the commissioners held their first formal meeting, thus beginning an endeavor that was to occupy them for more than six years.[15]

Before the commissioners started to examine individual cases, they consulted "the most respectable and most intelligent of the Committee or Agents of the American Loyalists" and other refugees as well in an attempt to gain information that "might tend to facilitate the investigation of each particular Claim." Wilmot later acknowledged that these preliminary discussions were "of great service" because they gave the commissioners "a very good general knowledge of the subject."[16]

The agents' contributions to the inquiry fell into two quite different categories. First, the members of the board, and other exiles acting at their instigation, supplied the commissioners with data on local property values, prices of household goods and foodstuffs, currency depreciation rates, and the confiscation policies of each of the states.[17] Second, and more important, the refugees offered numerous suggestions as to how the commissioners could best conduct their task. Not only did the exiles' assessments of possible pitfalls prove remarkably accurate, their proposals also became the basis for the lines of inquiry the commissioners eventually pursued.

In the statements they presented to the commission the agents began by stressing the wording of what George Chalmers called "the most significant clause in the whole act": that which restricted compensation to those persons injured "in consequence of loyalty." To the refugees' minds, this phraseology had a dual implication. It meant that incontestable proof of loyalty would have to be supplied by anyone who sought redress under the act. And, it meant that losses not specifically resulting from a claimant's fidelity to the crown should not be considered by the commission. Any losses "incidental to the War," caused by "the common Accidents or ravages thereof," would not fall within the scope of the investigation. A South Carolinian's formula was simple: loyalists should be reimbursed only for the property they would have held intact after the war had they been rebels.[18]

The agents' rationale for suggesting the first of these limitations is obvious: they wanted to prevent mendacious rebel sympathizers from submitting successful claims. But the second is more difficult to explain, because most of the refugees had indeed suffered losses that were not directly related to the fact of their loyalty. Soldiers of both sides had damaged their lands, expropriated their animals and crops, seized their ships, and lived in their houses, usually without payment.

Naturally the exiles wanted to obtain as much restitution as possible from the British government, yet their representatives consciously proposed a severe contraction in the scope of the inquiry. The resolution of this apparent paradox lies in the agents' entire approach to the subject of compensation. As was demonstrated by the diligence of the state committees in closely examining the claims of their constituents, the exile organizations wanted to reduce the total sum requested from the British government. By thwarting fraud and restricting claims to property lost directly as a consequence of loyalty, the agents hoped to ensure that Parliament would make full restitution of the remaining (and still sizable) amount. It was to their own advantage, they believed, to help the commissioners limit the size of claims, for the less that was distributed to the undeserving, the more that would be left for the truly worthy.

To this end, the agents warned the commissioners that they should trust no one. "Every mans claim be his Rank or Character what it will, ought to be enquired into as strictly as the lowest," admonished one southerner. This was all the more true because any man might value his property too highly simply because of "the prepossession and partiality with which mankind are apt to view their own acquirements." In fact, James Simpson correctly predicted, "the most intricate and difficult part" of the commissioners' task would be the assessment of the exact worth of a piece of property, not the determination of who had owned it.[19] To enable the commissioners to distinguish between accurate and inflated valuations, the agents suggested a long series of searching questions that could be asked of each supplicant for relief. The inquiries ranged from general requests for information about the claimant's background, birthplace, and so forth to very detailed queries concerning the amount of his indebtedness, the solvency of his creditors, and the exact status of the property under consideration (was it confiscated? was it sold? was it mortgaged? was it in the hands of relatives?) .[20] The loyalists covered nearly every imaginable contingency so thoroughly that the commission in later years rarely strayed from the pattern of questioning they established.

At the same time as the agents informed the commissioners of possible frauds, they also did their best to aid those among their honest constituents who would perhaps be unable to produce "such proofs, as might be necessary in a Court of law." Because of the circumstances of the war, said William Franklin, it was unlikely that all the refugees would have complete documentation to support their loss schedules. Urging the commissioners not to reject such cases out of hand, the agents suggested that the testimony of witnesses or evidence obtained directly from America could help to prove the validity of an otherwise questionable claim. Eventually, the commission recognized the wisdom of this advice and dispatched a representative to the United States to gather pertinent data.[21]

The agents' initial strategy, therefore, was to cooperate fully with the claims commissioners in the hope of bringing them to sympathize with the refugees' plight. During September 1783 the agents and the commissioners worked closely with each other, and the culmination of the relationship probably came with the publication of a pamphlet entitled *Directions to the American Loyalists, in order to enable them to State their Cases.* Although officially unattributed, the tract seems to have been produced jointly by the board of agents and the claims commission. It encouraged exiles to read the compensation act, advised them not to submit false claims, and provided sample forms for memorials, witness

lists, loss schedules, depositions, and powers of attorney. Although the commissioners later required claims to conform
on the whole to the conditions laid down in the *Directions,* it
is apparent from the contents of the pamphlet that they did
not draft it entirely by themselves.[22]

This cordial collaboration between the agents and the
commission could not long continue, if only because ulti-
mately the interests of the two groups were contradictory.
The commissioners, after all, were the investigators, and the
agents represented the persons being investigated. If the
agents were to fulfill their proper function, they could not
comfortably occupy a middle ground between their constituents and the commissioners. This they discovered when the
commissioners asked them to assist actively in the conduct of
the inquiry, either by handling preliminary examinations of
the claims or by appointing qualified persons to "digest"
cases and arrange evidence for persons needing help. The
agents' abrupt rebuff of both requests indicated that they had
recognized that their aims were not necessarily compatible
with the goals of the commission, and that they could best
serve their constituents by criticizing the claims process from
the outside rather than by participating fully in it.[23]

[2]

In early September the commissioners placed advertise-
ments in the London newspapers, instructing loyalists to
submit their claims for property loss to the commission's
offices in Lincoln's Inn Fields. For some the announcement
brought confusion, because a number of the exiles did not
understand the difference between the new investigation and
the pension hearings conducted previously by Wilmot and
Coke.[24] And even the refugees who knew they could now
submit more detailed requests for compensation sometimes

wondered whether it would be worth the effort. Polly Hutchinson, for one, expected little to result from the inquiry because of the British government's "parsimony." A young Pennsylvanian agreed that "the distracted situation of this Country" made the possibility of restitution "extremely slender indeed," and a New Yorker declared pessimistically, "I do not believe we shall ever get one Sixth part of our real losses."[25] But the loyalists' actions belied their words. Few eligible refugees failed to submit claims to the commissioners, and, although they continually denied any hope for complete redress, they balanced their explicit statements to that effect with an implicit assumption to the contrary.

An examination of a letter written in February 1784 by Isaac Low, a refugee from Manhattan who had served in the First Continental Congress, illuminates their pattern of thought. Low told his brother Nicholas that he was presenting a claim only out of "Duty," being "without Hope, that the desired Compensation to the Loyalists will terminate in any Degree equal to their Expectations." Yet elsewhere in the same letter Low asserted that his evidence was so complete it would "stand the Test of the strictest Examination."[26] Theoretically, he was willing to admit that most claimants would probably be reimbursed for only a small proportion of their actual losses. But he — like every other loyalist — clung to the belief that his award would amount to full compensation if the documentation was sufficiently convincing.

As a result, Low and his fellow exiles expended much time and effort in the preparation of their formal memorials to the commissioners. They assiduously collected written evidence of all sorts to support their claims, lined up series of witnesses to appear on their behalf, and besieged the commissioners with requests for early hearings. Since documents had to be submitted in quintuplicate, the copying chores alone took days, and many refugees, especially those who were poorly educated, had to have assistance in drafting their petitions.[27]

The loyalists' memorials followed a standard format. They usually began with a declaration of unswerving, eternal allegiance to Great Britain, which was followed by a detailed recitation of the applicant's contributions to the war effort. The purpose of this self-serving account was to demonstrate that the claimant had "done all that could reasonably be expected from an unsupported individual, whatever might have been his capacity and his vigour." Refugees took particular care to explain any circumstances that could be interpreted to their disadvantage: those who had not borne arms offered excuses for this apparent dereliction of duty; others defended their decision to remain in rebel-held territory; and those who had fled to safety in England early in the war stressed their attempts to avoid becoming a burden on government.[28]

More important than these subjective matters was the substance of the claim itself, the exile's listing of the exact amount of his losses. To make his account seem more reasonable, each loyalist did his best to convince the commissioners that he was requesting restitution for only a small percentage of his actual loss and that he had no intention of claiming "the uttermost farthing." Memorials habitually noted that "inconsiderable losses" or "extraordinary expenses" were generously being overlooked, and one New Jersey man even modestly decided that he would not ask to be reimbursed for "the future Value of his Estate."[29]

Despite the refugees' almost universal disclaimers, an examination of their memorials shows that they took advantage of every conceivable opportunity to increase the amount of their claims. In general, their efforts fell into two categories: first, the inflation of property values, and second, the inclusion of dubious items on their loss schedules.

An exchange of letters between Robert Leake, a New York refugee, and his brother John, who had remained in the United States, may serve to illustrate the first point. According to Robert, his estimate of loss was "thought by all who have seen it, to be the most reasonable one given in to the Office." But John, who found "many Errors" in his brother's account, took strong exception to that opinion. The property valuations, he told Robert with "no small degree of pain," were "in several instances far too high." In response, Robert admitted that the estimates were "in my opinion too high, but," he explained, "I was advised and overruled by the first Claimants in this Country." All he had done was to adopt land values comparable to those listed by men whose property had adjoined his; for obvious reasons he did not want his schedules to conflict with ones submitted by William Smith and Sir John Johnson. The only item that was really "extravagant," he informed John, was the listing of "loss of increase and profit, which I found charged by every other person."[30]

It was this latter sort of claim that was more commonly used to increase the size of loss accounts. Refugees regularly asked reimbursement for travel and living expenses, losses incurred when land was sold cheaply to avoid confiscation, damages done to their estates by troops of both sides, losses resulting from the depreciation of continental and provincial currency, and uncollectable debts, even when the debtors were admittedly insolvent.[31] Less often, but still not infrequently, the commissioners encountered claims for such blatantly inadmissible items as the £250 annual income a loyal law student expected from the practice he was never able to establish in Charleston, the £24,000 a Rhode Island merchant would have grossed had the war never occurred, and, in one extraordinary case, "the loss of the proper use of my Limbs," which, the applicant explained, is "of a much more valuable nature than any other species of property whatever."[32] In absolute terms, of course, he was correct, but by no stretch of the imagination was the compensation act intended to provide loyalists with that kind of relief.

The well-known fact that many exiles had by such means "magnified their Claims beyond the Bounds of strict Propriety" began to worry some of the more conscientious among them. One concerned New Jersey loyalist wrote in February 1784, "I fear from the enormous valuation that a great number of People have made, that Govermt not being able to pay the whole will be obliged to compound the matter and pay so much in the Pound, by that means those people who have had any concience and made a just estimate (which by the by I believe to be very few) will only receive in proportion to those that have charged three fold the value of their property."[33]

As this letter indicates, the refugees did not anticipate a serious inquiry into every item listed on their schedules. To them, the most important component of their claims was the total amount of their loss. They naïvely believed that the estimates would be accepted more or less as submitted, following a somewhat perfunctory investigation designed mainly to expose out-and-out fraud. They assumed that the more one claimed, the more he would receive; that deductions, if made at all, would fall evenly upon all claimants as a standard percentage of whatever amount had been originally requested. Even the loyalist agents, who had advised the commissioners to look closely at each memorial, operated under the same assumption. They too expected all reasonable claims to be accepted without much difficulty.[34]

Significantly, the claims commissioners had quite a different conception of their role. A refugee's total loss estimate, so

crucial to his mind, meant little to them. They were concerned rather with verifying each individual entry on the
schedules both as to the fact of loss and as to the amount of
loss involved. Demanding precision in written and oral evidence, they exhibited no qualms whatsoever about striking
unsupported items from exiles' accounts. From the outset
they defined the scope of their inquiry more narrowly than
the loyalists expected. Besides excluding "normal" wartime
damages (as the agents had suggested), they refused to consider claims for losses incurred outside the limits of the
United States or for any property acquired during the war in
territory then under rebel control. And, by the time of their
first report to Parliament in August 1784, the commissioners
had also declared inadmissible any claims for rents and incomes accrued during the war, offices acquired since 1775,
tracts of uncultivated land, uncollectable debts, depreciation
of currency, income that had not been habitual before the
war, and estimated income from trade. Only four categories
of acceptable claims remained. The first, and the one that
encompassed most of the eligible memorials submitted, the
commissioners described as losses of property within the
United States "sustained by Persons of undoubted Loyalty"
who had lived outside the United States before or during the
war, when those losses could be ascribed to their "Loyalty
and adherence to the British Government." The other three
admissible classes were losses of life appointments or positions
held during the pleasure of the king, if those posts had been
acquired before the war; losses of professional income to
which the claimants had been accustomed before 1775; and
claims submitted by heirs of loyalists, if the heirs were also
loyal.[35]

The commissioners had a good reason for excluding so
many classes of claims: on the whole, they either found it

impossible to evaluate such items accurately or did not consider them to be losses resulting from loyalty. But they never informed the board of agents of the restrictions thus established, regarding their procedures instead as requiring strict confidentiality. The policy was designed to prevent widespread objection to the exclusion of the claims items, but it succeeded only in creating misunderstandings and hard feelings. Although Wilmot later tried to shift the blame for the secrecy rule to the ministry, it was in fact the commissioners who first insisted that "great Inconveniencies to the future Conduct of the Inquiry may result from the making of the Contents of their Report public." In the end, the criteria for judging claims were revealed only to Members of Parliament and to government officials.[36]

Wilmot, Coke, Kingston, Dundas, and Marsh began hearing cases in October 1783, and the work proved to be so time-consuming that by August 1784 they had completed work on only 142 of the 2,063 claims that had been submitted before the March 1784 deadline. Their instructions from Parliament complicated their task, for they were required to place each claimant into one of six categories according to his degree of loyalty and service before they allotted him compensation. As Wilmot later put it, they had to mediate somehow "between the Nation on one side, and the Individual on the other, whose whole patrimony, as well as character, depended on their Verdict."[37] The task was far from easy. Only by subjecting claimants, witnesses, and documents to a searching scrutiny could the commissioners accomplish their goal.

As a consequence of the commission's dedication to uncovering the truth, the formal hearings became an ordeal for both claimants and their witnesses. Each person testified separately, in secret, and the examinations were "very particular." Many refugees later admitted to being "flutter'd" when they appeared before the commission, and more than one claimed that he had been "so agitated I could not properly answer to those questions you were pleased to ask me." The substantial number who thought it necessary to submit clarifying statements after their hearings amply attests to the difficulties they must have experienced.[38] All written material had to be presented to the commission in advance of the hearings, and if claimants could not produce several certificates from British army officers or leading American refugees describing their loyalty and services, their cases received short shrift. Even more important was the requirement that they supply definitive proof of the losses for which they claimed. This, as the agents had predicted, was a difficult assignment indeed, especially because at the time that many of the loyalists had fled their homes they had fully expected to return. Some had neglected to take their title papers with them, others had deliberately left their deeds behind in hopes that their property could be salvaged by friends and relatives, and many more had simply lost whatever documents they had once possessed.[39]

Occasionally, accurate supportive testimony could compensate for a lack of written evidence. Each loyalist called two types of witnesses to bolster his case: prestigious refugees, who could attest to his character and status, and former neighbors, who could usually describe his property in greater detail. According to Wilmot, most of the claimants testified with "the utmost honour, veracity, and candour," and any exiles who were less than honest were readily detected because "the opportunities were so many of comparing the information of such persons with that of others who could be depended upon, both for knowledge and integrity."[40]

As this statement implies, the commissioners were inclined to rely heavily upon the testimony of some persons whom they trusted implicitly, and the refugees seem to have sensed this fact. A few important men testified again and again, sometimes in cases of which they had only the most peripheral knowledge. James Simpson, the most popular witness, had forty-five appearances to his credit, but three or four persons from every state (usually former civil officials) each testified in more than twenty cases. The same rule applied to neighbors who served as witnesses. Fewer than half of the claimants ever testified for anyone else, even though each case was usually supported by three to seven witnesses. The group of twenty-six South Carolina claims examined between October and December, 1783, may serve as an example of this phenomenon. Seventeen of the claimants, more than the average, testified for one another; eleven of those appeared in several cases, and one man supported the claims of eight of his neighbors. There were ten instances of reciprocal testimony, and four of the claimants appeared only for persons who also testified for them.[41]

Such statistics suggest a definite possibility of collusion. Claimants often consulted their witnesses prior to drawing up their loss schedules, occasionally even requesting the witnesses' estimates of the value of their holdings. Other times they tried to persuade witnesses to include certain facts in their testimony or certificates, and still more frequently they showed their memorials and deeds to witnesses in advance of the hearings. But prior consultation could also backfire, as happened, for example, when one exile testified that the man for whom he appeared had told him that "there were some Articles he did not like and wished to expunge [from his account], and [he intended] to fill up the place with something to the same amount so as still to correspond with the Sum Total on the last page."[42]

Such blatant falsification was rare. Conscientious loyalists like Samuel Shoemaker refused to appear for persons with whom they were not well acquainted, and at times the poor quality of the supporting testimony was itself ample evidence that no collusion was involved. George Chalmers' scanty knowledge of a fellow Marylander's property was totally dependent upon what he had seen of it while "riding along the high Road," and a neighbor of a South Carolina blacksmith was only able to say that he "used to see many Negroes about the plant[atio]n which he took to be his — He lived in a very decent manner and appeared to be a man of some substance." Of the same type was testimony offered for a North Carolina farmer: the witness "knew he had Land at Crames Creek — but he can't speak to the value of it — Knew of no other Lands he had except that on which he lived — There were thereabouts 2 or 3 people who paid him rent."[43]

But even this minimal support was not always easy to obtain. Loyalists whose cases were heard after 1785 often complained that their key witnesses had already left to re-settle in Scotland, Ireland, or Nova Scotia. A few explained that none of their neighbors had come to the British Isles in the first place. Usually in such instances the commissioners themselves tried to locate witnesses who knew something about the claims in question, but on the whole they had no more success than the petitioners did.[44] It was all very well for the commission to require certificates, deeds, and witnesses to support each case, but in practice the established standards were seldom fully met. Most of the time the commissioners had to base their decisions on sketchy and fragmentary evidence, which did not make their task any simpler or less demanding. It also ensured that there would be unavoidable inequities in the awards they reported.

[*3*]

With the inquiry well under way, the agents in early 1784 began to consider further ways to aid their refugee constituents. At the recommendation of a committee that included the indefatigable Chalmers, they decided to press for the immediate payment of accepted claims. In trying to persuade the commission to agree to this demand, the agents argued both that the loyalists had a right to compensation that should not be negated through delay and that practical considerations favored rapid restitution. The board collected data to demonstrate that the American states were not enforcing the peace treaty, thus implying that Britain should not postpone her plans to recompense the loyalists in the expectation that the United States would soon act on their behalf. And the agents also hinted to William Pitt, the new first minister, that there were certain advantages to be gained by paying off the claims. "The sooner the intended compensation shall be made," they told him meaningfully, "the sooner government will get rid of the just complaints of these unfortunate men and be relieved from the burden of their present allowances."[45]

But Pitt stood firm in the face of these contentions, his adamancy based upon a not unreasonable desire to know the total extent of the demand upon his government before committing himself to paying it in full. The agents, stymied, decided to circumvent him by appealing directly to Parliament. In the spring of 1785 they published an official statement of their position, *The Summary Case of the American Loyalists,* which they distributed to the legislators in hopes of winning their support. But the tactic backfired. Although at this point the administration was well acquainted with the refugees' standard arguments, it was the first time Members of Parliament had been exposed directly to the agents' assertion that loyalist claims should be considered as "unfunded debts of the state," that is, that they constituted contractual obligations which Britain was legally required to pay. The legislators were not pleased, to say the least. One Member informed William Smith that the exiles "had only a Right to benign Consideration," and Pitt told the agents that "nothing . . . could be done till all the Losses were reported."[46]

Having no alternative but to accept failure in this endeavor, the agents then turned their undivided attention to two frequent complaints about debts that had come from their constituents. The first concerned debts owed by refugees to American citizens. Under the provisions of most of the state confiscation acts, the creditors of exiles were directed to apply for payment to the appropriate state governments, which were then to reimburse them out of funds received from the sale of the loyalists' property. Even under ideal conditions these applications were not always successful, and in certain cases the proceeds from the sale of the property were insufficient to cover the refugees' obligations. As a result, some American creditors began to file suit in British courts to recover their money. The refugees viewed these suits with resentment and dismay, for decisions favoring the Americans would in effect force loyalists whose property had been confiscated to pay the same debts twice.[47]

John Tabor Kempe, a New Yorker involved in just such a suit, tried in 1784 to obtain an English judicial decision freeing him from the obligation to pay his American creditors. John Antill, the refugee executor of the estate of Alexander Colden, an American subject, sued Kempe in the London chancery court for the £450 he owed Colden. Instead of contesting the suit, Kempe filed for an injunction in another court. He argued that "it is contrary to Equity and good

Conscience that any demand of the said Debt should be made upon your Orator by any Inhabitant of either of the said States [New York or New Jersey] unless your Orators Property should be restored to him of which there is no Probability." Antill responded merely that it would cause him "great Expense and trouble" to bring suit in New York and that his chance of success there would be "very uncertain." Although Kempe seemed to have equity and logic on his side, the second court refused to stay the judgment of the first, and Kempe was forced to pay the £450, plus court costs.[48]

In June 1785 the board of agents attempted to provide legislative redress for men like Kempe by drafting a bill to protect loyalists from suits brought in England by American creditors. Even though some refugees considered the board's proposal too weak, it and its successors in 1786 and 1787 encountered stiff opposition from the mercantile interests in Parliament. So strong was the feeling against the bills that none of them came to a vote.[49] Just as John Adams had predicted in 1782, the English merchants had been successfully separated from the loyalists by the terms of the treaty. Afraid that Congress would limit their rights to collect debts in America if Parliament restricted the Americans' right to sue in British courts, the merchants organized the resistance to the agents' efforts to win some protection for their constituents. In vain did Joseph Galloway contend that the passage of the bill would not violate the terms of the peace treaty. In theory he was correct, but the merchants knew only too well that the Americans had already proved to be notoriously disrespectful of technicalities.[50]

The agents had no more success in their efforts to deal with the other debt problem that beset the refugees, which was the question of whether the claims commission was going to compensate them for the sums they could not collect from

American debtors. Although the commission never officially informed the agents that it had excluded debts from its purview, the agents deduced that fact from loyalists' reports that they had not been examined on debt claims in their formal hearings. The agents repeatedly petitioned the commission on the subject, arguing that debts were "rights" lost because of loyalty and that as such they fell within the terms of the compensation act. The commissioners, though sympathetic, thought rather that the loyalists' debts were legally recoverable under the fourth article of the treaty, which provided that "creditors on either side shall meet with no lawful impediment to the recovery of the full value in sterling money, of all *bona fide* debts heretofore contracted." In response, the agents developed an ingenious argument contending that the fourth article did not apply to refugees because their debts had been transferred to the states by confiscation several years before the treaty was signed, but even this masterful effort was doomed to failure. The commission refused to alter its original decision not to accept claims for debt.[51]

All the agents' work did not go for naught, though. In the summer of 1785 the ministry finally made a significant concession to their demands for immediate payment. In June, Pitt proposed that £150,000 be distributed to those claimants whose cases already had been reported. Loyalists who had borne arms or rendered other services were to be paid 40 percent of their claims as liquidated by the commission, with all other refugees allotted 30 percent of the sums due them. After a spirited debate in which some Members of Parliament argued that "a fuller inquiry into the history and present circumstances of the loyalists" should be undertaken before the exiles were compensated, Pitt's plan was approved. The commission prepared a list of claimants eligible for shares of the £150,000, and the distribution began in early September.[52]

The loyalists welcomed the change of policy. The "handsome payment," John Watts commented, "exceedingly . . . rejoyces those who are partaking of it," and William Smith observed, "The good Humour it has created, cannot but give Pleasure even to those who don't share in the Benefaction." He approvingly remarked that the Treasury had managed the payments "so judiciously . . . as to free every Man's Mind from uneasy Anticipations; for he that recieves [*sic*], knows not of what Class he is, and so can't calculate upon the Appreciation of the Estimate he delivered in."[53]

Alas, Smith had vastly underestimated the refugees' deductive and mathematical capabilities. Soon the commission was inundated with complaints from dissatisfied claimants, who now realized for the first time how much was being deducted from their loss schedules. Many refugees, like Isaac Low, declared themselves "confounded and perplexed" by their "inadequate" allotments, most of them concluding with the New Yorker James DeLancey "either that I have not received my full proportion . . . or that my Claim has been decided upon mistaken principles." When assured that there had been no error, such men usually reasoned that they had "failed in point of proof." As a result they proceeded to dump additional documents in the laps of the commissioners, who were already overloaded with paperwork and who had no intention of reopening any of the cases they had decided.[54]

The first compensation act expired during the summer of 1785, and the law that replaced it reflected the experience of the preceding two years. The commission had realized that it was unreasonable to expect loyalists who had settled in Canada to come to England for claims hearings, so the new act authorized the sending of commissioners to Quebec and

Nova Scotia to examine cases there. It had also become apparent that the deadline of March 25, 1784, had excluded a large number of legitimate claims simply because many loyalists had not arrived in England by that time. Accordingly, the second act empowered the commission to receive claims until May 1, 1786, from persons who had been "utterly incapable" of submitting a memorial before the original deadline.[55]

The summer of 1785 also brought alterations in the personnel of the commission. After three years of dealing with the refugees, Daniel P. Coke decided to resign. In his place were appointed two new commissioners, Robert Mackenzie and Jeremy Pemberton, and they, plus the experienced Dundas, were dispatched to Canada, leaving Kingston, Marsh, and Wilmot to continue dealing with cases in England. In addition, the act of 1785 authorized the commissioners to send a representative to the United States to gather data on claims, and in August a young man named John Anstey was employed to perform that task. The commission instructed him to collect information about claimants' titles to property, the confiscation and sale of their possessions, the possibility of their estates being restored to them, and the debts they owed in America. Anstey left for the United States early in 1786, remaining there for nearly two years. The data he supplied caused the upward revision of many of the original claims reports.[56]

After the passage of the new act, the dispatching of Anstey, and the partial payment of some claims, the agents' objectives changed. They continued to call for protection from American creditors' suits and for restitution for uncollectable debts, but they abandoned their insistence on immediate reimbursement. Instead, they argued simply that refugees should be informed of the exact amounts of their liquidated claims and that they should be paid interest on the sums still outstanding. The board also requested that professional men, omitted from the distribution of funds in 1785 because of the nature of their claims (for income rather than property), be included in the similar distribution planned for 1786. As usual, though, their efforts were unsuccessful. Wilmot categorically rejected the agents' contentions on debts and professionals, and when Parliament considered granting the exiles interest on their remaining claims, the ministry quickly moved to squelch the idea. To allow interest on the sums due, the chancellor of the exchequer declared, "would pledge the House for the full payment of them at some future period, which was a principle not hitherto recognized."[57]

Thwarted in their attempts to gain additional concessions, the agents in late 1786 and 1787 largely ceased their complaints about procedures, awaiting instead the conclusion of the investigation. In March 1788, with the inquiry obviously drawing to a close, the board once again petitioned the king and Parliament. Although the memorials reiterated the usual arguments for compensation, they especially emphasized the "Wretchedness, and Woe" that characterized the lives of the refugees in England. Deprived of their property, denied redress, many of the loyalists had been "reduced from Affluence to Poverty — others, under the Pressure of Want, have died with broken Hearts — and some have been driven by their Distress into Insanity — and from Insanity to Suicide; leaving their helpless Widows, and Orphans to prolong their miserable Existence on the cold Charity of Strangers."[58]

Joseph Galloway contributed to the agents' final campaign by writing still another pamphlet. In it he repeated his contention that the loyalists' property had been *"the price and purchase of peace for the empire"* and that restitution was "due them by their birth-rights as British subjects." Besides being "fully compensated" for their property losses, the refugees deserved to be additionally "rewarded" for "extraordinary services." If the ministry did not accept this obligation, Galloway asserted, it would be "subverting the design of the union, and manifestly violating its solemn engagements, its duty, and the evident principles of reason, justice, and law."[59] Galloway's tract was joined in print by the agents' own concurrent publication, *Reasons why No Deductions ought to be Made from the Amount of Sums due to the American Loyalists.* Asserting that the refugees' great losses and the high standard of proof demanded by the commissioners had combined to make the official awards fall "very far short" of the actual amounts of loss, the agents argued that the liquidated claims should be paid in full. In April they supplemented the pamphlet with a formal memorial to the House of Commons, and James DeLancey, the vice-president of the board, wrote a lengthy letter to Pitt, explaining why no distinction should be made among various classes of refugees in the final settlement.[60]

But again the agents failed to achieve their objective, a circumstance that became evident when Pitt commented casually in a parliamentary debate in early May that the refugees' claims "amounted to so large a sum, that it would be utterly out of the power of this country to make them full compensation for their losses." His plan of payment, presented to Parliament on June 6, 1788, accordingly struck a compromise between partial and complete restitution. Pitt proposed that liquidated claims of less than £10,000 be paid in full, but that awards above that amount be reduced according to a proportional scale: 10 percent would be deducted from any excess over £10,000 but under £35,000; 15 percent from £35,000 to £50,000; and 20 percent from awards above that sum. In other words, the larger the amount reported by the commissioners, the greater the proportionate reduction in the sum a loyalist would actually receive. Of course, whatever compensation claimants had been allotted in the distribution of funds in 1785, 1786, or 1787 would be deducted from their final payment. Pitt described his plan as "a liberal and a handsome compensation" that "left the loyalists without a plea for complaining that they had been hardly dealt by."[61]

Most Members of Parliament agreed with him. Many recorded their approval of the scheme, among them Edmund Burke, who declared that he had never voted for a bill "with more satisfaction," for he thought the compensation "both liberal and prudent, neither too large on the one hand, nor too small on the other." But there were two significant exceptions to the general chorus of approbation: Daniel P. Coke and John Wilmot. Both men argued that every loyalist should be paid the full amount of his liquidated claim. Coke cited specific cases of refugees who would be adversely affected by the deductions Pitt had proposed, and, although Wilmot reluctantly agreed to bow to the will of the majority, he "owned he had ever expected, that what the commissioners reported, was to be the amount of the sums paid to the loyalists."[62]

In spite of the obvious drawbacks of Pitt's plan, the loyalists were so pleased at the settlement of their claims that initially they did not criticize the details of the arrangement. In a formal petition of thanks to the king, the agents on July 2 poured forth "the ardent effusions of their grateful hearts" and asserted that their constituents would ever be ready to "devote their lives and properties to your Majesty's service, and the preservation of the British Constitution."[63] Although the compensation scheme fell short of the loyalists' expectations, Parliament had not drawn distinctions among different descriptions of exiles. Moreover, since 1785 the

John Eardley-Wilmot, by Benjamin West (1812). The picture in the background, painted by West in the 1780's, symbolically portrays the loyalists' gratitude to Great Britain for offering them compensation and a refuge. At right are West and his wife; at the head of the refugees stand William Franklin and Sir William Pepperrell. (Wilmot took the additional surname Eardley in 1812.)

refugees had become accustomed to the idea that their awards would be far less than they thought they deserved. They felt only gratitude and relief that their fight for restitution had finally culminated in a victory of sorts.

[*4*]

The claims commission's final report, issued in 1790, revealed that 3,225 claims had been submitted in England and Canada, with 2,291 loyalists receiving a compensation of £3,033,091. The figures were impressive, but the 2,291 refugees had originally estimated their losses at £8,216,126, and their awards consequently represented an average return of only 37 percent on their claims. Furthermore, 343 claims were completely disallowed by the commissioners, and those loyalists received no property compensation whatsoever.[64] Therefore, although the total amount disbursed by the British government seemed generous, some individual loyalists did not necessarily fare very well.

Because of the endemic deficiencies of documentation and testimony, the commissioners' awards rested largely upon their estimate of the truthfulness of each claimant and his witnesses. As a result, refugees whose integrity was questionable — especially those who had supported the rebel cause in any way — found themselves being closely examined by the commissioners.[65] Although the commission did not automatically disallow the claims of men who had switched sides, it did award them proportionately less restitution. A convenient means of demonstrating this fact is to compare the amount of compensation allotted to South Carolina refugees whose loyalty was doubtful with the awards to Carolinians whose allegiance was undeniable. Of 44 problematical loyalists whose cases were heard in England, only 17 (or 39 percent) received more than a 30 percent return on their claims. By contrast, of 98 known loyalists, 54 (or 55 percent) were awarded more than 30 percent of their estimated loss, with 19 (20 percent) of these receiving over one-half of the amount they requested. Only 6 (13 percent) of the other group of refugees were awarded as much.[66] Perhaps the commissioners did not consciously discriminate against vacillating exiles, but they were less inclined to believe the specific details of the testimony of a man who had changed his allegiance during the war. When the evidence was incomplete, as it was in many cases, they tended to decide against a claimant whose fidelity was questionable.

Despite the large number of loss schedules that were consciously or unconsciously inflated by the loyalists who submitted them, the commission rarely decided that a memorial had been prepared with a deliberate intent to defraud the government. Under the terms of the 1783 act, the commissioners' determination that a claim was fraudulent automatically excluded its author from receiving further compensation of any sort. The commissioners were genuinely reluctant to impose this sanction on persons whom they regarded as loyal, even if those persons had apparently submitted a false estimate of loss. Of all the property claims considered in England, the commissioners cited only the ten most flagrantly spurious as fraudulent. Two were cited because the claimants had charged for property they had sold during the war; one because its author had knowingly substituted sterling valuations for estimates originally drawn in terms of a depreciated colonial currency; one because the merchant who submitted it had been insolvent before the war; and the remaining six because the claimants had declared large losses even though they owned little or no property.[67]

The most incredible of the fraudulent claims was submitted by John F. D. Smyth of Maryland. Smyth represented himself as a wealthy physician with an annual income of £1900 and plantations worth £37,841, not to mention large tracts of valuable Ohio lands. But witnesses called by the commission testified that Smyth's practice had been small, his one plantation rented, and his reputation "so notorious as a liar that nobody would believe him." When confronted with this evidence, Smyth adopted a pose of injured innocence, explaining to the commissioners that he did not "presume" to claim any exact sum from the government. Rather, the only compensation he solicited was "what I conceived I had a right to expect without having sustained any Loss at all." Smyth was mistaken if he expected this disclaimer to protect him from charges of fraud; the commissioners decided that he had been guilty of "gross wilful perjury" and reported his case immediately to the Lords of the Treasury.[68]

When both the intent and the lies were less obvious, the commission was inclined to be lenient. Several times it merely disallowed claims, even when it decided that their authors had "prevaricated grossly" at the hearings. Disallowal carried with it no stigma of fraud, for that designation was commonly applied to items inadmissible under the commission's rules. Anyone's claim might be disallowed in whole or in part, and not even men like William Franklin were immune from such a determination. Most of the 343 disqualified claims simply fell outside the guidelines the commission had established for admissible losses, but a few do indeed appear to have been fraudulent.[69]

On the whole, it seems that the vast majority of claims were relatively honest. The commission rarely uncovered deliberate lies, most of their deductions resulting rather from the fact that inadmissible items were usually included on loss schedules. Unquestionably, some — perhaps even many — loyalists inflated the value of their estates, but few tried to claim for property they had not owned. And, because of the commissioners' strict rules, it is highly unlikely that any claimants were allocated more compensation than they deserved. In fact, an analysis of the distribution of the awards reveals that a majority of the exiles were allotted less than half the amount they originally requested. Moreover, the larger a refugee's claim, the smaller was his proportionate return, which demonstrates that the commissioners themselves had reduced the relative size of the awards even before Pitt officially proposed such deductions. No wonder both Wilmot and Coke opposed Pitt's plan in Parliament.[70]

A further conclusion that can be drawn from the pattern of claims awards is that certain types of claimants were likely to receive better compensation than others. Small landowners (if their lands were cultivated) received a higher percentage return on their claims than did artisans, tradesmen, and professional men, the bulk of whose property consisted of furniture, houses, books, tools, and the like. Since the same low percentages held for both obscure laborers and well-known clerics and lawyers, the difference in awards seems to have derived from the kind of loss claimed. The reason was simple: it was far easier for the commissioners to evaluate landed property than it was for them to estimate the worth of personal possessions. Witnesses, deeds, and titles could help to pinpoint the value of a farm, but the precise worth of personal property was difficult to determine. And when the commission was uncertain of its awards, it preferred to err on the low side.[71]

The group of claimants that suffered the most in relative terms was the merchants. Since much of their business was conducted on credit, the commission's decision to exclude claims for uncollectable debts hit them particularly hard. A majority of refugee merchants received less than a 30 percent return on their loss estimates, whereas a majority of all other claimants received more than a 30 percent return. As George Erving, a Bostonian and mandamus councilor who was allotted only £500 on a claim of approximately £20,000, accurately declared, "Those who have lost *dirt* are paid in gold, and those who have lost gold are paid in *dirt*."[72]

Appropriately enough, therefore, it was the merchants who most severely criticized the claims settlement. Contending that the board of agents, "being composed principaly [*sic*] by men of the learned Professions," had failed to protect their interests properly, a sizable number of refugee merchants organized their own pressure group in late 1788. Led by such men as John Hamilton and Cumberland Wilson of North Carolina, Robert Gilmour of Virginia, and John Jamieson of Georgia, the American merchants' committee repeatedly petitioned the ministry and Parliament for compensation for confiscated debts. But despite their conviction that they had been " (for reasons we cannot comprehend) . . . singled out and doomed to hardships unknown to any other class of his Majesties Subjects," it was not until 1802 that the merchants received even partial restitution for their debt losses.[73]

Other claimants soon followed the merchants' lead. The revelations of the preliminary fund distributions had not fully prepared some exiles for the proportionately small amounts they received, and they complained both long and loudly. One New Jersey loyalist commented on his allotment, "Justice if such a being existed would blush on hearing that publick confidance could be so much violated," and, he continued in utter bewilderment, "if the Commissioners of American Claims saw fraud in the representation I made of my losses, why not punish me as the Act of Parliament in that case directs, for willful and corrupt perjury; if on the contrary, no imposition, fallacy, or imposture appeared on my side; why dismiss me by the payment of so pitiful a sum." The exiles' dissatisfaction with their awards caused the board of agents once again to seek disclosure of the commissioners' "General Rules, and Principles," but without success. The loyalists in fact did not learn the exact basis on which the claims had been decided until Wilmot published his account of the inquiry in 1815.[74]

The secrecy issue, though important, was an old one, and the agents found a new concern in the months following the acceptance of Pitt's plan: the method of payment adopted by Parliament. Instead of being allocated one lump sum, claimants were issued government debentures bearing only 3½ percent interest. Furthermore, the principal was to be paid off in sixteen equal installments spread over eight years, an arrangement so complex as to make the debentures (in the words of James DeLancey) "utterly unfit for circulation, and so unmarketable, that a heavy Discount can alone force the Sale of them." Loyalists who wanted to realize cash in December 1788, the agents reported, were compelled to sell their bonds at a 5 or 6 percent discount from face value, with no allowance for future interest. Although the agents for several years sought a more favorable scheme for retiring the debentures, the most they could achieve was the prompt payment of the installments, which at least brought the discount rate down to 3 percent.[75]

In the end, it must be concluded that the loyalists were not, in a strict sense, reimbursed for their losses in America. They did receive partial compensation for those losses, a compensation that bore at least a loose relationship to the amount they had claimed, but their awards probably fell far short of what they had actually sacrificed by remaining faithful to the crown. Of course, seen from the standpoint of the

British government, the provisions made for them were indeed generous, perhaps even beyond what the loyalists had any right to expect. It is also obvious that the *pro forma* investigation and full restitution advocated by the board of agents would never have been implemented under any circumstances. In 1788, the refugees owned less than they had in 1775, but on the other hand they had more than they had possessed in 1783. Thanks to the compensation act and the claims commission, they had now the means to begin a new life. Finally, five years after the war's close, they were able to put it behind them and to plan for the future.

8

Finishing Their Days Among Strangers

> Once I thought to have spent my last breath there [in America], but since providence has otherwise ordain'd it, I am content, and must finish my days amongst strangers.
> — JOHN WATTS, 1785[1]

THE final settlement of loyalist claims, effected between 1788 and 1790, brought to an end the uncertainty that had afflicted the refugees since 1775. At long last their lives had begun to acquire a measure of permanence. The alternatives open to them were clear: they could remain in England, emigrate to British provinces in Canada or the West Indies, or return to the United States to live under the independent republican governments they had so strongly opposed. Each of these courses of action had its advantages and its drawbacks, and the exiles assessed the relative merits differently. Some stayed in the mother country, little changing the mode of existence they had adopted during the war years. A few decided to brave the lingering wrath of their rebel fellow countrymen in order to rebuild their lives in the United States. But most chose instead to begin anew in the wilderness of Nova Scotia or the uninhabited islands of the

Bahamas. For all, the financial support they received from the British government was of crucial importance. Without the reimbursement for losses of income or property, without the continuation of subsistence allowances, most of the loyalists would have been unable to make viable plans for their future.

[*1*]

After Pitt's proposal for paying the liquidated claims had been accepted, the ministry turned its attention to two types of cases that had previously been neglected: demands against the British army or navy, and losses of property in Florida as a result of the cession of that territory to Spain. Hearings to determine the extent and value of the Florida property were conducted by independent commissioners in 1786 and 1787, and the records reveal that most of the claimants were southerners who had settled in Florida after the evacuation of Charleston, in the mistaken belief that the area would remain in British hands. Consequently, many of them had endured two confiscations, first in the Carolinas or Georgia, then in Florida. Since these cases were comparable to the regular property claims, they were decided on approximately the same grounds.[2]

The army and navy cases, by contrast, involved a completely different kind of loss. They consisted of demands for reimbursement for property seized or destroyed by British forces during the war, and claimants with proof of the exact value of their losses were entitled to full restitution. Although preliminary examinations of these claims had been conducted in New York in 1783 and in London two years later, the three commissioners (Dundas, Pemberton, and Mackenzie) assigned to hear them still took two years to reach a final decision. In 1790 they recommended that more than £66,000 be distributed among 210 refugees.[3]

During the six years that property claims were being investigated, the commissioners had also continued to allot pensions to refugee Americans. But, in the years following Wilmot and Coke's revision of the allowance system, the criteria for awarding stipends changed significantly. In the first place, petitioners arriving in England after the final evacuation of America usually had no intention of remaining in the mother country longer than it took to press their claims for property loss. To the commissioners it seemed as though many had applied for temporary support simply as an "Experiment" to see if they could thereby obtain more money from the government than they would otherwise have deserved. As a result the commission began to stress need as the primary prerequisite for assistance. Loyalty and the amount of loss still entered into the commissioners' decisions, but increasingly they based the size of their awards upon their estimate of an applicant's ability to support himself. They commented that a New Jersey teen-ager was "a strong hearty young man . . . able to get his own Bread," that a Pennsylvania porter's "only misfortune (if it can be called so) is the being obliged to labour for his Bread in England instead of America," and they concluded that "in these Cases we think the parties, especially if they are young, should contribute to their own Livelihood, by their Industry in this Country as well as they before did in America."[4]

The commissioners proved particularly reluctant to award allowances to refugees whose status or prospects had actually been improved by the war. After hearing the testimony of a Philadelphia waiter, they observed, "It has been his Misfortune that the Troubles put him for a time into the Situation of a Gentleman and he is probably unwilling to return to his former Occupation which certainly is as open to him here as it was in that Country." And in the case of a North Carolinian they wrote, "If he is now without Property he is only in the Situation that he was in before the War." They especially applied this line of reasoning to the few blacks who submitted requests for pensions. Such men, the commissioners noted repeatedly, came "with a very ill grace to ask for the bounty of Government." Because of the war, they were "in a much better Country," where they would "never more be Slaves." What more could they want or deserve?[5]

A second alteration in allowance-granting procedures that occurred after 1783 was a new emphasis on applicants' merit and steadfast loyalty. Whereas Wilmot and Coke had been relatively sympathetic to men who had, under pressure, renounced their allegiance to the king, the commission as a whole — and especially Dundas and Marsh, it appears — was openly hostile to supplicants whose wartime role had been ambiguous. The commissioners expressed contempt for the men, mainly southerners, who had "played with their Allegiance" and "put it on or shaken it off as they thought it would best answer the Purpose of saving their Property." Such vacillation, they declared, "does not deserve the Name of Loyalty"; in fact, any persons who thus "played the double part" were "the worst Enemies of Great Britain."[6] Particularly culpable were the natives of the British Isles who, however briefly, had flirted with the rebels. Of an Irish gunsmith who had worked for the American troops until 1780, they wrote, "He ought to be ashamed of making this application and deserves to be punished rather than rewarded by this Country." They described a Scotsman who had taken a Virginia loyalty oath as a "Traytor" and commented on a former member of the Georgia provincial assembly: "As an Englishman he is much more to blame than

if he had been an American." Concluding that "Great
Britain must protect such people but she ought not to reward
them," they rarely recommended more than miniscule
stipends even for the most indigent loyalists of this description.[7]

The commissioners, then, went to great lengths to ensure
that refugees given allowances after 1783 truly deserved and
needed government assistance. But in spite of their careful
examination of applicants, the smaller size of the allotments
they awarded (most pensions now fell between £30 and £60
annually), and a constant review of previously granted
stipends, the pension list expanded rapidly. At the end of
1784, 643 loyalists were receiving £52,695; a year later, even
after reductions resulting from the preliminary distribution
of property compensation, it was 840 refugees and £57,528.[8]
One of the reasons for the vast increase in the number of
pensioners was the fact that by 1785 the commissioners had
begun to use the allowance system as a means of assisting
propertyless refugees who were not eligible for relief under
the acts of 1783 and 1785. Since such persons had been indigent in America, there was no way for the commissioners to
aid them within the framework of the official compensation
law. But, feeling an obligation to help support the deserving
loyal poor, the commissioners adopted a practice of awarding
them stipends of perhaps £10 or £20 a year. In consequence,
20 percent of the persons on the pension rolls in the spring of
1787 had not claimed a property loss.[9]

At the time of the final settlement of the claims, allowances
were being paid to three widely differing groups of refugees.
First, there were loyalists who had lost property and who
would need little or no assistance once they had been issued
their debentures. Second, there were merchants and other
persons who had not incurred losses falling within the scope

of the compensation acts. Finally, there were professional men who had suffered in terms of income, not property. These pensioners were permanently provided for (to varying degrees) by a dual allowance system established in early 1789.

One component of the system was simply the continuation of the regular pension list, with allotments completely revised in light of the property settlement. After loyalists who had received a sizable compensation were dropped from the rolls, two categories of pensioners remained. The first was composed of widows and orphans, the elderly and the sick, wounded veterans, and the like: those exiles whose indigency enlisted the commissioners' sympathy. The second was the merchants who could not be reimbursed under the relief acts because of the commissioners' exclusion of uncollectable debts from their investigation. All together, the revised temporary support list included 588 names and represented an annual outlay of £28,673.[10]

The other part of the dual system resulted from the section of Pitt's compensation plan that dealt with professional income. Under his formula, loyalists with a certifiable annual loss of £400 or less were awarded a yearly stipend of one-half their regular income. Any amount above £400 was adjusted according to a sliding scale similar to that adopted for property claims, and the allowances, of whatever size, were regarded as permanent and unalterable. They were not, however, awarded irrespective of other variables. If a pensioner had an outside income equal to or greater than his allotted sum, he received nothing. If he had some additional support, he was granted an allowance sufficient to bring his total income to the permissible level. In either case it was understood that future changes in outside income would cause suitable adjustments in the size of pension payments. The

204 exiles on the list were awarded allotments totaling £25,785 a year.[11]

These annuities provided some loyalists with the financial security that all of them had been seeking for years. According to Thomas Hutchinson, Jr., many of the lawyers and other professionals included on the rolls "were never so well off before," and a Rhode Islander rejoiced that he had not previously found employment, because "the *certainty* of a decent support of which we *cannot* be *deprived*" was not to be taken lightly under the circumstances.[12] The merchants, relegated to the more precarious temporary support list, looked upon the professionals with undisguised envy, and through the medium of their organized committee they tried to convince the ministry that only "arbitrary Grammatical definitions" had prevented them from being classed with the more fortunate lawyers and clergymen. In fact, they argued, commerce had been "the most honourable calling" in America prior to the war, and their income had been just as "secure" as if it had been invested in land or obtained from a law practice. The distinction between them and those who had been awarded permanent annuities was "verbal but not substantial"; they had been discriminated against only because the board of loyalist agents had "failed to represent, the Merchants Situation."[13]

Predictably, the merchants' appeal fell on deaf ears. Pitt and the commissioners, having worked so hard to limit the number of persons who could claim a right to a government allowance, had no intention of admitting the merchants to that exclusive group. Furthermore, they had before them in 1789 a prime example of how one innocent, well-meaning concession to the refugees could lead both to incredible confusion and to enormous cost. This was the half-pay system for provincial officers that had been set up immediately after

the war, even before the passage of the regular compensation
act.

Originally, commissioned officers in loyalist regiments had
been warned "neither to expect Rank in the Army, after
their Reduction, in consequence of such Commissions, or to
be entitled to half pay." But in January 1779 lagging recruitment had led Germain to alter this policy. He had directed
that the officers of "such Provincial Regiments as shall be
compleated to the same number and proportion of Men and
officers as the present Establishment of the British Regiments
of Foot" would be allowed half pay and rank "in the same
manner as the officers of British reduced Regiments are
paid." By the end of the war, only three loyalist corps had
qualified for half pay under these standards, and interested
refugee officers (Benjamin Thompson foremost among
them) pressed the ministry to loosen the requirements. In
mid-June 1783 Lord North succumbed to their pleas, formally extending the benefits of half pay to loyalists "who by
their Services and their Exertions have rendered themselves
deserving of those advantages and honorable marks of His
Majesty's Favor set forth in that Letter [Germain's] altho'
they may not have literally complied with the Engagements
which entitle them to it."[14]

Two weeks later North accordingly proposed to the House
of Commons that the officers of all twenty-one provincial
regiments on the British establishment be allowed half pay,
arguing as a justification that the spirit of Germain's policy
was more important than its specific wording. A number of
Members of Parliament, including the future first minister
William Pitt, questioned the wisdom of the idea, contending
instead that restitution of all sorts could best be left to the
planned claims commission. Pitt and others opposed the
scheme on the grounds that it would merely add to the

"profuse and wasteful system that had characterized the whole of the American war," but, notwithstanding "a very long and warm debate," the motion carried without a division.[15]

Unlike the property compensation act approved the following month, the half-pay bill established no special machinery to handle the loyalists' applications for benefits. Instead, half-pay petitions submitted to the ministry were simply routed to the offices of Sir George Yonge, the secretary at war. Yonge allowed the memorials to accumulate for months before taking any action, and it was not until August 1784 that he forwarded his first recommendations to the Treasury. Yonge's report indicated that he had had little difficulty in identifying the refugees eligible for half pay under the conditions outlined by Germain and North. But, he noted significantly, a number of other persons had also applied for relief under the act. Since these loyalists had "rendered very material Services during the War," he thought them "deserving the consideration of Government."[16] The Lords of the Treasury after some delay asked two generals, William Fawcett and William Roy, for their advice on the marginal petitions singled out by Yonge. Fawcett and Roy immediately undertook the "very complicated business" of reviewing the memorials, and their report agreed with Yonge's in pointing out that many exiles who did not qualify for half pay appeared to have "strong pretensions to some provision from the Public." The generals, well intentioned and seemingly unaware of the claims commissioners' attempts to award compensation to refugees in an orderly and controlled manner, recommended that worthy loyalists be given "particular allowances, not however to be under the denomination of Half-Pay, nor to give Rank."[17]

With this innocent and generous suggestion the work of

the commissioners was undone. Once it was admitted that persons with no claim whatsoever to half pay could receive :nilitary pensions, all efforts to limit the total outlay to refugees were doomed to failure. The exiles quickly learned that it was possible for men with only minimal military pretensions to qualify for allowances, and they soon came to regard the half-pay system as nothing more than another kind of compensation for their sufferings and losses in America. The scheme originally proposed to reward a small number of refugee officers for faithful service during the war was therefore transformed through ignorance and confusion into a general pension system paralleling, and in many cases contradicting, the one administered by the claims commissioners.

The loose interpretation of eligibility requirements for military compensation was the source of the problem, but it was further compounded by the lack of standard procedures for reaching decisions on the refugees' applications. Ordinarily, petitions were passed upon separately by Yonge, the Treasury, and Fawcett and Roy. Occasionally Howe, Clinton, Cornwallis, and Carleton were consulted as well. By the time memorials came before the Treasury for final decisions, they usually had at least one favorable recommendation attached to them. The Lords were always reluctant to disregard the opinions of the experts on any subject, and so many loyalists were allotted assistance on the strength of one general's vague statement on their behalf. Moreover, unlike the claims commissioners, the military authorities did not keep good records of their past proceedings. Exiles who had been denied allowances could simply apply again, not mentioning their earlier failure, and sometimes achieve success on the second try.[18]

As such cases imply, the generals paid little attention to precedent. No sooner would they establish a rule than they would break it. For example, militia officers were usually denied half pay because they had not served in regular regiments, but a lieutenant colonel of the North Carolina militia was awarded a pension after he argued that he had "run the same Risks, and made the same Sacrifises" as officers in established corps. Occasionally refugees who had been promised commissions but had never actually served in the army were given half pay, other times they were not; some loyalist guerrilla leaders received allowances, others did not; and although a few civilians were awarded both rank and half pay, most were not. The only way to describe the system accurately is to call it chaotic.[19]

The complete collapse of reasonable standards for awarding military compensation is apparent in the decisions involving loyalists who could not claim even peripheral connections with the war effort. A South Carolinian told Clinton, "*Good God* sure none can have a better claim to half pay, than a Man who lost a large property, took an Early, Active, and decisive part in the War suffered every hardship under Lord Dunmore in the Year 75 and part of 76 in Virginia — taken prisoner there Chained Handcuffed, and pinioned to two Negroes and in that Situation marched in the dead of Winter from Hampton to Williamsburg without shoe or Hatt being plunder'd of every thing and it snowing all the Way." Although nothing in this recitation indicated that he had rendered military services, much less that he deserved half pay, he was awarded £60 a year. Even more incredibly, Thomas Macknight, who had fled to England in 1776 and could only assert that he had "exerted his utmost endeavours as a citizen, as a magistrate, and a member of the Legislature" to support the British cause, was awarded £50 annually after he argued that, since most of his acquaintances had military pensions, the fact that he did not receive one "affixes a stigma on his character which he has not deserved." It is hardly surprising that by the end of 1785 the outlay for military allowances was already double North's original estimate.[20]

In February 1788 the Lords of the Treasury realized that somehow they had to put a stop to the steady stream of half-pay applications that continued to flood their offices. This resolve was strengthened several months later when Fawcett and Roy revealed that "as they happened not to serve in America during the late War . . . they find it difficult if not impossible to discriminate between those who are justly entitled or are real objects of Compassion, and those who are not." Early the following year the generals made the further damaging admission that they were "apprehensive" that they had recommended pensions for unqualified persons, observing in passing that "they cannot help fearing that they are still more liable to be mislead [*sic*] in future on account of the Length of Time which has elapsed since the Close of the War." The Lords thereupon decided that, as of January 3, 1789, they would accept no more half-pay applications. And that rule they did not break.[21]

By the spring of 1789, therefore, final compensation for the loyalists had been arranged. The first debentures were being issued for property losses, permanent annuities had been apportioned, an equitable system of charity was being continued, and military allowances assisted those who had been fortunate enough to qualify for them. But, even before all of these provisions had been made for their support, many of the exiles had begun the slow process of making new lives for themselves. In fact, some had started when the ink on the peace treaty was scarcely dry.

[2]

The end of the war left the refugees (as Mrs. Henry Barnes said) in "a very unsettled state, not knowing where, or how, to dispose of themselves." She assessed the alternatives accurately: "Few of them wish, (even were they allowed that libberty) to return to Boston, and (after injoying the sweets of old England for Eight Years,) they shuder at the thoughts, of repairing to the Wilds of Nova Scotia." It seemed to Mrs. Jacob Duché, as it did to many other exiles, that the only solution to their problem was to remain in England, "a good Land, where we have not only every necessary and Comfort, but likewise . . . an agreeable and affectionate sett of friends."[22]

The decision was easiest for the younger Americans, those who had been brought to the British Isles as children by their refugee parents. They had grown to maturity in the mother country, and by the mid-1780's they were marrying into English families. Older exiles, many of whom had been unwilling to commit themselves to a permanent residence in Great Britain while the war continued, finally began to consider reestablishing themselves in business. "Tired of being Idle," they embarked upon new careers, and like Isaac Low they found that "the Gloom which oppressed me begins to dispel as the Prospect opens of earning a Subsistence."[23] Doctors sought places in which to practice; refugee merchants settled in Liverpool or Glasgow or perhaps Ireland; the more well-to-do exiles purchased country homes with the proceeds of their property compensation; the less wealthy opened shops or taverns or tried to find regular employment.[24] The possible variations were endless: for example, the Wells sisters of Charleston established "a residence for those young gentlewomen of fortune who are without female relations to introduce them into life," and two enterprising young refugee artists, Thomas Duché and Mather Brown, busily gathered commissions to paint portraits of their fellow Americans to be sent to relatives in the United States.[25]

A few of the loyalists were fortunate enough to obtain minor appointments from the British government, but only George Chalmers, who became first clerk to the Committee on Trade, acquired an influential post. Even a man with the stature of Anthony Stokes could do no better than to be named agent for the Bahama Islands. As a result, most of the exiles would have agreed wholeheartedly with Benjamin Thompson, who, after having "solicited in vain" for a job in the British Isles, concluded that "England is not a place for a Loyalist to make his way." Thompson, whom a Massachusetts exile described as "one of the wonders really of the age," eventually became an aide-de-camp to the elector of Bavaria and a count of the Holy Roman Empire.[26]

Not many loyalists went that far afield in their search for employment, but they did find it easier to obtain positions outside the confines of Great Britain. Most of these posts were located, as might well be expected, in the remaining British colonies. In the 1780's, several southern refugees were rewarded with jobs in the customs or civil services of the islands in the West Indies.[27] But in such established colonial governments only a few jobs fell vacant each year, and for that reason the most fertile ground for loyalist job hunters was the Canadian provinces, where the large number of new refugee settlers eventually created the need for an expansion of the bureaucracy.

In the months following the signing of the peace treaty, more than twenty-eight thousand loyalists left New York City to settle in Canada, which Jonathan Sewall termed "the american New Jerusalem." Many of the exiles who had been living in England also sailed for Canada, and the settlers, most of whom were destitute on their arrival in their new homes, were supplied with free land, provisions, and tools by the Treasury.[28] Despite this assistance the future prospects of ordinary loyalists in Canada were bleak, and the circumstances of unemployed professionals were still worse. In the words of a young attorney, Nova Scotia was "overstocked with starved Lawyers" — and he could have added clerics, doctors, and former civil officials as well. The only way a professional man could ensure himself an adequate income in Canada was to acquire a government post, which, as a New Yorker observed, required "interest, Money, and friends." Not only that: it also required available jobs and there were few vacancies in the existing bureaucracies. Indeed, it was reported, "For every Place . . . there were 40 Appliers."[29]

Few loyalists found immediate employment in Nova Scotia or Quebec, despite the massive migration of refugees to those provinces. William Smith was named chief justice of Quebec, largely because Sir Guy Carleton, who was appointed governor general of Canada in 1785, insisted that he replace Peter Livius, with whom Carleton had been feuding for years. Sampson Salter Blowers received the much-sought-after post of attorney general of Nova Scotia, but few other loyalists were given positions in the hierarchy of that colony until after John Wentworth took over as governor in 1792.[30] The chief source of the Nova Scotia bottleneck was Governor John Parr. He and the refugees disliked each other intensely: the exiles thought him unsympathetic to their plight, and he regarded them as "impossible to satisfy." A campaign the loyalists organized to have Parr replaced with William Franklin naturally antagonized the governor, and he frequently complained to the colonial office that the refugees had given him "many anxious disagreable and distressing hours."[31] In

1785, when the then chief justice of Nova Scotia died, Parr made it clear to the authorities in London that he wanted "a good and proper Man," namely, "an *Englishman*," to fill the position. Although such refugees as Stokes, Galloway, Andrew Allen, Daniel Coxe, and James Hume were considered for the job, it eventually was awarded (to Parr's satisfaction) to Jeremy Pemberton of the claims commission.[32]

With Parr so antagonistic to their aspirations, the loyalists could obtain only lesser posts within his jurisdiction. David Mathews, the former mayor of New York City and a disappointed applicant for Blowers' job, had to settle for an appointment as attorney general of Cape Breton Island, which was an administrative dependency of Nova Scotia. The salary for the position was low, and Mathews soon discovered to his dismay that he could not supplement it with outside fees because the "distressed" residents of the island had neither the need for legal services nor the money to pay for them. In June 1790 he complained that he simply could not support his large family on his limited income and declared piteously that the only fresh meat they had eaten for three months was "a little moose meat which at this season is extreamly poor and bad."[33]

The only Nova Scotia job seekers who did not have to contend with Governor Parr were the Anglican clerics who hoped to be named bishop of the province. Although the establishment of a bishopric in the area had been discussed seriously as early as 1783, it was not until 1787 that final arrangements for the post were made. In the interim just about every exiled Anglican clergyman of stature continually jockeyed for position, each man attempting simultaneously to reinforce his own claims and to undercut those of his competitors. Initially, Thomas Bradbury Chandler was the leading candidate for the miter, but because his health was poor the other contenders saw nothing unethical in advancing their own names as alternatives to his. Both Samuel Seabury and Myles Cooper disclaimed any desire to compete with Chandler but suggested that if his candidacy were withdrawn theirs might be considered. Samuel Peters viciously attacked still another hopeful, Charles Inglis, in a series of pamphlets, and it was reported that Seabury had been persuaded to concentrate on seeking appointment as bishop of Connecticut so that he "might not be in the way of others more arch than himself" in the Nova Scotia race. Among the other divines interested in the coveted position were Boucher, Duché, Vardill, East Apthorp, Mather Byles, Jr., Thomas Coombe, and William Walter.[34]

The process of attack and counterattack went on until the spring of 1785, when Chandler, his health steadily worsening, returned to New Jersey and relinquished his claims to the post. Jonathan Boucher, the next in line, set conditions the church would not meet, and, despite Peters' hopes of being appointed, the choice eventually fell on Inglis.[35] It was not a popular decision. Smith termed him a "Prigg Parson" who would "ill support that Humility necessary to recommend him either to Men in Civil Office or to the lower Clergy and especially of other Persuasions," and Peters commented to an American relative, "We appoint the worst men we have or can find out in any Country to be Consuls, Bishops, Governors, Commissaries, Judges Collectors and Lawyers in our Colonies and in your States."[36] Even when a loyalist won an important position, it seemed, he was not the person the refugees themselves would have selected for the job.

The Americans' continuing difficulties with Governor Parr led them to seek a means of circumventing his authority. Since many of the loyalists had settled in the western part of

Nova Scotia, they concluded that partitioning the province would achieve the ends they desired. Not only would they thereby be freed from Parr's domination, they would also acquire additional opportunities for employment, since any new colony would presumably have to be administered by exiles. Under heavy pressure from refugees in both Canada and England, the ministry in June 1784 finally agreed to divide the former territory of Nova Scotia into two sections, with the inland region designated as the separate province of New Brunswick.[37]

With one stroke of the pen, therefore, a myriad of new jobs was created. Although the man appointed governor of New Brunswick, Thomas Carleton, was an Englishman (and the younger brother of Sir Guy), almost every other post in the province was awarded to a refugee. But the jobs were not handed out indiscriminately. One exile had predicted that a "preference" would be given to "the principal Loyalists of New York and other places who have borne the heat and Burthen of the day, that is who have been in arms."[38] He was correct, though not for the reason he supposed. Such men received the appointments not because of their services but rather as a result of their connections with the elder Carleton and with Brook Watson, a London merchant and politician who had served as commissary general in New York. Because of the combined influence of Carleton, Watson, and Sir William Pepperrell, with whom the ministry cleared potential appointees from Massachusetts, the New Brunswick hierarchy was dominated by New Englanders, New Yorkers, and men who had been in some way connected with the British army in Manhattan.

For example, Jonathan Odell of New Jersey, Carleton's former secretary, was named secretary to the province. Joshua Upham of Massachusetts, who founded his application on

"Sir Guy Carletons Friendship for me" and gave Pepperrell's name as a reference, became an assistant judge. He was joined on the bench by James Putnam of Massachusetts and Colonel Isaac Allen of Pennsylvania, who had served under Carleton. The post of chief justice went to George Duncan Ludlow of New York, whose brother Gabriel was appointed to the council. Ward Chipman of Massachusetts, who had the support of Carleton in his quest for an appointment, found that the post he wanted, attorney general of New Brunswick, had been awarded to Sampson Blowers "thro' the interest of Sir Wm. Pepperrell." When Blowers refused the job to accept a comparable post in Nova Scotia, the New Brunswick position was awarded to Jonathan Bliss, another favorite of Pepperrell's, but Chipman's influence was sufficient to obtain for him the appointment as solicitor general of the new province. Although the post was not equal to his expectations, Chipman's connection with Carleton had served him well.[39]

Brook Watson, who was to become sheriff and then lord mayor of the City of London, also came to the aid of Americans who sought employment in Canada. His close relationship with the exiles is evidenced not only by the frequent mention of him in the diaries of William Smith and Samuel Shoemaker, but also by the fact that he was the subject of one of Copley's most famous paintings. After the war Watson's recommendations won allowance increases for several refugees, and he tried (unsuccessfully but not unenthusiastically) to obtain half pay for the American commissaries who had worked with him in New York.[40] Two of his associates were named to the New Brunswick council, and a third, Christopher Sower, became king's printer for the province. Watson saw to it that Sower's commission fees were remitted and provided him with a printing press and other equipment. Sower was so grateful that he named his only son after his benefactor.[41]

[*3*]

During the war the loyalists had talked constantly of going home but few had actually ventured to return to rebel-held territory. Since those who were bold enough to make the attempt were most often arrested, mistreated, and deported,[42] the refugees who considered settling in the United States after the war had an unwelcome precedent before them. Their sentiment on the subject was concisely expressed by a New Yorker: "However much I wish to live among you . . . I will not do it unless I can meet with the same cordiality I have been accustomed to from my friends, and those I have been used to live with." Other exiles agreed that they would not return "in a Sculking manner, as if I had been guilty of some crime," nor become "an humble Sollicitor . . . merely to breathe my native air." As Polly Hutchinson wrote of her husband Elisha's decision to remain in England, "Better to be a beggar in a land where there is some appearance of humanity than in affluence in a country where he cou'd have no expectation but of continu[e]d persecution."[43]

As a consequence of their fears of being badly treated upon arrival in the United States, most of the loyalists who thought seriously of returning home in 1783 first consulted rebel acquaintances about their probable reception. The replies were consistently disheartening. "Be assured my dear Sir!" John Gardiner told his father Silvester, "that no Refugee can come here at present." One of Robert Auchmuty's correspondents warned him not to come to Boston until "a different temper prevails among the people at large, and in our General Court in particular," and a Virginian cautioned an exiled friend, "I'm afraid it will be long before the temper of the people here will be such as to acquiesce" in the provisions of the peace treaty.[44]

The advice the refugees received was well founded, because although Americans expressed general satisfaction with the treaty, the articles pertaining to loyalists and debts "excite[d] much ferment." Members of the Continental Congress concluded that the recommendations in favor of the loyalists must have been a "matter of form" only, for "if they should be serious . . . we should be Involved in very Great Difficulties Indeed." They assumed that "the Refugees, have nothing to expect of Right": the exiles would have to depend upon the "lenity and compassion" of the state legislatures. And they made it clear that they thought "the Chance for the Adherents to their gracious sovereign is but a blue one." After all, the Congressmen asked, "Does Justice require that we should shew them lenity?" The loyalists were "no small cause of the burthens and Distresses that we shall feel for many years to come. . . . Does Policy then dictate to us a revision of our Laws, Retribution and a free admission of them amongst us?"[45]

The legislators had correctly assessed the mood of the nation. Their constituents were "extremely opposed" to allowing the "Tory Villains" to return "while filial Tears are fresh upon our Cheeks and our murdered Brethren scarcely cold in their Graves." At town meetings and special gatherings throughout the country the Americans declared themselves determined to prevent this awful eventuality, believing, with a group of Baltimore residents, that "an universal attachment to the present government of this state, is essential to the harmony and tranquility of the good citizens thereof; and . . . that such an uniformity cannot possibly be obtained in this town, if those who have abandoned the cause of America, are permitted to return to, and remain among us as citizens."[46] These opinions were reflected at the state level, where legislatures not only refused to repeal acts of attainder and confiscation but also continued to enforce them in defiance of the specific prohibitions in the treaty. Even where state laws were repealed (as in Connecticut), towns often acted independently to exclude loyalists from their boundaries.[47]

The refugees who had impetuously embarked for America upon learning the terms of the treaty bore the brunt of this fury. Tales circulating in England in the fall of 1783 asserted that returnees had been "whipt Imprisoned Fined — or Hanged," and the stories were not overly exaggerated. A Virginian was greeted with "a New England Jacket (Tar and feathers) and sent back, tho he had the Govr's permission in his pocket"; a New Jerseyite was "apprehended by a party of armed men who insulted and abused him very much and obliged him to leave the province"; and it was reported (perhaps not very reliably) that three loyalist soldiers were "on their immediate arrival in No Carolina, murder'd without the form of even a mock trial."[48]

More common than such vigilantism was quasi-legal action against the refugees. Usually it took one of two forms: either the returning loyalists were not permitted to enter the state in the first place, or they were arrested as soon as they did. Four South Carolinians who arrived in Charleston in the spring "were not allowed to Land if they had Landed they would have been confined and Banished again." A number of New Englanders were refused readmittance to Massachusetts, and southerners who had managed to disembark unnoticed in the United States were warned to leave again immediately. A Rhode Islander's experience was typical: relying on the preliminary articles, he went home to try to recover his property. But instead of succeeding he "was seized as soon as he Landed and put into Prison, where he remained untill they sent him off."[49]

In the midst of the outpouring of hostility, there were some moderates who argued that the treaty should be obeyed. They did not adopt this conciliatory line out of sympathy for the exiles, but rather because they believed that the "indiscriminate punishment" of loyalists was not a wise policy for the United States to pursue. Generally, the critics of "avowed implacability" took two different tacks. Some thought that "certain descriptions of the Refugees" should be allowed to return, that "a line [should be] drawn between those who are gone from us," so that persons who had not taken an active role in the fighting could be permitted to resume their lives in America.[50] Others emphasized the importance of enforcing the treaty, "the faithful observance of which so deeply interests the United States." The "national character" was at stake, for the "intemperate" measures taken by the states were "holding us up as a vindictive persecuting People" to the countries of Europe, which were sympathetic to the loyalists' plight. "Will foreign nations be willing to undertake any thing with us or for us," asked Alexander Hamilton, "when they find that the nature of our governments will allow no dependence to be placed on our engagements?"[51]

Fortunately for the refugees who wished to return to their homes, such sentiments represented the wave of the future. As time passed, the intense passions of the immediate postwar period subsided. In December 1784 a Connecticut resident informed Samuel Peters, "The vindictive Spirit of the Country is almost totally altered in the space of one year past . . . I can assure you that the fierce Spirit of Whiggism is Dead." A few months later Benjamin Franklin asserted, "The Circumstances of the Royalists in the United States are daily mending, as the Minds of the People irritated by the Burning of their Towns and Massacre of their Friends, begin to cool."[52]

In accordance with the new mood, state legislatures began to modify the harsh wartime statutes directed at loyalists. Encouraged by the Continental Congress's formal recommendation in favor of the refugees (as stipulated by the fifth article), states like Massachusetts and New York relaxed their universal prohibitions against the return of exiles. Although Massachusetts asserted that it had the right to expel "all aliens who . . . hold principles incompatible with the safety and sovereignty of the state," and New York declared that "persons holding principles inimical to the constitution should not be admitted into office or places of public trust," both states in the spring of 1784 agreed that certain types of loyalists could live within their jurisdiction. In general, they continued to exclude only persons who had taken an active part in attempting to suppress the rebellion or who had been identified by name in the earlier confiscation acts. In Massachusetts, less obnoxious refugees were allowed to return if they obtained permission from the governor and council; in New York, loyalists were disfranchised and barred from office but were not otherwise penalized. Other states took comparable actions, and even in New Jersey and South Carolina, where hostility towards loyalists persisted for a longer period than elsewhere, antagonism had to a large extent dissipated by the later years of the decade.[53]

Although refugees who returned in 1784 and thereafter consequently met with less persecution than did their predecessors, one class of loyalists still uniformly aroused the Americans' ire. These were the men who came to the United States not to become citizens of the republic but instead to try to collect debts or to sell their remaining property. Their efforts invariably failed. One Virginia merchant claimed that the courts "laughed" at his attempts to force his debtors to discharge their obligations, and a frustrated New England loyalist commented from Boston in 1785 that "there seems almost a fixd determination amongst all Ranks of People here to withhold from the Loyalists whatever they have taken from them." Carolinians as well complained that they found it "impossible" to obtain satisfaction under the fourth and fifth articles of the treaty, and a returned resident of Camden told his brother, "Although they at present treat me very well, yet was I to go into the Country, and enter any action to recover any Debts, there are many many, if they could do it privately, would put an End to my Existance."[54]

The one group of refugees who retained their British nationality and who were not molested were those who came to the United States as British consuls after 1786. Phineas Bond, John Hamilton, and George Miller were able to function relatively well under the protection of diplomatic immunity, even though a New Yorker observed of Bond, "But for his appointment from Great Britain he would have mounted the Ladder had he ever been found in that State [Pennsylvania]."[55]

Loyalists who recanted and repented of their errors were treated rather well once the initial hostility had faded. In fact, it appears that a loyalist's willingness to admit he had been mistaken in his allegiance was more important than the passage of time in winning him eventual acceptance by his former neighbors. Even before Massachusetts officially altered its laws, John Amory was allowed to take up residence in Boston after he had assured the General Court that "there is no form of Government upon earth, that he so much desires to live under" as a republic. In the spring of 1784, the repeal of the restrictive acts encouraged other New England exiles to follow Amory's lead, and what happened then must have been typical of other areas as well. Isaac Smith was one of the first returnees to arrive in Boston, and his discovery that "the temper of the people is much soften'd" started a chain reaction among his acquaintances in London. Smith assured the Boston merchant John Atkinson that "you need not . . . be under any apprehension of danger, in consequence of returning here immediately," and he cited the experience of Amory and others to prove his point.[56] Smith's good friend Samuel Curwen, relying on assurances that he was seen "not as an enemy but as a timid friend," sailed for America a few months later. Joseph Taylor, an associate of all three men, ventured forth to Boston in October and met with "a most Cordial Reception" that led him to add his voice to those urging Atkinson to return. Thus heartened, Atkinson embarked with his family for Massachusetts, arriving at the end of November 1785 to find his friends "overjoy'd to see us."[57]

In other states the pattern was the same. Peter Van Schaack went back to New York; Thomas Bradbury Chandler was treated "with remarkable kindness and respect" when he reappeared in New Jersey; and Samuel Shoemaker and Jacob Duché returned to Philadelphia in 1789 and 1790, respectively. On the other hand, although Galloway asked Pennsylvania for permission to return, the legislature would not allow him to enter the state. And many others (like members of the Hutchinson family) never even submitted such requests, knowing their efforts to be futile from the very beginning. Moreover, most of the returnees would have agreed with a Virginian who commented to a relative that he was glad to be back in his native land, "but it is so much chang'd that I hardly know it and I am sorry to say very little for the better or more properly for the worse."[58]

Some of the exiles had indeed managed to go home again.

But most had not: the vast majority of the loyalists remained outside of the independent United States, whether as a result of choice or necessity. Wherever these men settled, they continued to cherish the hope that England and America would one day be reunited. They refused to accept the verdict of the Revolution as final, nursing instead the belief that the force of tradition and the exigencies of world politics would eventually bring the two countries together in a lasting coalition.

Epilogue
A British-American Empire

The time draws nigh when Britain and America
will be again united and the greatest Empire that
ever was on Earth will be formed, which will in
due time be removed to the West, where the
English Laws, Language Manners and Customs
will prevail and at no distant day prove the most
formidable in the World.

— JOHN CRUDEN, 1785[1]

SINCE the earliest days of the Revolution, the loyalists
had believed that independence would prove ruinous to
the United States, and the events of the 1780's did little to
make them change their minds. They found in the interstate
quarrels, in Shays' Rebellion, in the problems of the Confederation government, all the evidence they needed to
confirm the truth of their predictions. They saw no reason to
alter their original opinion that America would have been
far better off within the empire. Their inability to recognize
the Americans' commitment to independence combined with
an exaggerated emphasis on the vicissitudes of the United
States to produce in them the firm belief not only that a
complete reconciliation was desirable but also that it would
eventually be achieved. The exiles' futile hopes for reunification may therefore be taken as a final, forlorn symbol of their
failure to comprehend fully the concatenation of forces that
had ejected them from their homes.

[*1*]

The loyalists had long been convinced that, as Curwen put it, "the colonies will never find any good purpose answered by independence." After all, their belief that America gained more than it lost by inclusion in the British Empire was one of the reasons why they had remained faithful to the crown. They foresaw only "ruin and Destruction" for a free United States, because they expected that the "clashing interests, prejudices and principles" suppressed under royal rule would "burst out with destructive violence" once independence was achieved. The rebels would soon "cutt each others Throats," and "America would be a scene of bloody discord and desolation for ages — the most miserable distracted country on earth."[2] The refugees were particularly concerned about the influence of the "lower, illiterate classes" in the new American governments. It seemed to a New England physician, for example, that the "general principle of the lower Orders" was "a desire of being free from all Restraints of Government, and this principle still continues to operate under the Independency." Although Jonathan Sewall expressed the hope that such fears were "Chimerical and imaginary," he asked pessimistically, "Will ye independent Americans tamely submit to be dragooned into Submission and Compliance, by their fellow Citizens and Countrymen?"[3]

The exiles' gloomy expectations colored their every pronouncement on the United States in the 1780's. Each time they learned of a new disaster — whether it was clashes over boundaries, internal disputes, or widespread inflation — they renewed their predictions that the republican experiment was doomed.[4] Yet their comments were characterized by a curious ambivalence: although on the one hand they were inclined to gloat over the Americans' difficulties, on the other their lingering affection for the United States prevented them from being altogether pleased by her problems. Nowhere was this contradictory attitude more clearly displayed than in the correspondence of George Erving. In March 1786 he told his brother that America was "the destin'd Country — where Liberty and Science promise to bless and enlighten mankind." But just four months later he criticized the "bad Stamina . . . in the Governing power" of the United States, declaring that "the Laws wear a very sperious [sic] aspect of liberty and security." Throughout the rest of the decade he continued his inconsistent observations on America, rejoicing when matters went well for his former compatriots while simultaneously retaining his skepticism about the wisdom of independence. In 1790 he explained, "I feel truly interested in every thing that regards the prosperity and welfare of my Country; nor is my attachment to it the least weaken'd by my seperation [sic], or the unmerited doom I am sentenced to by my Countrymen."[5]

In the refugees' writings on the United States there was no small element of an attitude that was best expressed by Thomas Coffin. "They chose to be independent, let them suffer the Inconvenience of it." Or, to put it another way, the Americans deserved whatever troubles they were experiencing. Partly for this reason, influential exiles like George Chalmers and William Smith vigorously opposed allowing the Americans to trade with the British West Indies. Like Elias Ball, they were determined that the United States should not "throw off Britan [sic] and still Retain the Privaledge of subjects." Furthermore, the refugees wanted their fellow loyalists in Canada to acquire a monopoly of the lucrative West Indian commerce previously enjoyed by New England. The exiles' opinions were accurately summed up in Ball's simile: "I compare America to a boy of Eight or ten years of age who has quarrild and thrown of[f] his parents. If you was to see such a boy abus'd and buffeted by other people you would say that Chap deserves it I think its applycable to the Case in view."[6]

By August 1785 Smith and a number of other refugees had concluded, "Every thing hastens to another Revolution in America." A New Brunswick resident declared, "The foederal union of the United States[,] totally destitute of energy, is verging to dissolution," because in America "commerce languishes, credit is annihilated, morals destroyed, and all faith between man and man seems wholly to have disappeared." Shays' Rebellion then confirmed the loyalists in their opinion. One exile sarcastically told a friend in New York, "I find you begin to enjoy a *little* the Blessings of Independance — Strange that the ungrateful Multitude should turn upon the illustrious Patriots, who led them to seek such Happiness!"[7] Not even the adoption of the Constitution, which the loyalists at least thought superior to the Articles of Confederation, sufficed to make them alter their assessment of America's future. The new government might "do well enough for a time," admitted a New Englander, but, he added, "I do not think much of its Continuance." Ball described the new scheme as "the bubble of the Day that will soon vanish into nothing," and although Jonathan Boucher conceded that the Americans displayed a "partiality" for the Constitution, he noted that they "set out on principles incompatible with stability; and of course it is natural to suppose that their people, following the example of their founders, will always be prone to revolt and rebellion."[8]

As a consequence of their persistent pessimism about America's chances for survival as an independent republic, the refugees continued to nurture the hope that a reunification of Britain and America could be effected. When

Boucher published a book of sermons in 1797, he noted that his "sincere aim" was to bring about "a perfect reconciliation" between the two countries. As a proof of his intentions, he dedicated the book to George Washington and went on to assert that the interests of Britain and America were "demonstrably the same." For the hundredth time he contended that "it was never the serious wish either of the one or the other to separate." Indeed, "the settled persuasion of their judgments, and the most cordial wish of their hearts, [was] to unite again." The Americans and Britons would combine to create "one great and happy people" divided between "two distant, distinct, and completely independent states" that would be linked by political and economic ties, as well as by those of culture.[9]

Boucher was not the only loyalist who dreamed of a renewed connection between America and Great Britain. The southerner John Cruden predicted in 1784 that "both Countries will yet embrace each other . . . The tender Ties of Blood, the same Religion, Laws, and Manners . . . will come in to aid the Union, cement the Friendship, and make us one People again." Smith continued to believe that the United States could be "reclaimed" if Britain took the proper steps, and in 1785 he wrote seriously of the possibility that Congress might be planning to negotiate a reunification. Samuel Peters, convinced that New England could be separated from the rest of the states, suggested to the lieutenant governor of Connecticut that the northerners abandon their southern allies, who were merely "a Composition of Renegadoes, Africans, Convicts and the Refuse of all Nations," in order to rejoin the empire. And, in a supreme show of confidence in 1787, a Bostonian volunteered to serve as an "impartial and unequivocal" channel of communications between the ministry and the Americans in the event of an attempt to reach agreement on "any sort of Union."[10]

Just as during the war the refugees had found evidence for their beliefs in reports from America, so too now what they heard from the United States encouraged them to think that the empire could yet be salvaged. When John Rapelje of New York arrived in England in June 1784, he told Smith that the Americans "hate those who have led them to the Separation from Great Britain and long for a Restoration." Rapelje insisted that the most disaffected were former Whigs, who were "free and impetuous ag[ains]t their Leaders beyond Description." Upon his return to New Jersey, Thomas Bradbury Chandler talked with "some persons who made themselves conspicuous in the late rebellion," and he reported that "all of them feel, that the exchange of British protection for independency has been ruinous to the Country." In Chandler's opinion, "a very large majority are disposed to adopt the language of the repenting Prodigal in the Parable, towards the *Parent* Country."[11]

The pattern of self-deception that had been characteristic of loyalist thinking since 1774 thus persisted into the first decades following independence. The exiles had long before convinced themselves that the Revolution lacked majority support, and the fact that it had succeeded did not necessarily indicate to them that they had been mistaken. On the contrary, it seemed as though the Americans' victory had been "one of those extraordinary and unexpected events . . . which bid defiance to all human foresight and calculation." The refugees still thought it possible that the results of the Revolution could be reversed, and they persisted in their efforts to produce reconciliation plans that would resolve the differences that divided Britain and the United States. But if the proposals they had drawn up during the war were hopelessly outdated at their very inception, then the postwar plans were still more ineffectual and uncomprehending.[12] Motivated by a deep concern and affection for both nations, the refugees simply could not understand that their former compatriots did not share their sentiments.

[2]

In 1815 John Eardley-Wilmot excused the loyalists for their erroneous interpretation of the Revolution by observing that they were "too much interested, and too much inflamed, perhaps, by their sufferings or resentments, to form a cool and impartial judgment."[13] True enough: but Eardley-Wilmot's comment failed to explain sufficiently either the sources of the refugees' bias or the reasons for its peculiar configuration. Hatred of the rebels, though obviously endemic among the exiles, does not provide an adequate explanation of the rigid and unrealistic manner in which they perceived the events of the revolutionary era. The loyalists counted among their number many of the political and social leaders of prewar America, men who had not gained their positions through stupidity or lack of intellectual attributes. Some of them had even been the chief participants in the colonies' most notable success stories. Yet all were dumbfounded and confused by what happened to their homeland in the 1770's, and the explanation for their confusion appears to lie in the nature of the Revolution itself rather than in their own perceptual shortcomings.

As is well known, the rebels used the language of conservatism, arguing that the British government was the innovator, that all they wanted (at least initially) was the reversal of certain oppressive acts that had altered the normal imperial relationship. But, although the revolutionaries' ends were perhaps conservative, their means were not. Despite their rhetoric, the Americans were engaged in a most radical endeavor. They were remaking and reshaping their politics, their society, their culture. The full implication of their ideology was not immediately apparent; indeed, much of their innovation was achieved unconsciously. But innovation it undeniably was. And the testimony of the loyalists is the key to understanding the radical character of that innovation.

As long as the debate with Great Britain remained within traditional lines, future loyalists were in the forefront of the American cause. Daniel Dulany, Robert Alexander, Jacob Duché: all made significant contributions to the colonists' struggle for greater autonomy within the empire. Joseph Galloway, William Smith, and others equally learned tried to work out compromises that would give the Americans a greater voice in their own governance. Some men who chose in the end to adhere to the crown even took up arms with their compatriots in the hectic days following Lexington and Concord. But, when the dispute jumped outside of the accepted boundaries, when the issue became that of independence, the loyalists refused to go any further.

For independence was indeed a radical solution to the problems that had arisen inside the imperial structure. In effect, the revolutionaries were telling their fellow Americans that the only way they could attain the rights of Englishmen was to abandon their connection with England. To the loyalists, this seemed both contradictory and incomprehensible. Change within the empire? Yes, answered Robert Alexander, who freely admitted to the claims commission that he believed that "the inhabitants of America were not liable to Taxation by the British Parliament." But independence? Never! His goal had been to promote "every Constitutional Connection between the two Countries."[14]

The loyalists' inability to understand the dynamics of the

Revolution acquires new significance when seen in this context. The issue of independence was what first irreversibly divided them from their rebellious fellow countrymen, but it was not the sole question raised by the revolt. In order to defend their right to seek a separation from Great Britain, the Americans adopted new notions about the nature of politics and society, and these ideas the refugees found especially perplexing. What gave legitimacy to government, argued the revolutionaries, was the consent of the governed, not the force of tradition or the canonical pronouncements of interpreters of the British constitution. Theoretically at least, all men were created equal: and if that statement had little immediate impact upon actual practice, it was eventually to more than compensate for its modest beginnings. Both themes, it is true, had deep roots in the shared Anglo-American heritage, but never before had they been expressed with such vigor and persuasive power. Never before had they so completely seized the imagination of a large proportion of the American population. And never before had they deliberately, consciously been acted upon by political leaders.

This was not conservatism. If it had been, the loyalists could have comprehended it, analyzed it, and in the end perhaps dissented from it. Rather, the revolutionary ideology was truly revolutionary — though the rebels did not view it as such — and that was why the loyalists had a difficult time in coming to terms with its realities. Thoroughly conversant with imperial ways of thinking, they could not make the break with the past that the Revolution required: not in order to join the rebels, not even in order to understand their motives and actions. What was happening in America after 1774 was so new, so alien to them that they were bewildered, confused, even unhinged by the experience. The only way they could retain some semblance of certainty in their lives was to deny, in effect, the very existence of a true revolution. Thus the insistence that the conflict had been fomented by a small disgruntled minority. Thus the clinging to hopes for victory or reconciliation. Thus their refusal to accept the finality of their exile. And thus Thomas Hutchinson's pathetic 1778 characterization of the last few years of his life as "a dream or other delusion."[15]

With his talent for graphic analogy, Peter Oliver once described the Revolution as a volcano. If his metaphor can be extended, then the lava flow from the crater was the revolutionary movement itself, consuming everything in its inexorable path. And the loyalists were the debris scattered across the countryside by successive eruptions. Men of all descriptions — rich and poor, celebrated and unknown — they were what was left when the lava moved on; they were the rocks thrown hither and yon by the force of the explosions. And, almost as uncomprehending as their inanimate counterparts, they held fast to the America, to the empire, they had known and loved. In London, in Bristol, in Halifax, their thoughts were the same. They lamented the loss of a Utopian empire that had never existed and longed for its rejuvenation. They did what they could to re-create their former lives, but it proved impossible to reverse the flow of time. Their chief virtue was a steadfast loyalty to a governmental system they revered, their chief shortcoming an inability to recognize a need for change. In the end, it might accurately have been said of each of them, as it was of one: "He loved God, honoured his King, esteemed his friends, and hated rebellion."[16]

Essay on Sources

This bibliographical essay does not pretend to be a comprehensive survey of the materials available for the study of loyalism. Rather, its purpose is to provide the interested reader with a brief guide to the existing literature of the field, the major printed primary works, and the most important collections of documents pertinent to the refugees. More detailed references may be found in the notes (pages 275–317).

Secondary Sources

The logical starting point for a study of the literature of loyalism is Wallace Brown, "The View at Two Hundred Years: The Loyalists of the American Revolution," *American Antiquarian Society Proceedings,* LXXX (April 1970), 25–47. In this article Brown discusses trends in loyalist scholarship since the nineteenth century, making it unnecessary for me to supply additional comments upon some of the major works in the field. Suffice it to say that, despite their age, such studies as Claude H. Van Tyne, *Loyalists in the American Revolution* (New York, 1902); Moses C. Tyler, "The Party of the Loyalists in the American Revolution," *American Historical Review,* I (1895), 24–45; Egerton Ryerson, *The Loyalists of America and Their Times* (2 vols., Toronto, 1880); and Lorenzo Sabine, *Biographical Sketches of Loyalists of the American Revolution* (2 vols., Boston, 1864), still deserve the careful attention of researchers.

Brown's own work has done much to correct the erroneous impression (received from these earlier scholars) that the loyalists were almost to a man wealthy colonial aristocrats. Brown's examination of the refugees' claims in *The King's Friends* (Providence, 1965) proves beyond a doubt that most of the loyalists were ordinary Americans, but, as Eugene Fingerhut has shown in "Uses and Abuses of the American Loyalists' Claims: A Critique of Quantitative Analyses,"*William and Mary Quarterly*, 3rd ser., XXV (1968), 245–58, Brown's statistical conclusions are based upon a number of incorrect assumptions and must therefore be regarded as questionable. Brown's more recent book, *The Good Americans* (New York, 1969), a much broader survey, is the most comprehensive single-volume treatment of the loyalists available at this time.

In contrast to Brown, whose major concern has been the social and economic background of the loyalists, William H. Nelson has concentrated upon the development of their ideology. The publication of his *The American Tory* (New York, 1961) marked the beginning of the current wave of loyalist studies. Nelson's work is useful for many reasons, not the least of which is his suggestive analysis of possible motivations for loyalism, but it is flawed by his overemphasis upon Thomas Hutchinson and Joseph Galloway and by his failure to consult any but the most obvious published sources. Another recent book dealing with ideology is William A. Benton, *Whig-Loyalism* (Rutherford, N.J., 1969), which discusses the middle ground between "Whigs" and "Tories." Although it contains information not found elsewhere, Benton's study is narrowly focused on nine individuals and so is not as useful as it might perhaps have been.

Of works dealing more specifically with the refugees and the war, North Callahan's *Flight from the Republic* (Indianapolis, 1967) is little more than an undigested narration of facts and incidents. Far more useful are Paul H. Smith's excellent *Loyalists and Redcoats* (Chapel Hill, 1964), which examines loyalist participation in the British war effort, and his "The American Loyalists: Notes on Their Organization and Numerical Strength," *William and Mary Quarterly*, 3rd ser., XXV (1968), 259–77. One book that treats the exile experience at some length is Lewis Einstein, *Divided Loyalties: Americans in England during the*

War of Independence (Boston, 1933), but he concentrates solely on the lives of a few leading refugees, especially those involved in the British espionage service.

Much of loyalist scholarship has been concerned with the loyalists from particular areas, and some of this plethora of state studies contain information pertinent to the exiles. Among the most useful publications are Richard D. Brown, "The Confiscation and Disposition of Loyalists' Estates in Suffolk County, Massachusetts," *William and Mary Quarterly*, 3rd ser., XXI (1964), 534–50; Robert S. Lambert, "The Confiscation of Loyalist Property in Georgia, 1782–1786," *William and Mary Quarterly*, 3rd ser., XX (1963), 80–94; James H. Stark, *The Loyalists of Massachusetts* (Boston, 1907); E. Alfred Jones, *The Loyalists of New Jersey* (*Collections of the New Jersey Historical Society*, X [1927]); and two articles by Oscar Zeichner: "The Rehabilitation of the Loyalists in Connecticut," *New England Quarterly*, XI (1938), 308–30; and "The Loyalist Problem in New York after the Revolution," *New York History*, XXI (1940), 284–302. The most prolific practitioner of this sort of local analysis was Wilbur H. Siebert, who wrote innumerable articles about various aspects of loyalism. His relevant works include "The Dispersion of the American Tories," *Mississippi Valley Historical Review*, I (1914), 185–97; "The Refugee Loyalists of Connecticut," *Transactions of the Royal Society of Canada*, 3rd ser., X (1916), 75–92; *The Loyalists of Pennsylvania* (Columbus, O., 1920); and *Loyalist Refugees of New Hampshire* (Columbus, O., 1916).

Information about the more famous refugees may, of course, be found in biographies. Unfortunately, however, many of the book-length studies of individual loyalists date from the nineteenth century and are of the "life and times" variety. These works contain long quotations from the correspondence or journals of their subjects but cast little analytical light upon their lives. Into this category fall such works as Henry C. Van Schaack, *The Life of Peter Van Schaack* (New York, 1842), and E. Edwards Beardsley, *Life and Correspondence of the Right Reverend*

Samuel Seabury, D.D. (Boston, 1881). Biographies of more recent vintage are accordingly of greater value to modern scholars; numbered among the best of these are Grace Cockcroft, *The Public Life of George Chalmers* (New York, 1939); Oliver Kuntzleman, *Joseph Galloway, Loyalist* ([Philadelphia], 1941); and L. S. F. Upton, *The Loyal Whig: Chief Justice William Smith of New York and Quebec* (Toronto, 1969). Also useful in this regard are biographical articles, the more important of which include Catherine Fennelly, "William Franklin of New Jersey," *William and Mary Quarterly*, 3rd ser., VI (1949), 361–82; Catherine S. Crary, "The American Dream: John Tabor Kempe's Rise from Poverty to Riches," *William and Mary Quarterly*, 3rd ser., XIV (1957), 176–95; the essays on Anthony Stokes and Sir James Wright in Horace Montgomery, ed., *Georgians in Profile* (Athens, 1958); Michael D. Clark, "Jonathan Boucher: The Mirror of Reaction," *Huntington Library Quarterly*, XXXIII (Nov. 1969), 19–32; and the articles in Lawrence H. Leder, ed., *The Colonial Legacy*, vol. I: *Loyalist Historians* (New York, 1971).

Printed Primary Sources

Published primary materials relevant to the refugees are both copious and significant. Many of their own writings have been printed in the years since the Revolution, and in addition the papers of many of the British officials who dealt with them have been at least partially published. Clarence E. Carter, ed., *The Correspondence of General Thomas Gage, 1763–1775* (2 vols., New Haven, 1931–1933), supplies important information concerning affairs in Massachusetts in 1774–1775. John Eardley-Wilmot, *Historical View of the Commission for Enquiring into the Losses, Services, and Claims, of the American Loyalists* (London, 1815), and Daniel P. Coke, *The Royal Commission on the Losses and Services of American Loyalists*, ed. Hugh E. Egerton (Oxford, 1915), which prints Coke's notes on cases heard in London in 1783–1785, together provide an introduction to the workings of the claims commission. The British Historical Manuscripts Commission's publications are also useful, though incomplete: *The Manuscripts of the Earl of Dartmouth* (2 vols., London, 1881, 1895), *Report on Manuscripts of Mrs. Stopford-Sackville* [Lord George Germain] (2 vols., London, 1904), and *Report on Manuscripts in Various Collections,* VI [William Knox] (Dublin, 1909), make readily available some of the papers of the most important British politicians who came into regular contact with the refugees. Further, there is the incomparable and invaluable Benjamin F. Stevens, ed., *Facsimiles of Manuscripts in European Archives Relating to America, 1773–1783* (25 vols., London, 1889–1895), which reproduces a number of Galloway's letters and includes many other documents pertinent to the study of the loyalists and the war as a whole.

The exiles were not reluctant to express their views about the Revolution in print, so the historian has ample sources to draw upon for a study of their thought. Galloway alone wrote more than ten pamphlets during the war, the most important of which are *A Candid Examination of the Mutual Claims of Great-Britain and the Colonies . . .* (New York, 1775; repr. London, 1780), *Historical and Political Reflections on the Rise and Progress of the American Rebellion* (London, 1780), and *Political Reflections on the late Colonial Governments* (London, 1783). Other significant contemporary publications include Jonathan Boucher, *A View of the Causes and Consequences of the American Revolution* (London, 1797); George Chalmers, *Political Annals of the Present United Colonies* (London, 1780; repr. New York, 1968); Myles Cooper, *National Humiliation and Repentance recommended, and the Causes of the present Rebellion in America assigned* (Oxford, 1777); [Thomas Hutchinson], *Strictures upon the Declaration of the Congress at Philadelphia* (London, 1776); and Alexander Hewatt, *An Historical Account of the Rise and Progress of the Colonies of South Carolina and Georgia* (2 vols., London, 1779; repr. Spartanburg, 1962). In addition, some loyalist writings were published only after the deaths of their authors; among these are Chalmers' *An Introduction to the History of the Revolt of the American Colonies* (2 vols., Boston, 1845; repr. New York, 1971) ; Thomas Jones, *History of New York during the Revolutionary War,* ed. Edward F. De-Lancey (2 vols., New York, 1879) ; and Peter Oliver, *Origin & Progress of the American Rebellion,* ed. Douglass Adair and John A. Schutz (San Marino, Calif., 1961) .

Of equal interest and importance are the published journals and memoirs of the loyalist exiles. These works contain much information concerning the refugees' daily lives — information that can be found nowhere else. The most significant collection of this nature is Peter O. Hutchinson, ed., *The Diary and Letters of Thomas Hutchinson* (2 vols., Boston, 1884) . Although the first volume is a nearly complete edition of Hutchinson's diary for 1774–1775, the second abridges the entries for succeeding years, and Hutchinson's correspondence is scattered through both volumes with little attention to chronology. George A. Ward, ed., *Journal and Letters of the late Samuel Curwen,* 3rd ed. (New York, 1845), is better organized but still an abridgment of the original; it will soon be replaced by a new edition prepared by Andrew Oliver. Curwen's comments are always interesting and quotable, but he was by no means representative of his fellows. The ready availability of his diary has therefore caused an unfortunate distortion in the work of men like William Nelson who have relied heavily upon it.

Another diary of some importance is that of Edward Oxnard, extracts from which were published in the *New England Historical and Genealogical Register,* XXVI (1872) , 8–10, 115–21, 254–59. The printed version is so inaccurate, though, that it is necessary to consult the original in the Maine Historical Society in Portland in order not only to verify the exact wording of entries but also to determine the correct dates. L. S. F. Upton's edition of *The Diary and Selected Papers of Chief Justice William Smith 1784–1793* (2 vols., Toronto, 1963) avoids the above-mentioned problems and provides a vivid picture of life in London during 1784–1785. More sketchy and fragmentary but still useful are the following diaries: *The Journal of Mrs. John Amory, 1775–*

1777, ed. Martha C. Codman (Boston, 1923) ; Louisa Wells Aikman, *The Journal of a Voyage from Charleston, S.C. to London* (New York, 1906) ; *The Diary and Letters of Benjamin Pickman (1740–1819) of Salem, Massachusetts* (Newport, 1928) ; Samuel Quincy, "Diary Oct. 9, 1776 — March 30, 1777," *Proceedings of the Massachusetts Historical Society,* XIX (1881–1882), 211–23; and "Journal of Rev. Joshua Wingate Weeks, Loyalist Rector of St. Michael's Church, Marblehead, 1778–1779," *Essex Institute Historical Collections,* LII (1916), 1–16, 161–76, 197–208, 345–56.

Less reliable than the foregoing, because they were written years after the Revolution, are Jonathan Boucher, *Reminiscences of an American Loyalist, 1738–1789,* ed. Jonathan Bouchier (Boston, 1925) ; *The Journal of Alexander Chesney, a South Carolina Loyalist,* ed. E. Alfred Jones (Columbus, O., 1921) ; and Elizabeth Johnston, *Recollections of a Georgia Loyalist* (New York, 1901). Also of interest are a few valuable collections of loyalist letters: W. O. Raymond, ed., *Winslow Papers 1776–1826* (St. John, N.B., 1901) ; Anne Hulton, *Letters of a Loyalist Lady* (Cambridge, 1927) ; and Nina M. Tiffany, ed., *Letters of James Murray, Loyalist* (Boston, 1901). The pamphlets published by individual loyalists as part of their campaigns to win compensation from the British government were clearly self-serving, but they too contain useful material. Typical of the genre are *An Account of the Sufferings and Persecution of John Champneys* (London, 1778) ; *The Case of James Christie, jun. Late of the Province of Maryland, Merchant* (n.p., n.d.) ; John McAlpine, *Genuine Narratives, and Concise Memoirs . . .* (n.p., 1788) ; *Narrative of the Exertions and Sufferings of Lieut. James Moody,* ed. Charles Bushnell (New York, 1865) ; and *A Narrative of the Official Conduct of Anthony Stokes . . .* [London, 1784].

Manuscripts

The manuscript sources on the loyalist refugees are of two major types: government records and personal papers. British archival collections provide information about individual loyalists and about their collective attempts to influence the administration, and the exiles' letters and diaries give insight into the day-to-day existence of particular families. Both kinds of materials should be used in conjunction if a coherent picture of the loyalist experience is to be obtained.

The single most important repository of manuscripts for the study of the loyalists is the Public Record Office in London, and the most useful of its many series are Audit Office 12 and 13, in which are deposited the documents utilized by the claims commission. Audit Office 12 is composed for the most part of the official record books of the commission, which contain copies of the loyalists' memorials and notes on their hearings before the board. The series also includes documentary material collected by John Anstey on his trip to the United States in 1786–1788 and the records of the refugees' pension hearings. Audit Office 13 duplicates this series to a certain extent, in that it contains many of the original documents copied in the volumes of 12, but it also includes much additional material not found elsewhere. In 13 are deposited the loyalists' claims memorials, certificates, and deeds; correspondence relating to their claims; and many of the pension petitions they submitted to the government during the war years.

Several other series in the Public Record Office contain significant manuscripts pertinent to the loyalists. Many volumes of Colonial Office 5 include correspondence with and about the refugees; of particular importance are the collections of miscellaneous petitions to Lord George Germain, vols. 115–117 and 156–158. Similar memorials from the period after 1783 are contained in the first volumes of the Foreign Office 4 series. Other Colonial Office papers relevant to the loyalists may be found in the series devoted to the Canadian provinces: 42 (Quebec), 188 (New Brunswick), and 217 (Nova Scotia). Also of special interest are the record books of interoffice correspondence, in the Home Office 36 and Colonial Office 5 groups; the two volumes of the Foreign Office series relating to the Paris peace negotiations,

FO 97/157 and FO 95/511; and the multivolumed private papers
of William Pitt.

The various Treasury series provide another major source of
information about the loyalists. T 1, miscellaneous in-letters to
the Treasury, contains many communications from and relevant
to the refugees, particularly half-pay petitions from the period
1783–1789. The minute books of the Lords of the Treasury
(T 29) record the decisions of the Lords on pensions and other
types of compensation for the exiles, and deposited in Treasury
50 are the loyalist pension rolls from 1782 to 1839. The series
Treasury 79 includes both the reports of the claims commissioners
and documentation pertaining to loyalists' claims under the Jay
Treaty and the disposition of their property in the first half of
the nineteenth century.

The other significant repository in London for the study of the
loyalists is the British Museum. The most important collection
here is the Hutchinson family papers, Egerton Manuscripts 2659–
2674. In these volumes are the diaries of Thomas Hutchinson, his
son Elisha, Chief Justice Peter Oliver, and his son Dr. Peter
Oliver. The collection also contains the family correspondence
and several letterbooks. Likewise deposited in the British Museum are the papers of Lord Hardwicke, who corresponded
extensively with both Thomas Hutchinson and Joseph Galloway,
and the papers of Charles Jenkinson (Lord Liverpool), who was
secretary at war in the North administration. Both collections include letters from refugees, as do the papers of General Frederick
Haldimand. Also of interest in the British Museum are the more
than two hundred volumes of transcripts of documents relating
to the Revolution prepared under the direction of Benjamin F.
Stevens.

Other libraries in England have material of similar importance.
The very valuable letters of Jonathan Boucher may be consulted
at the East Sussex Record Office in Lewes, where they have
been deposited by their owner, Mr. Jonathan Locker-Lampson.
(A portion of this collection has been published as "Letters of

Rev. Jonathan Boucher, 1759–1777," *Maryland Historical Magazine,* VII [1912], 1–26 *et seq.*) In the William Salt Library, Stafford, are the personal papers of Lord Dartmouth, which contain many communications from loyalists. The small collection of the papers of Henry Rugeley of South Carolina in the Bedfordshire County Record Office is of some interest, and the letter-book of the Reverend Henry Caner of Massachusetts in the University of Bristol Library provides a vivid account of the siege and evacuation of Boston. Two useful larger collections are the Parker family papers, in the Liverpool Record Office, and the papers of Charles Steuart, in the National Library of Scotland, Edinburgh.

There are also many important repositories of relevant manuscripts in the United States. In particular, the William L. Clements Library, in Ann Arbor, Michigan, possesses the personal papers of a number of the British officials who came into contact with the loyalists. Of greatest significance are the papers of Lord George Germain and Lord Shelburne. Included in both collections are many letters and petitions from Americans and documents revealing the British government's policy towards the refugees. Also of great value are the papers of William Knox, Sir Henry Clinton, and General Thomas Gage. The Clements Library, moreover, owns four small but useful collections of loyalists' private papers: the Dering, Perkins, John Calef, and Atkinson MSS.

The Massachusetts Historical Society in Boston houses the largest quantity of refugees' personal papers to be found under one roof. Its holdings are too extensive to describe in detail, but the most important collections are the following: Coffin MSS (Thomas and Francis Coffin), Gardiner-Whipple-Allen MSS (Silvester Gardiner), David Greenough MSS (George Erving), Jeffries MSS (John Jeffries), Samuel Quincy MSS, J. M. Robbins MSS (Henry Barnes), S. P. Savage MSS II (Arthur Savage), Robie-Sewall MSS (Jonathan Sewall), Smith-Carter MSS (Isaac Smith), and Winslow MSS (Sir William Pepperrell). In addition, the Massachusetts Historical Society has several small collections of Hutchinson family papers, and it owns a microfilm of the Hutchinson papers in the British Museum. The MHS also possesses a film of the letterbook of William Browne (part of which has been published in *Essex Institute Historical Collections,* XCVI [1960], 1–46).

Of only slightly lesser significance are the collections of the New-York Historical Society. The Robert Watts and Leake papers both contain many letters from the loyalist members of those families, and they should be used in conjunction with the papers of Samuel Peters (now on microfilm only), John Peters, James DeLancey, and the Colden family. In addition to the Historical Society, there are four other libraries in New York City that possess manuscripts relevant to the study of the refugees. In the New York Public Library are several small collections of loyalists' letters (the Chandler, Balch, and Bayard-Campbell-Pearsall papers), and twenty volumes of documents collected by George Chalmers. Also in the Public Library are the Bancroft Transcripts of parts of the Audit Office 12 series from the Public Record Office. The Library of the Museum of the City of New York houses two limited but informative collections of manuscripts, the Harry Munro and Thomas Jones papers, in addition to an interesting miscellaneous group of letters. In the Columbia University Library are the papers of Peter Van Schaack, and in the library of the General Theological Seminary are deposited the cursory diary of Thomas B. Chandler and the somewhat more valuable papers of Samuel Seabury.

The Historical Society of Pennsylvania also owns numerous collections of loyalists' personal letters. Of particular importance is the diary of Samuel Shoemaker, which provides a detailed account of life in London in 1784 and 1785. The letters of Joseph Galloway and his daughter Elizabeth may be found in the Dreer and Thompson collections, those of Phineas Bond in the Cadwalader Collection, and those of Mr. and Mrs. Jacob Duché in the Redwood Papers. Also of interest are the John Warder letterbooks, 1776–1778, the letters of Thomas Coombe, Jr., in the

Coombe MSS, and the journal of Samuel R. Fisher (microfilm). Another Philadelphia library, that of the American Philosophical Society, has a small collection of material pertinent to the loyalists in addition to the Franklin Papers, which contain some of William Franklin's correspondence.

Although the Manuscript Division of the Library of Congress does not have a large number of original manuscripts relevant to the loyalists, its holdings are of major importance. The Nicholas Low Papers contain many letters from that American's loyal relatives, and the recently acquired personal letters of Joseph and Elizabeth Galloway are particularly useful in illuminating aspects of the refugees' daily lives in London. The letters of Mrs. Henry Barnes describe the details of life in the Massachusetts colony at Bristol. Further, the brief diary of Thomas Moffat (1775–1777), the Andrew Bell MSS, the Peter Van Schaack MSS, and the John Singleton Copley MSS include material of interest. In addition, the LCMD owns forty-two volumes labeled "Proceedings of the Loyalist Commissioners," which are for the most part notes pertaining to claims cases heard in Canada.

It should be pointed out that the Library of Congress Manuscript Division is also the repository for a large number of transcripts and reproductions of documents from the Public Record Office in London. Most of the important volumes of Colonial Office 5 have been transcribed or filmed for the division, which also has microfilms of all of Audit Office 12 and 13, as well as parts of T 29. In addition, the LCMD has extensive transcripts from the papers of the Society for the Propagation of the Gospel in Foreign Parts and photostats of some of the Hutchinson papers from the British Museum.

Other American libraries have limited but significant holdings on the loyalists. In the Harvard University Library are the Jared Sparks MSS, the most relevant component of which is the George Chalmers collection. Here may be found information concerning both the Loyalist Association of 1779 and the board of loyalist agents. Also deposited in the Harvard University Library are the journal of George Inman, which is owned by the Cambridge Historical Society, and a microfilm of the letterbook of William Vassall. At the Yale University Library is the Knollenberg Collection, a group of exceptionally useful letters written during the war by Anglican clergymen in London to a friend in New York. The Virginia Historical Society in Richmond possesses a number of interesting letters of the Harrison Grays, father and son (published in the *Virginia Magazine of History and Biography,* VIII [1901], 225–36), and the Maryland Historical Society in Baltimore has several small collections of pertinent documents: the Murray (MS. 1376), Dulany (MS. 1265), and Addison (MS. 3) papers. At the Maine Historical Society in Portland are the valuable diary of Edward Oxnard and fragments from the papers of Silvester Gardiner, John Wiswall, and Thomas Flucker. In the South Caroliniana Library, Columbia, may be found the interesting papers of Elias Ball, a refugee, and Gabriel Manigault, a young American rebel resident in London during the 1770's. Two repositories in Hartford, the Connecticut State Library and the Connecticut Historical Society, have extensive collections of Samuel Peters' correspondence, and at the historical society in Newport, Rhode Island, are the informative letters of George Rome and Charles Dudley, and the Hunter family papers.

Chapter References

Abbreviations
Appearing in the Notes

Add. MSS: Additional Manuscripts, British Museum, London.
AO: Audit Office series, Public Record Office, London.
APSL: American Philosophical Society Library, Philadelphia.
BRO: Bedfordshire County Record Office, Bedford, England.
CHS: Connecticut Historical Society, Hartford.
CL: Columbia University Library, New York.
CO: Colonial Office series, Public Record Office, London.
CSL: Connecticut State Library, Hartford.
Eg. MSS: Egerton Manuscripts, British Museum, London.
ESRO: East Sussex Record Office, Pelham House, Lewes, England.
FO: Foreign Office series, Public Record Office, London.
GTS: General Theological Seminary, New York.
HL: Harvard University Library, Cambridge, Mass.
HO: Home Office series, Public Record Office, London.
HSP: Historical Society of Pennsylvania, Philadelphia.
LCMD: Library of Congress Manuscript Division, Washington, D.C.
LRO: Liverpool Record Office, Liverpool City Libraries, Liverpool, England.
MCNY: Museum of the City of New York Library.
MdHS: Maryland Historical Society, Baltimore.
MeHS: Maine Historical Society, Portland.
MHS: Massachusetts Historical Society, Boston.
MHS Procs.: *Proceedings of the Massachusetts Historical Society.*
NHS: Newport Historical Society, Newport, R.I.
NLS: National Library of Scotland, Edinburgh.
NYHS: New-York Historical Society.
NYPL: Manuscript Division, New York Public Library; Astor, Tilden and Lenox Foundations.
PRO: Public Record Office, London.
SCL: South Caroliniana Library, University of South Carolina, Columbia.
S.P.G. MSS: Society for the Propagation of the Gospel Papers, Library of Congress Manuscript Division, Washington, D.C.
T: Treasury series, Public Record Office, London.

UBL: University of Bristol Library, Bristol, England.
VHS: Virginia Historical Society, Richmond.
WLC: William L. Clements Library, Ann Arbor, Mich.
WMQ: *William and Mary Quarterly.*
WSL: William Salt Library, Stafford, England.
YL: Yale University Library, New Haven, Conn.

Notes

PROLOGUE

1. See, e.g., Wallace Brown, *The Good Americans* (New York, 1969), 30ff; and William A. Benton, *Whig-Loyalism* (Rutherford, N.J., 1969), 42ff.
2. Jonathan Mayhew, *The Snare Broken, A Thanks-giving Discourse* (Boston, 1766), 16.
3. See Thomas C. Barrow, "The American Revolution as a Colonial War for Independence," *WMQ*, 3rd ser., XXV (1968), 452–64.
4. Both this paragraph and the prologue as a whole draw heavily upon Pauline Maier, *From Resistance to Revolution: Colonial Radicals and the Development of American Opposition to Britain, 1765–1776* (New York, 1972).
5. See [Thomas B. Chandler], *What Think ye of the Congress Now?* (New York, 1775), esp. 31; and Samuel Seabury, *Letters of a Westchester Farmer,* ed. Clarence Vance (White Plains, 1930), *passim.*
6. William Nelson, in *The American Tory* (New York, 1961), discusses both ideological and nonideological factors that impelled men toward loyalism.

1: A CERTAIN PLACE OF SAFETY

1. Caner to the Archbishop of London, Aug. 16, 1775, Caner Letterbook, UBL.
2. Hutchinson to Francis Bernard, March 9, 1774, Eg. MSS 2661, f 13. And see Peter O. Hutchinson, ed., *The Diary and Letters of Thomas Hutchinson* (Boston, 1884), I, 114–7, 152–4.
3. Clarence E. Carter, ed., *The Correspondence of General Thomas Gage, 1763–1775* (New Haven, 1931–1933), I, 380. For an account of the Tea Party and its aftermath: Merrill Jensen, *The Founding of a Nation* (New York, 1968), 447–60.
4. Hutchinson was critical of the acts (Hutchinson, *Diary and Letters,* I, 175–8, 402), some of the details of which seem to have been suggested to Lord Dartmouth by an American, John Vardill (see his "Thoughts on the State of the Colonies," 1774, Dartmouth Papers, I, 2, no. 1219, WSL).
5. Lechmere to Lane Son and Fraser, May 30, 1774, Miscellaneous Manuscripts, MHS. Copies of addresses to Hutchinson and Gage may be conveniently found in James H. Stark, *The Loyalists of Massachusetts* (Boston, 1907), 123–32.
6. *Boston Gazette,* July 8, and Sept. 16, 1765; Carter, ed., *Gage Corres.,* I, 363. For Lechmere's comments on the reaction to his signing the Address: Lechmere to Lane Son and Fraser, Sept. 28, 1774, Misc. MSS, MHS.
7. On the role of the council, see Francis G. Walett, "The Massachusetts

Council, 1766–1774: The Transformation of a Conservative Institution," *WMQ*, 3rd ser., VI (1949), 605–27.

8. On intimidation of councilors: Carter, ed., *Gage Corres.*, I, 364; Albert Matthews, "Documents Relating to the Last Meetings of the Massachusetts Royal Council, 1774–1776," *Publications of the Colonial Society of Massachusetts*, XXXII (1937), 476–83.

9. Matthews, "Documents," *Pubs. Col. Soc. Mass.*, XXXII, 485–6.

10. A summary of the resignations, refusals, and acceptances may be found in *ibid.*, 472, 496. Also, Carter, ed., *Gage Corres.*, I, 370–1; "Letters of John Andrews, Esq., of Boston, 1772–1776," *MHS Procs.*, VIII (1864–1865), 352–3; and Daniel P. Coke, *The Royal Commission on the Losses and Services of American Loyalists*, ed. Hugh E. Egerton (Oxford, 1915), 186.

11. Carter, ed., *Gage Corres.*, I, 374. Also, Coke, *Royal Commission*, 231; Daniel Oliver, claims memorial, 1784, Hutchinson-Oliver Papers, MHS; and "Andrews Letters," *MHS Procs.*, VIII, 357–8.

12. See Arthur M. Schlesinger, *The Colonial Merchants and the American Revolution* (New York, 1918), 325–33, 341–7, 360ff.

13. Samuel Seabury, claims memorial, AO 12/19, f 356.

14. [Thomas B. Chandler], *A Friendly Address to All Reasonable Americans* . . . (New York, 1774), 4, 47; [Joseph Galloway], *A Candid Examination of the Mutual Claims of Great-Britain and the Colonies* . . . (London, repr., 1780), 8; [Charles Inglis], *The True Interest of America impartially stated* . . . (Philadelphia, 1776), 70; Jonathan Sewall to Thomas Hutchinson, Dec. 11, 1774, Dartmouth MSS, Amer. ser., no. 1018.

15. Chandler, *Friendly Address*, 6–7, 15, 19, 23, 46; Samuel Seabury, *Letters of a Westchester Farmer*, ed. Clarence Vance (White Plains, 1930), 45–60, 155, 62.

16. Chandler, *Friendly Address*, 47–8; John Adams and Jonathan Sewall (i.e., Daniel Leonard), *Novanglus and Massachusettensis* (New York, 1968: 1st ed., 1819), 144–5.

17. Seabury, *Letters*, 116–7; [Thomas B. Chandler], *What Think ye of the Congress Now?* (New York, 1775), 25; [Isaac Wilkins], *Short Advice to the Counties of New-York* (New York, 1774), 5; [Joseph Galloway], *A Candid Examination of the Mutual Claims of Great-Britain and the Colonies* . . . (New York, 1775), 32–3. Also, [James Chalmers], *Plain Truth* . . . (London, repr., 1776), 36–7; and Peter Oliver, *Origin & Progress of the American Rebellion*, ed. Douglass Adair and John A. Schutz (San Marino, Calif., 1961), 167–8.

18. Chandler, *Congress*, 44. See also Jensen, *Founding of Nation*, 501–2, 508ff.

19. "Some Letters of Joseph Galloway, 1774–1775," *Pennsylvania Magazine of History and Biography*, XXI (1897), 484.

20. On the limited functions of committees: Jensen, *Founding of Nation*, 516–34; and Schlesinger, *Colonial Merchants*, 476–540. On the failure of counterassociations: Bernard Mason, *The Road to Independence: The Revolutionary Movement in New York, 1773–1777* (Lexington, Ky., 1966), 85–6; Kenneth Scott, "Tory Associators of Portsmouth," *WMQ*, 3rd ser., XVII (1960), 507–9; Wilbur H. Siebert, "Loyalist Troops of New England,"

New England Quarterly, IV (1931), 108–10. On men who took the middle ground: William A. Benton, *Whig-Loyalism* (Rutherford, N.J., 1969).

21. Jacob Duché, *The Duty of Standing Fast in our Spiritual and Temporal Liberties* (Philadelphia, 1775), 18; Worthington C. Ford, ed., *The Washington-Duché Letters* (Brooklyn, 1890), 11. Boucher's sermon is printed in his *A View of the Causes and Consequences of the American Revolution* (London, 1797).

22. Order of Provincial Congress, Georgia, Dec. 6, 1775, CO 5/115, f 223. Gordon Wood discusses the Americans' intolerance of dissent in *The Creation of the American Republic, 1776–1789* (Chapel Hill, 1968), 62–3.

23. See Schlesinger, *Colonial Merchants*, 552–9, for a general account of committee activities in this period.

24. S.P.G. Journal, XX, 273, S.P.G. MSS; E. M. Saunders, "The Life and Times of the Rev. John Wiswall, M.A.," *Nova Scotia Historical Society Collections*, XIII (1908), 8, 13–7. Similar experiences are recounted in Coke, *Royal Commission,* 69; S.P.G. Journal, XX, 448–9, S.P.G. MSS; and Samuel Porter to Lords of Treasury, Feb. 23, 1776, T 1/520.

25. See, e.g., G. A. Gilbert, "The Connecticut Loyalists," *American Historical Review*, IV (1899), 281–2; David S. Lovejoy, *Rhode Island Politics and the American Revolution, 1760–1776* (Providence, 1958), 189; Alexander C. Flick, ed., *History of the State of New York* (New York, 1933–1937), III, 336–40; and "Journal of the Committee of Observation of the Middle District of Frederick County, Maryland," *Maryland Historical Magazine*, X, 301–21; XI, 50–66, 157–75, 237–60, 304–21; XII, 10–21.

26. Accounts of the use of these tactics may be found in Jonathan Watson, claims memorial, n.d., AO 12/56, f 266; Janet Schaw, *Journal of a Lady of Quality . . . in the years 1774 to 1776*, ed. Evangeline Andrews (New Haven, 1923), 187–99, *passim*; and Hutchinson, *Diary and Letters*, I, 433.

27. Nicholas Cresswell, *The Journal of Nicholas Cresswell* (Port Washington, N.Y., 1958), 131 (also, 165–200, *passim*, esp. 172, 186, 191). And, S.P.G. Journal, XXI, 167–8, S.P.G. MSS; Ralph Earl to Lords of Treasury, Feb. 6, 1779, AO 13/41, f 245; and [Thomas Gilpin], *Exiles in Virginia . . .* (Philadelphia, 1848).

28. John Agnew, claims memorial, March 24, 1784, AO 12/56, f 403; George Meserve to customs commissioners, Feb. 8, 1776, T 1/520.

29. George Milligan [Johnston], "Report of the State of South Carolina," Sept. 15, 1775, CO 5/396, ff 211–3; Macknight to Lord George Germain, Nov. 1776, CO 5/147, f 830. Also, Schaw, *Journal*, 181, 190–1. A rare instance of tarring and feathering is recounted in Anthony Warwick, claims memorial, n.d., AO 12/56, f 228.

30. Anthony Stewart to Lords of Treasury, March 10, 1777, T 1/533. Also, Thomas Buffton to Lords of Treasury, Oct. 14, 1777, AO 13/43, f 631; "Extract of a letter from Mr Anthony Lechmere of Newport Rhode Island Dated, Jamaica 14 Octob. 1776," AO 13/68, pt. 2, ff 235–6.

31. James Parker to Charles Steuart, Sept. 25, 1775, Steuart Papers, 5029, f 104, NLS.

32. Hutchinson, *Diary and Letters*, I, 469; Henry Caner to [Richard Hind], July 15, 1775, S.P.G. MSS, ser. B, XXII, 133; Sewall to Thomas Robie, July

15, 1775, Robie-Sewall Papers, MHS; John Wiswall to Richard Hind, Dec.
1, 1775, Miscellaneous Massachusetts Manuscripts, S.P.G. MSS; Henry
Caner to Richard Hind, July 13, 1775, Caner Letterbook.

33. Hutchinson, *Diary and Letters*, I, 457–8, 573; S.P.G. Journal, XXI, 70,
S.P.G. MSS; Peter Oliver, Journal, March 27, 1776, Eg. MSS 2672, ff 4–5.

34. Henry Caner to Bishop of London, April 24, 1776, Caner Letterbook;
Thomas Oliver to Lord George Germain, April 21, 1776, CO 5/175, f 161;
Peter Oliver journal, April 3, 1776, Eg. MSS 2672, ff 6–7. Also, Silvester
Gardiner to ———, May 9, 1776, Gardiner-Whipple-Allen Papers, MHS;
and Emily P. Weaver, "Nova Scotia and New England during the Revolu-
tion," *Amer. Hist. Rev.*, X (1904–1905) , 67.

35. Henry Hulton to his sister, June 18, 1776, Hulton Letterbook, II, 5, HL;
Thomas Oliver to Thomas Hutchinson, April 28, 1776, CO 5/175, f 168.

36. Of 278 families (927 persons) evacuated to Halifax, 73 families (including
three-fourths of the civil officials and one-third of the customs officers)
eventually went to England. A list of the evacuees may be found in Stark,
Loyalists of Massachusetts, 133–6.

37. Thomas Hutchinson to Lord Hardwicke, July 19, 1776, Add. MSS 35427,
f 86; Oscar T. Barck, *New York City during the War for Independence*
(New York, 1931) , 74–8.

38. John Potts to Joseph Galloway, Dec. 17, 1778, Balch Papers, NYPL; Cresswell, *Journal*, 219–21, 244–5; Galloway to his wife, Sept. [1778], Galloway
Papers, LCMD. See Barck, *New York City*, 49–56, 79–86.

39. Clinton to John Robinson, Dec. 20, 1781, T 1/572; Clinton to [Germain],
Dec. 15, 1779, CO 5/237, ff 239–40. On recruitment of troops: Barck, *New
York City*, 192–200.

40. Cresswell, *Journal, passim*, esp. 165–7, 226–7, describes the difficulties of a
suspected person in the South during this period. And see Hugh F. Rankin, "The Moore's Creek Bridge Campaign, 1776," *North Carolina Historical Review*, XXX (1953) , 23–60.

41. Richard P. McCormick, *Experiment in Independence: New Jersey in the
Critical Period, 1781–1789* (New Brunswick, 1950) , 35–6; Gilbert, "Conn.
Loyalists," *Amer. Hist. Rev.*, IV, 286; *Documents and Records relating to
the State of New Hampshire . . .*, ed. Nathaniel Bouton (Concord, N.H.,
1874) , VIII, 713–4; and *Pennsylvania Archives* (Harrisburg, 1876) , 2nd
ser., III, 4–5, contain examples of state loyalty oaths. Also of interest is
the account of a Virginian's arrival in Scotland, in Edward Penman to
George Maxwell, Aug. 31, 1775, T 1/514.

42. Edward McGrady, *South Carolina in the Revolution, 1775–1780* (New
York, 1901) , 213–4, 266–7; Isaac Harrell, "North Carolina Loyalists," *N.C.
Hist. Rev.*, III (1926) , 580–1.

43. Banished loyalists: Edmund Head, Thomas Knox Gordon, *et al.*, memorial,
Nov. 3, 1778, T 1/540; Robert Brailsford, memorial, 1778, T 1/547. Eva-
sive loyalists: Alexander Garden, testimony, Nov. 9, 1786, AO 12/50,
ff 164–8; James Simpson, testimony, Feb. 2, 1785, AO 12/47, f 274. The
quote is from Robert W. Powell, testimony, Nov. 19, 1785, AO 12/48, f 43.

44. Anthony Stokes, *A View of the Constitution of the British Colonies, in North-America and the West Indies* (London, 1783), 117.
45. The evacuation records of Charleston (Shelburne Papers, LXIX, 213–6, WLC) show that most of the civilian evacuees sailed to Jamaica. At the evacuation of New York, most of the loyalists went to Nova Scotia: see CO 5/111, f 471; and Barck, *New York City*, 210–5.
46. Wallace Brown, *The King's Friends* (Providence, 1965), 253, 257–8.

2: *VAIN HOPES*

1. George A. Ward, ed., *Journal and Letters of the late Samuel Curwen*, 3rd ed. (New York, 1845), 59.
2. Louisa Wells Aikman, *The Journal of a Voyage from Charleston, S.C. to London* (New York, 1906), 61–2. For Peter Oliver's similar comments: Peter O. Hutchinson, ed., *The Diary and Letters of Thomas Hutchinson* (Boston, 1884), II, 53; and Peter Oliver, Journal, June 1, 13, 1776, Eg. MSS 2672, ff 16, 61.
3. The radicals' expectations are discussed at length in chapter 8 of Pauline Maier's recent book, *From Resistance to Revolution* (New York, 1972).
4. William Laight to his father, Nov. 16, 1775, Miscellaneous Letters, MCNY. And, in general, Isaac Smith's letters to his family, 1775, Smith-Carter Papers, MHS, esp. to his father, July 27.
5. John Vardill to Peter Van Schaack, Feb. 12, 1775, Van Schaack Papers, CL; Isaac Smith to his father, Sept. 26, 1775, Smith-Carter MSS; Samuel Quincy to Henry Hill, Aug. 18, 1775, S. Quincy Papers, MHS.
6. Harrison Gray, Jr., to Harrison Gray, Oct. 6, 1775, Gray Papers, VHS; Isaac Smith to William Smith, Aug. 2, 1775, Smith-Carter MSS; Samuel Quincy to Henry Hill, Aug. 18, 1775, S. Quincy MSS; Isaac Smith to Mr. Gannett, Dec. 6 [1775], CO 5/40, f 324. The loyalists' accounts of the government's policy were accurate; see Sir John Fortesque, ed., *The Correspondence of King George III* (New York, 1967), III, 131, 153–4; and the discussion in Ira Gruber, "Lord Howe and Lord George Germain: British Politics and the Winning of American Independence," *WMQ*, 3rd ser., XXII (1965), 226.
7. Ward, ed., *Curwen Journal*, 31; John Maunsell to Peter Van Schaack, July 5, 1775, Van Schaack MSS; William Laight to John Jay, Oct. 3, 1775, Misc. Letters, MCNY.
8. For accounts of loyalists' futile attempts to talk with various ministers: Henry Barnes to James Murray, April 28, 1776, Miscellaneous Manuscripts, MHS; John Amory, petition to Massachusetts General Court, c. 1783, LCMD; and Isaac Royall to James Bowdoin, Sept. 8, 1779, Bowdoin-Temple Papers, III, 99, MHS.
9. Chandler: Thomas B. Chandler, Diary, July 1775, *passim*, esp. 14, GTS. Vardill: John Vardill, claims memorial, Nov. 16, 1783, AO 12/20, f 23; and his letters to Peter Van Schaack, 1774–1775, Van Schaack MSS. Boucher: Jonathan Boucher, claims testimony, Jan. 16, 1787, AO 12/8, f 87. Johnston: [George Johnston] to Germain, July 26, 1776, AO 13/79, f 459.

Moffat: Thomas Moffat, Diary, Jan.–Mar., 1776, *passim*, LCMD; and Moffat to Lords of Treasury, Dec. 10, 1778, T 1/541.

10. Hutchinson to Thomas Flucker, July 7, 1774, Eg. MSS 2661, f 31; to James Murray, July 23, 1774, Misc. MSS, MHS. And, in general, Hutchinson, *Diary and Letters*, I, 153–95, *passim*.

11. Hutchinson, *Diary and Letters*, I, 190; Hutchinson to James Murray, July 23, 1774, Misc. MSS, MHS; to his son Thomas Jr., Sept. 29, 1774, Eg. MSS 2661, f 61.

12. Cf. Hutchinson, *Diary and Letters*, I, 158; Hutchinson to Thomas Flucker, July 7, 1774, Eg. MSS 2661, f 31; and Fortesque, ed., *Corres. George III*, III, 116.

13. Hutchinson to Mr. Gambier, Oct. 20, 1774, Eg. MSS 2661, f 70; to Israel Williams, Sept. 29, 1774, Williams Papers, MHS.

14. Hutchinson, *Diary and Letters*, I, 526; Hutchinson to Lord Hardwicke, Aug. 23, July 7, 1775, Add. MSS 35427, ff 39, 26.

15. Nina M. Tiffany, ed., *Letters of James Murray, Loyalist* (Boston, 1901), 257–8; Hutchinson to Abijah Willard, Sept. 7, 1775, Eg. MSS 2661, f 165.

16. Hutchinson to Mr. Hooper, March 10, 1775, Eg. MSS 2661, f 132; to Lord Hardwicke, Sept. 6b, 24, 1775, Add. MSS 35427, ff 43, 46.

17. Hutchinson to ———, Nov. 4, 1774, Eg. MSS 2661, f 76; to Charles Paxton, Feb. 16, 1776, *ibid.*, f 172, printed with modified punctuation in Hutchinson, *Diary and Letters*, II, 40.

18. George Rome, claims memorial, [March 1784], AO 13/69, f 60; Jane Gordon to Charles Steuart, Jan. 28, 1778, Steuart Papers, 5030, f 210, NLS.

19. William Vassall to Dr. James Lloyd, Dec. 20, 1775, Vassall Letterbook, I, 105, HL (microfilm). On disruption of incomes: Sir William Pepperrell to Isaac Winslow, Aug. 19, 1781, Winslow Papers, MHS.

20. See, e.g., the cases of Thomas Harper, Francis Thomas, and James Tory (AO 12/100, ff 89, 165, 342); Richard F. Pitt (AO 12/102, f 117); and Samuel Garnett (AO 12/105, f 126). Also, Anthony Stokes, *A View of the Constitution of the British Colonies, in North-America and the West Indies* (London, 1783), 269–70.

21. William Rugeley to his father, c. Dec. 1778 (draft), Rugeley Papers, BRO; Hutchinson, *Diary and Letters*, II, 245. For further on Hutchinson's job search: *ibid.*, I, 437, 449, 482–3; II, 80; and Hutchinson to [Lord North?], May 22, 1778, Eg. MSS 2661, ff 180–2. And see Dorothy Marshall, *Dr. Johnson's London* (New York, 1968), 137–40, on the general problem of job hunting in eighteenth-century London.

22. On salaries: Thomas B. Chandler to George Panton, Dec. 3, 1777, Knollenberg Collection, YL; S.P.G. Journal, XXI, f 390, S.P.G. MSS. On the relief fund: Chandler diary, Dec. 7, 1775, April 6, 1776; Chandler to Samuel Seabury, April 8, 1776, Seabury Papers, GTS; Chandler to William Samuel Johnson, Feb. 17, 1786, William Samuel Johnson Papers, CHS.

23. See Isaac Hunt, claims memorial, n.d., AO 12/42, f 313; Lord Percy to George Rose, Dec. 9, 1782, Add. MSS 42774A, f 19; John Wiswall to Samuel Peters, Feb. 19, 1782, Peters Papers, I, 59, NYHS (microfilm).

24. "Letters of Rev. Jonathan Boucher, 1759–1777," *Maryland Historical Magazine*, VIII (1913), 344; Boucher, *Reminiscences of an American Loyalist*,

1738–1789, ed. Jonathan Bouchier (Boston, 1925), 144; Boucher to John James, April 27, 1780, Boucher Papers, ESRO. Also, Boucher, *Reminiscences*, 147–52.

25. Isaac Smith to his father, Oct. 14, 1782, Smith-Carter MSS. Many letters in this collection describe Smith's life in Sidmouth.
26. Caner to Dr. Breynton, July 1, 1776, to Mather Byles, Jr., Dec. 26, 1776, to John Jeffries, July 17, 1776, to Mather Byles, Jr., July 1, 1776, all in Caner Letterbook, UBL. For an identical observation: Thomas B. Chandler to George Panton, June 25, 1779, Knollenberg MSS.
27. Henry Caner to Lady Agnes Frankland, Aug. 19, 1776, to Dr. Breynton, Aug. 5, 1777, both in Caner Letterbook; S.P.G. Journal, XXI, 136, 176, S.P.G. MSS.
28. Thomas Danforth to Evan Nepean, June 20, 1786, CO 188/2, f 67.
29. The four men were Ebenezer Richardson, George Wilmot, David Ingersoll, and Samuel Peters. On Richardson and Wilmot: their memorials to Dartmouth, Jan. 19, 1775, and John Pownall to Grey Cooper, Jan. 20, 1775, all in T 1/517; Wilmot to Dartmouth, Richardson to Dartmouth, April 13, 14, 1775, Dartmouth Papers, Amer. ser., nos. 1217, 1219, WSL. On Ingersoll: his memorials to Dartmouth, Feb. 7, Oct. 14, 1775, *ibid.*, nos. 1136, 1551. On Peters: Peters to Dartmouth, Feb. 27, 1775, *ibid.*, no. 1166; S.P.G. Journal, XX, 292, 355–6, S.P.G. MSS; and Peters to Dr. Markham, April 18, 1775, Peters MSS, I, 14. Peters was given twenty guineas by the S.P.G. but apparently received nothing from the government at this time.
30. Hutchinson to James Murray, Feb. 24, 1775, Misc. MSS, MHS; Hutchinson to [Richard] Clarke, July 24, 1775, Eg. MSS 2661, f 159. He was replying to a letter from Clarke, April 18, 1775, which is in the Alexander Wedderburn Papers, II, 49, WLC. The one person who was granted additional assistance was David Ingersoll (Treasury minutes, Nov. 3, 1775, T 29/44).
31. Treasury minutes, Feb. 27, May 30, 1776, T 29/45. Boucher received part of the £177 (Boucher, *Reminiscences*, 144). On the distribution of the £5000: William Browne to John Robinson, July 2, 1777, AO 13/43, f 650. And see "An Account of Monies paid for the Relief and Benefit of Sundry American Officers and Others who have suffered on Account of their Attachment to his Majesty's Government," in Benjamin F. Stevens, ed., *Facsimiles of Manuscripts in European Archives Relating to America, 1773–1783* (London, 1889–1895), 2024.
32. William Knox to John Robinson, July 19, 1776, HO 36/1, f 10. On continuing civil salaries, see the memorial that perhaps prompted Knox's letter, Thomas Oliver to Germain, July 18, 1776, CO 5/115, ff 285–8; and Anthony Stokes to Lords of Treasury, Jan. 5, 1778, CO 5/116, ff 335–43. On postmasters: Treasury minutes, Aug. 27, 1779, T 29/48; and Postmaster General to Lords of Treasury, June 2, 1784, T 1/604. For customs officers, chapter 4, notes 53–6; admiralty judges, chapter 4, note 41.
33. Caner to William Lee Perkins, July 15, 1776, Caner Letterbook; "Account of Monies paid," in Stevens, ed., *Facsimiles*, 2024; Massachusetts loyalists to Germain, n.d., AO 13/46, f 24; Massachusetts councilors to Germain, n.d. but c. Dec. 24, 1776, *ibid.*, ff 20–1. Although the general petition is undated,

there are references placing it in October 1776 in Ward, ed., *Curwen Journal*, 85–6; and John Sargent to Germain, March 7, 1777, AO 13/49, f 274.

34. Edward Oxnard, Diary, Dec. 23, 1776, MeHS. The original pension list is apparently no longer extant, and it has been reconstituted by comparing the names of exiles receiving pensions in 1782 with the names of those whose cases were heard by the Treasury between 1777 and 1782. The ones included in the 1782 list but not considered by the Treasury after July 1777 must have been on the first list. Eighty-eight persons can be identified by this method, but since some pensioners were struck off before 1782, there must have been about one hundred names on the original rolls. For comments on the first list: Ward, ed., *Curwen Journal*, 103; Note on Paxton Hatch, April 29, 1778, AO 13/46, f 311. Before final decisions on the pension amounts were made, Hutchinson was asked for his opinion on some of the applicants (Thomas Hutchinson, Diary, Jan. 18, 1777, Eg. MSS 2663, f 130).

35. Treasury minutes, July 22, 24, 29, Aug. 16, 19, 1777, T 29/46; "Account of Monies paid," in Stevens, ed., *Facsimiles*, 2024.

36. *The Gentleman's Magazine*, LII (Feb. 1782), 57. For other debates on the same topic, see *ibid.*, XLIX (Jan. 1779), 42, and LIII (Jan. 1783), 71. There is another, somewhat different account of the 1781 debate in *The Political Magazine*, II (April 1781), 239–40.

37. *The Political Magazine*, III (April 1782), 236; Myles Cooper to George Panton, July 31, 1778, Knollenberg MSS; George Boyd to John Robinson, April 8, 1778, T 1/546; John Randolph to ———, July 16, 1777, AO 13/32, f 339.

38. E.g., Arthur Savage to Samuel Savage, Feb. 25, 1778, S. P. Savage Papers II, MHS; George Erving to John Wilmot and Daniel Coke, Nov. 1, 1782, AO 13/44, f 529; James Wright to Lord North, Dec. 16, 1778, AO 13/37, ff 490–1.

39. There are a few household bills in the Silvester Gardiner Papers, MeHS, and the Waldo-Knox-Flucker Papers, MeHS. Rents (as recorded, e.g., in Samuel Shoemaker, Diary, May 20, July 6, Sept. 24, 1784, HSP) averaged 12 to 15 shillings a week, or approximately £30 to £40 annually. Comments indicating that £100 was sufficient may be found in Thomas Hutchinson, Jr., to Elisha Hutchinson, March 5, 1783, Eg. MSS 2659, f 399; and Samuel Peters to Dr. Markham, March 7, 1775, Peters MSS, I, 10. On a large family's problems: case of Philip Van Cortland, Nov. 27, 1783, AO 12/100, f 84.

40. William Vans Murray to Henry Maynadier, Feb. 8, 1784, Murray Papers, MdHS, referring to Philip B. Key. And see Polly Hutchinson to her father, c. Aug. 1783 (draft), Hutchinson-Watson Papers, MHS. These estimates jibe roughly with the figures in Jackson T. Main, *The Social Structure of Revolutionary America* (Princeton, 1965), 118, 123.

41. *The Examination of Joseph Galloway, Esq; . . . Before the House of Commons* (London, 1779), 79; Galloway to Lord [Germain?], n.d., Galloway Papers, LCMD. He admitted his allowance put him "in a Condition above want" in a letter to his wife, Feb. 4, 1779, *ibid.*

42. George Erving to claims commissioners, Feb. 1, 1786, AO 13/137, f 196. Also, Galloway to Lord [Germain?], n.d., Galloway MSS; "Boucher Letters," *Md. Hist. Mag.*, IX, 62; John McAlpine, *Genuine Narratives, and Concise Memoirs . . .* (n.p., 1788), 59.

43. For example, the five refugee colonial attorneys general (presumably of comparable status) received allowances ranging from £150 to £500, only two of which were for the same amount. For an instance of influence peddling: Richard Rigby to Henry Barnes, July 20, 1778, AO 13/43, ff 359–60; Treasury minutes, July 23, 1778, T 29/47; Daniel P. Coke, *The Royal Commission on the Losses and Services of American Loyalists*, ed. Hugh E. Egerton (Oxford, 1915), 239.

44. Otis G. Hammond, *Tories of New Hampshire in the War of the Revolution* (Concord, 1917), 32–5; Allen French, *General Gage's Informers* (Ann Arbor, 1932), 132–43.

45. See Egon Lehrberger, *An American in Europe* (London, 1953), 15–6, 36–7; Alan Valentine, *Lord George Germain* (Oxford, 1962), 272–4; Piers Mackesy, *The War for America, 1775–1783* (Cambridge, Mass., 1964), 51. Thompson's "Observations" are in the Germain Papers, WLC.

46. Sir William Pepperrell to Isaac Winslow, Oct. 2, 1781, Winslow MSS; case of William L. Perkins, AO 12/105, f 78; Hannah Winslow to [Germain], July 31, [1779], CO 5/117, ff 133–5; Treasury minutes, July 19, 1780, T 29/49; Pepperrell to Winslow, Sept. 29, 1780, Winslow MSS. On the others: Thompson to Silvester Gardiner, Feb. 24, 1780, Gardiner-Whipple-Allen Papers, MHS (hereafter Gardiner MSS); Thompson to John Robinson, Dec. 28, 1780, AO 13/43, ff 639–40; Thompson to William Knox, Aug. 30, 1780, CO 5/157, f 392; Knox to Grey Cooper, Jan. 25, 1777, HO 36/1, f 38; Germain to Lords of Treasury, May 14, 1778, *ibid.*, f 158.

47. Batwell to George Panton, Nov. 1, 1780, Knollenberg MSS; Jane Gordon to Charles Steuart, Nov. 3, 1777, Steuart MSS, 5030, f 132. Also, Sir William Pepperrell to Silvester Gardiner, July 20, 1780, Gardiner MSS. A comparison of the times petitions were referred to the Treasury (from HO 36/1–3) with the times they were considered (from T 29) shows an average waiting period of five to six months, though some were acted upon immediately and others took more than two years to gain a hearing.

48. Hutchinson to Elisha Hutchinson, Aug. 28, 1780, Eg. MSS 2659, f 306; Ward, ed., *Curwen Journal*, 279. And, on the practices discussed in the text, Thomas Hutchinson, Jr., to Elisha Hutchinson, Nov. 19, 1782, Eg. MSS 2659, f 390; John Maclean to Charles Steuart, Jan. 15, 1778, Steuart MSS, 5030, f 186; Thomas Jack to Steuart, Aug. 28, 1778, *ibid.*, 5031, f 48.

49. Ward, ed., *Curwen Journal*, 212; E[lizabeth] G[alloway] to Polly Hutchinson, Oct. 5, 1781, Hutchinson-Watson MSS. Also, Oxnard diary, Dec. 23, 1776.

50. Henry Barnes to James Murray, Feb. 10, 1781, J. M. Robbins Papers, MHS; Hutchinson, *Diary and Letters*, II, 408–9.

51. Extract of a letter from Connecticut, [Sept. 1774], Dartmouth MSS, Amer. ser., no. 974; Samuel Peters to John Robinson, Feb. 7, 1777, AO 13/42, f 351.

3: *AMERICA TRANSPLANTED TO LONDON*

1. Samuel Quincy to his wife, Jan. 1, 1777, S. Quincy Papers, MHS.
2. Peter O. Hutchinson, ed., *The Diary and Letters of Thomas Hutchinson* (Boston, 1884) , I, 281. Also, *ibid.*, 201; and Elisha Hutchinson to his wife Polly, Nov. 4, 1776, Eg. MSS 2668, f 105.
3. The information on addresses has been drawn from many sources, mainly letters, diaries, and memorials. And see Samuel Shoemaker, Diary, July 1784, HSP; and John Watts to Robert Watts, Aug. 5, 1789, Robert Watts Papers, NYHS.
4. Peter Oliver to Polly Hutchinson, April 2, 1777, Hutchinson-Watson Papers, MHS; Arthur Savage to Samuel P. Savage, April 23, 1777, S. P. Savage Papers II, MHS. On Highgate: Edward Oxnard, Diary, July 11, 1776, Oct. 23, 1777, MeHS. On Brompton: Harrison Gray, Jr., to Harrison Gray, Oct. 6, 1775, Gray Letters, VHS.
5. Hannah Winslow to Mr. Winslow, Jan. 4, 1779, Winslow Papers, MHS; Colden to his wife, June 27, 1784, Miscellaneous Manuscripts, NYHS; Colden to Elizabeth DeLancey, June 28, 1784, Colden Papers, NYHS; William Bayard to Betsy Cornel, Sept. 20, 1783, Misc. MSS, NYHS; Isaac Low to Nicholas Low, March 3, 1784, Nicholas Low Papers, box 67, LCMD.
6. Samuel Quincy, "Diary, Oct. 9, 1776 – March 30, 1777," *MHS Procs.*, XIX (1881–1882) , *passim*, esp. 215. George A. Ward, ed., *Journal and Letters of the late Samuel Curwen*, 3rd ed. (New York, 1845) , 45, describes a lengthy circumnambulation among the lodgings of various New Englanders in the area.
7. Hutchinson, *Diary and Letters*, II, 59; Oxnard diary, March 21, 1777; Samuel Quincy to his wife, Jan. 1, 1777, S. Quincy MSS.
8. Samuel Sparhawk to Isaac Winslow, Sept. 11, 1778, Winslow Papers, MHS; Elisha Hutchinson, Diary, Aug. 11, 1779, Eg. MSS 2669, f 64.
9. Hutchinson's moves may be traced in Hutchinson to his son Thomas Jr., Nov. 11, 1774, Eg. MSS 2661, f 79; and Hutchinson, *Diary and Letters*, II, 90–1, 157, 160. The frequent address changes caused Mrs. Elisha (Polly) Hutchinson to have a hard time locating the family when she arrived in London in September 1777 (*ibid.*, 159) .
10. See Shoemaker diary, *passim*, for frequent visits to the New York and Pennsylvania coffeehouses, and Ward, ed., *Curwen Journal*, 42, 294, 318, and *passim*, for similar accounts of the New England coffeehouse. When Curwen stopped going to the coffeehouse in 1784, he remarked that he was as a result "rarely in the way of Americans" (*ibid.*, 403) .
11. On clergymen, e.g.: "Journal of Rev. Joshua Wingate Weeks, Loyalist Rector of St. Michael's Church, Marblehead, 1778–1779," *Essex Institute Historical Collections*, LII (1916) , 1–16, 161–76, 197–208, 345–56, *passim*, esp. 347; and "Letters of Rev. Jonathan Boucher, 1759–1777," *Maryland Historical Magazine*, VIII (1913) , 344. On Copley and West: Ward, ed., *Curwen Journal*, 51. The quotations are from Shoemaker diary, Nov. 12, 1784; and Daniel P. Coke, *The Royal Commission on the Losses and Services of American Loyalists*, ed. Hugh E. Egerton (Oxford, 1915) , 201.

12. Shoemaker diary, *passim*, esp. May 7, 1785.
13. Hutchinson, *Diary and Letters*, II, 226, records the first meeting of Hutchinson and Galloway. See Elisha's diary, 1779 *passim*, Eg. MSS 2669, for accounts of his association with the Galloways. The New Yorker John Watts made the mistake about Hutchinson in his letter to Andrew Elliot, July 4, 1775, Ms 71820, CHS.
14. Quincy to his wife, March 12, 1777, S. Quincy MSS; Arthur Savage to Samuel P. Savage, Aug. 6, 1779, S. P. Savage MSS II. Burgwin, it should be noted, was a friend of Mrs. Quincy's cousin, so the families were previously acquainted. On the lack of interprovincial contacts at Brompton, see, e.g., the Elias Ball Papers, SCL, which never mention New Englanders, or Ward, ed., *Curwen Journal*, which mentions only Savage and John Randolph, and then very infrequently.
15. On Randolph: Mary Beth Norton, "John Randolph's 'Plan of Accommodations,'" *WMQ*, 3rd ser., XXVIII (1971), 104. On Bull: Gabriel Manigault to Francis Kinloch, March 12, 1778, [William L. Smith] to Gabriel Manigault, Nov. 3, 1779, both in Manigault Papers, SCL; William Rugeley to his father, July 11, 1780, Rugeley Papers, BRO. Elizabeth Galloway found that her father's position had its drawbacks; her rueful comments are contained in a letter to her mother, Jan. 4, 1779, Dreer Collection, HSP.
16. The New England diarists are Katherine (Mrs. John) Amory, Mather Byles, Jr., Samuel Curwen, Elisha Hutchinson, Thomas Hutchinson, George Inman, John Jeffries, Chief Justice Peter Oliver, Dr. Peter Oliver, Edward Oxnard, Benjamin Pickman, Samuel Quincy, and Joshua W. Weeks.
17. Typical Hutchinson dinner parties are described in Hutchinson, *Diary and Letters*, I, 198, 508, 575. On Pepperrell, see George Inman, Diary, Dec. 11, 1782–Jan. 1, 1783, *passim*, HL; and Mather Byles, Diary, Dec. 17, 1784, Byles Papers, I, 145, MHS.
18. Tabulated from Hutchinson, *Diary and Letters*, *passim*. Cf. Elisha Hutchinson, Diary, Eg. MSS 2669, *passim*.
19. Ward, ed., *Curwen Journal*, *passim*; Martha C. Codman, ed., *The Journal of Mrs. John Amory, 1775–1777* (Boston, 1923), *passim*; Oxnard diary, *passim*.
20. "Refugees in London 1775," *New England Historical and Genealogical Register*, III (1849), 82–3.
21. *Ibid.*, 83; Ward, ed., *Curwen Journal*, 45. There are accounts of meetings in *ibid.*, 48, 52, 56; and Oxnard diary, Oct. 12, 1775, Feb. 8, 15, 22, March 14, 28, April 4, 1776.
22. The list is on the front paper of vol. IV of Oxnard's diary (Sept.–Dec. 1776). For accounts of meetings: *ibid.*, Oct. 1776–Mar. 1777, *passim*. Curwen attended some of the sessions (Ward, ed., *Curwen Journal*, 104–6).
23. Ward, ed., *Curwen Journal*, 348–9.
24. See, e.g., William Pepperrell to Isaac Winslow, Oct. 1, 1779, Winslow MSS; Samuel Quincy to his wife, Oct. 15, 1777, S. Quincy MSS; Mather Byles, 3rd, to Katherine Byles, May 5, 1784, Byles MSS, I, 128.
25. Oxnard diary, Feb. 24, 1777. Also, Codman, ed., *Amory Journal*, 5; Ward,

ed., *Curwen Journal*, 31; Benjamin Pickman, *The Diary and Letters of Benjamin Pickman (1740–1819) of Salem, Massachusetts* (Newport, 1928), 95; Samuel Quincy to his wife, Oct. 15, 1777, March 11, 1779, S. Quincy MSS.

26. Thomas A. Coffin to his mother, Feb. 5, 1785, Coffin Family Papers, MHS. For a comment by a rebel on the firm's sympathies, see Glenn Weaver, *Jonathan Trumbull* (Hartford, 1956), 147.

27. Information on many of these lower-class loyalists may be found in AO 12/99–101. For some Massachusetts exiles never mentioned by the diarists, see AO 12/99, ff 26, 119, 208, 291; and AO 12/100, f 272.

28. Ward, ed., *Curwen Journal*, 318.

29. Arthur Savage to Samuel P. Savage, Jan. 9, 1781, S. P. Savage MSS II. On life in eighteenth-century London, see Dorothy Marshall, *Dr. Johnson's London* (New York, 1968); and George Rudé, *Hanoverian London* (London, 1971).

30. Catherine Goldthwait to Mrs. Forbes, July 31, 1781, J. M. Robbins Papers, MHS; Oxnard diary, April 27, 1777. Also, Elias Ball to [E. Ball], April 29, 1785, Ball MSS; Thomas Chandler, Diary, Sept. 28, 1775, GTS; John Jeffries, Diary, June 30, 1779, Aug. 17, 1784, MHS; Ward, ed., *Curwen Journal*, 342; Pickman, *Diary*, 99.

31. Shoemaker diary, Feb. 7, 1784; Jeffries diary, March 30, 1779; "Weeks Journal," *Essex Inst. Hist. Colls.*, LII, 354; L. S. F. Upton, ed., *The Diary and Selected Papers of Chief Justice William Smith 1784–1793* (Toronto, 1963), I, 171. On Westminster Abbey and St. Paul's Cathedral: Peter Van Schaack, Notes on Arrival in England, 1779, Van Schaack Papers, CL.

32. Upton, ed., *Smith Diary*, I, 204–5. And Jeffries diary, June 14, 1783; Peter Oliver, Journal, July 23, 1776, Eg. MSS 2672, f 96; Shoemaker diary, Jan. 9, 1784; Ward, ed., *Curwen Journal*, 56, 313, 378.

33. William L. Perkins to his brother Isaac, April 4, 1788, Perkins Papers, WLC; Upton, ed., *Smith Diary*, I, 204–5; Jeffries diary, May 5, July 4, 1781. Also, Oxnard diary, May 29, 1776; Elisha Hutchinson diary, March–June 1781, *passim*, Eg. MSS 2669.

34. Thomas A. Coffin to his mother, Dec. 26, 1785, Coffin MSS, MHS. A similar experience is described in Upton, ed., *Smith Diary*, II, 12.

35. Oxnard diary, Oct. 25, 1775; Jeffries diary, Aug. 29, 1783, July 27, 1781.

36. Oxnard diary, Sept. 3, 1775, Aug. 19, 1776; Byles diary, July 6, 1785, Byles MSS, I, 173; Jeffries diary, July 21, 1779.

37. Oxnard diary, Sept. 15, 1775; Upton, ed., *Smith Diary*, I, 225–6; Ward, ed., *Curwen Journal*, 280–95, *passim*. Also, Jeffries diary, Jan. 3, 1783, Oct. 11, 1784; Oliver journal, July 9, 1776, March 11, 1777, Eg. MSS 2672, ff 88, 265.

38. See Ward, ed., *Curwen Journal*, 55. A detailed discussion of London theaters of the period may be found in Charles A. Hogan, ed., *The London Stage 1660–1800: pt. 5, 1776–1800* (Carbondale, Ill., 1968), I, xix–ccxviii.

39. Oxnard diary, Nov. 6, 1775; Jeffries diary, Nov. 16, 1782, April 8, 1783.

40. Ward, ed., *Curwen Journal*, 239, 299; Oxnard diary, Oct. 20, 1775.

41. Upton, ed., *Smith Diary*, II, 31. And, Marshall, *Dr. Johnson's London*, 150.

42. Marshall, *Dr. Johnson's London*, 158–66. E. B. Chancellor, *The Pleasure Haunts of London* (London, 1925), and Warwick Wroth, *The London Pleasure Gardens of the Eighteenth Century* (London, 1896), discuss these attractions at length.

43. Upton, ed., *Smith Diary*, I, 232; Oxnard diary, Aug. 29, 1776. Jeffries described another final night of the season in his diary, Aug. 26, 1779. For more usual visits: Chandler diary, July 27, 1775; and Francis Coffin to his mother, July 16, 1781, Coffin MSS.

44. Oxnard diary, May 11, 1776. And see his earlier, less complimentary opinion, Sept. 12, 1775. William Smith comments on Ranelagh in Upton, ed., *Smith Diary*, I, 83, 89.

45. Jeffries diary, April 10, 1782, July 28, 1784, July 28 or 29, 1781. And, Jan. 15, 1781, May 12, 1783. Also, Oxnard diary, Nov. 12, 1775; and William Vans Murray to Henry Maynadier, May 20, 1784, Murray Papers, MdHS.

46. Upton, ed., *Smith Diary*, I, 146, 148. Also Shoemaker diary, Sept. 15, Oct. 19, Nov. 30, 1784; Ward, ed., *Curwen Journal*, 393; William Vans Murray to Henry Maynadier, Feb. 8, 1784, Murray MSS.

47. For a more complete account of the flight: Mary Beth Norton, "America's First Aeronaut: Dr. John Jeffries," *History Today*, XVIII (Oct. 1968), 722–9. Jeffries carried the first airmail letters with him to France.

48. Thomas A. Coffin to his mother, Dec. 15, 1785, Coffin MSS; Polly Hutchinson to her sister, Feb. 18, 1785, Hutchinson-Watson-Oliver Papers, MHS; Codman, ed., *Amory Journal*, 28–9.

49. Oliver journal, Aug. 30, 1776, Eg. MSS 2672, f 219. Also, Isaac Low to his brother Nicholas, Nov. 3, 1790, Low MSS, box 67; Elizabeth Duché to her mother, Dec. 3, 1789, Redwood Papers, HSP. For typical journeys, see Ward, ed., *Curwen Journal*, 64–78, 115–42.

50. Samuel Sparhawk to Isaac Winslow, Sept. 11, 1778, Winslow MSS. Sir William Pepperrell (Sparhawk's brother) expressed a similar view to Winslow, July 18, 1778, *ibid.*

51. Thomas Hutchinson to Mr. Green, Jan. 11, 1775, Eg. MSS 2661, f 107; Oxnard diary, May 23, 1777. On Brighton: Thomas Hutchinson, Jr., to Elisha Hutchinson, Aug. 19, 1783, Eg. MSS 2659, f 417. On Margate: Thomas A. Coffin to his mother, Sept. 16, 1784, Coffin MSS. On Bristol Wells: Catherine Goldthwait to Elizabeth [Murray?], Sept. 17, 1781, Robbins MSS; and Oliver journal, July 29, 1777, Eg. MSS 2673, f 483.

52. Gabriel Manigault to his grandmother, Dec. 21, 1777, Manigault MSS; Thomas Hutchinson to Sarah Oliver, March 13, 1775, Eg. MSS 2661, f 133; Jacob Ellegood to James Parker, Jan. 19, 1785, Parker Papers, pt. 5, no. 16, LRO. And see Gabriel Manigault, journal of a trip to Bath, Dec. 1777–Jan. 1778, Manigault MSS.

53. Oxnard diary, Aug. 4, 1777; Hutchinson, *Diary and Letters*, II, 170–1.

4: A DISTRESSING CONDITION

1. George A. Ward, ed., *Journal and Letters of the late Samuel Curwen*, 3rd ed. (New York, 1845), 161.

2. Thomas B. Chandler to Samuel Seabury, March 5, 1777, Samuel Seabury Papers, GTS; Robert Auchmuty to Lord Hardwicke, Aug. 15, 1777, Silvester Gardiner to Hardwicke, Oct. 29, 1777, both in Add. MSS 35614, ff 30, 84; "Letters of Rev. Jonathan Boucher, 1759–1777," *Maryland Historical Magazine*, IX (1914), 335.

3. George Chalmers to Charles Steuart, Nov. 13, 1777, Steuart Papers, 5030, f 143, NLS; Thomas B. Chandler to Samuel Seabury, Dec. 9, 1777, Seabury MSS; Jonathan Boucher to John James, Dec. 23, 1777, Boucher Papers, ESRO.

4. Browne to F. B. Winthrop, May 12, 1778, Browne Letterbook, I, 7, MHS (film); Peter O. Hutchinson, ed., *The Diary and Letters of Thomas Hutchinson* (Boston, 1884), II, 235. Also, Thomas Hutchinson, Jr., to Elisha Hutchinson, June 5, 1778, Eg. MSS 2659, f 224.

5. Elias Ball to [Elias Ball?], Nov. 22, 1784, Ball Papers, SCL. On Shrewsbury: Ward, ed., *Curwen Journal*, 243, 269. On Glasgow: John Maclean to Charles Steuart, Jan. 15, 1778, Steuart MSS, 5030, f 186. On Chester: John Watts to Robert Watts, Sept. 10, 1785, Robert Watts Papers, NYHS; and several 1785 letters in the Andrew Bell Papers, LCMD.

6. Hutchinson to Lord Hardwicke, Aug. 3, 1778, Add. MSS 35427, f 136; Coffin to his mother, Feb. 5, 1786, Coffin Family Papers, MHS.

7. Hutchinson, *Diary and Letters*, II, 203; Oliver to Polly Hutchinson, Aug. 28, 1779, Eg. MSS 2659, f 264. On the Birmingham group: Benjamin Pickman, *The Diary and Letters of Benjamin Pickman (1740–1819) of Salem, Massachusetts* (Newport, 1928), 152–63, *passim*; Elisha Hutchinson, Diary, 1782 *passim*, Eg. MSS 2669. And, Peter Oliver, Journal, Aug. 22, 1776, Eg. MSS 2672, ff 182–5, for Oliver's first impressions of the city.

8. Pickman, *Diary*, 157; Elisha Hutchinson diary, Jan. 23, May 20, 1782, Eg. MSS 2669, ff 108, 117.

9. Oliver to Elisha Hutchinson, July 27, 1784, Eg. MSS 2660, f 21; Coffin to Thomas A. Coffin, July 24, 1786, Coffin MSS. See also Samuel R. Fisher's account of his visit to Pennsylvanians and Quakers in Birmingham, November 1783, in his journal, HSP.

10. Browne to Peter Oliver, Dec. 30, 1778, to Joseph Wanton, May 11, 1778, to F. B. Winthrop, May 12, 1778, all in Browne Letterbook, I, 15, 1–2, 6–7; Caner to Rev. Jones, April 22, 1778, to William Apthorp, April 28, 1778, both in Caner Letterbook, UBL.

11. Browne to James Putnam, Nov. 1780, Browne Letterbook, II, 31; Caner to William Morrice, June 23, 1781, S.P.G. MSS, ser. B, XXII, f 137; Browne to F. B. Winthrop, May 6, 1779, Browne Letterbook, I, 30. Browne listed his neighbors in a letter to his mother, Aug. 22, 1780, *ibid.*, II, 26–7.

12. Browne to Thomas Hutchinson, March 31, 1780, Browne Letterbook, II, 10; Mrs. John Erving, Jr., to Mrs. James Bowdoin, March 13, 1783, Bowdoin-Temple Papers, VI, 12, MHS; case of Mr. Thomson, April 4, 1783, AO 12/99, f 158. On the refugee residents of Wales, see E. Alfred Jones, "American Loyalists in South Wales," *Americana*, XIII (April 1919), 146–55.

13. L. S. F. Upton, ed., *The Diary and Selected Papers of Chief Justice William Smith 1784–1793* (Toronto, 1963), I, 241; Leake to John Leake, Feb. 3,

1788, Leake Family Papers, II, 51, NYHS. For other information on the New Yorkers resident in Wales in the late 1780's: same to same, Sept. 2, 1787, *ibid.,* II, 44; and John Watts to Robert Watts, July 11, 1787, Watts MSS.

14. Hutchinson, *Diary and Letters,* II, 148. For the names of Americans in Bristol, see *ibid.,* 18, 82; and Ward, ed., *Curwen Journal,* 156. One of the resident Americans was Joseph Waldo, a pro-rebel merchant and Harvard graduate (*ibid.,* 276) .

15. Barnes to James Murray, Aug. 14, 1776, to Gilbert Deblois, Dec. 6, 1778, Royall to Edmund Quincy, May 29, 1779, all in Miscellaneous Manuscripts, MHS. For further information on Bristol residents: Jonathan Sewall to Mrs. Higginson, March 4, 1778, to Thomas Robie, Feb. 11, 1780, both in Robie-Sewall Papers, ff 43, 60, MHS; Ward, ed., *Curwen Journal,* 237–8. Also, Wilbur H. Siebert, "The Colony of Massachusetts Loyalists at Bristol, England," *MHS Procs.,* XLV (1912) , 409–14.

16. Henry Barnes to James Murray, Dec. 7, 1779, Misc. MSS, MHS; George Inman, Diary, retrospective section, April 1780, HL.

17. Nina M. Tiffany, ed., *Letters of James Murray, Loyalist* (Boston, 1901) , 259. On daily life in Bristol, see Inman diary, 1782 *passim;* and Mrs. Henry (Christian) Barnes Papers, LCMD.

18. Elizabeth Duché to her mother, Dec. 3, 1789, Redwood Papers, HSP; Elias Ball to [Elias Ball], June 6, 1785, Ball MSS. Also, William Bull to William Knox, July 3, 1779, Germain Papers, WLC; and Elias Ball to Elias Ball, May 28, 1788, Ball MSS.

19. Mrs. Henry Barnes to Catherine Goldthwait, July 11, 1781, Barnes MSS; Fisher journal, Sept. 11–3, 1783; Samuel Shoemaker, Diary, June 29–July 2, 1784, HSP. For an exception to this rule: Hutchinson, *Diary and Letters,* II, 269.

20. Hume to Germain, May 23, 1778, CO 5/155, f 120; William Knox to Philip Stephens, Aug. 31, 1779, CO 5/254, f 292; Samuel Quincy to his wife, March 11, 1779, S. Quincy Papers, MHS. Also, Memo on [S.] Quincy, [June 1780?], CO 5/157, f 327.

21. On Browne: Browne to Thompson, Dec. 2, 1780, Browne Letterbook, II, 39; Grey Elliott to Thompson, March 20, 1781, CO 5/249, f 218; Thompson to Elliott, May 28, 1781, CO 5/252, f 74; Treasury minutes, May 19, 24, 1781, T 29/50. On Leonard: Thompson to John Robinson, Feb. 6, 1781, HO 36/2, f 253; case of Daniel Leonard, AO 12/105, f 39; Treasury minutes, Aug. 9, 10, 1781, T 29/50; "Memorial of Daniel Leonard," *MHS Procs.,* 2nd ser., VI (1890–1891) , 255–7. Browne returned to Great Britain in 1790, Leonard in 1806.

22. S.P.G. Journal, XXII, 182, 436–9, 507–8; XXIII, 228, 403–6, S.P.G. MSS.

23. *Ibid.,* XXI, 448; XXII, 192–3, 321–3.

24. *Ibid.,* XXII, 191, 381–2; XXIII, 101–2; Mather Byles to ———, Nov. 19, 1781, to William Morrice, May 7, 1782, to [Morrice], Oct. 25, 1782, all in S.P.G. MSS, ser. B, XXV, 251, 260, 265.

25. Nutting to [Germain], Jan. 17, 1778, CO 5/155, f 88; North to William Knox, Aug. 6, 1778, Knox Papers, WLC. There are many petitions in favor of the plan in the Shelburne Papers, LXVI, 413–528, WLC; and the John Calef Papers, WLC.

26. Germain to Clinton, Sept. 2, 1778, Clinton Papers, WLC.

27. Hutchinson, *Diary and Letters*, II, 217–8, 239, 290–1. Wentworth's ideas are contained in his "Suggested Regulations for Preserving Masts and Other Timber," Oct. 12, 1778, CO 5/175, ff 81–98. The news of the plans spread rapidly; Edward Oxnard learned of the proposal in Bristol in November (Oxnard, Diary, Nov. 1, 1778, MeHS).

28. William Knox, Plan of Government of New Ireland, Aug. 1780, Shelburne MSS, LXVI, 513–28.

29. Germain to Knox, Aug. 7, 11, 1780, Knox MSS; Oliver to Knox, Aug. 19, 1780, CO 5/175, ff 171–3. For Thompson's efforts, Thompson to Knox, Aug. 30, 1780, CO 5/157, ff 391–4.

30. Germain to Knox, Sept. 18, 1780, Knox MSS; "Enquiry into the application for Lands on Sahagadahock [*sic*] River by Captain Coram in 1717 etc. Taken in 1780," CO 5/8, f 87.

31. Batwell to George Panton, Feb. 6, 1781, Knollenberg Collection, YL; Pepperrell to Isaac Winslow, Oct. 2, 1781, Winslow Papers, MHS; John Jeffries, Diary, Feb. 28, 1781, MHS. See also Winslow to Pepperrell, Jan. 22, 1781, Winslow MSS; Tiffany, ed., *Murray Letters*, 284; E. M. Saunders, "The Life and Times of the Rev. John Wiswall, M.A.," *Nova Scotia Historical Society Collections*, XIII (1908), 35. There are accounts of the attempts to form the colony in Paul Smith, *Loyalists and Redcoats* (Chapel Hill, 1964), 175–7; and Wilbur Siebert, "The Exodus of the Loyalists from Penobscot and the Loyalist Settlements at Passamaquoddy," *New Brunswick Historical Society Collections*, III (1914), 485–529.

32. Knox to Grey Cooper, Jan. 13, 1779, HO 36/1, ff 239–40; [Sir James Wright], "Points on Matters which it Seems Necessary to have some directions about," [1779], Germain MSS; Germain to Knox, March 12, 1779, Knox MSS. And see Wright's account of Georgia refugees in England, March 9, 1779, CO 5/665, ff 114–5.

33. *A Narrative of the Official Conduct of Anthony Stokes . . .* [London, 1784], 51–3; Simpson, "Reasons humbly suggested to show . . . that the Kings Forces should take possession of . . . Charles Town," Sept. 1, 1778, Germain MSS. Kenneth Coleman, *The American Revolution in Georgia* (Athens, 1958), 147–55, discusses the workings of the restored provincial government.

34. Simpson to Germain, June 9, 1780, CO 5/230, f 101; Irving to General Leslie, Jan. 31, 1782, T 1/571; Germain to Knox, Sept. 5, 1780, Knox MSS.

35. Bull to Germain, Feb. 16, 1781, Germain MSS; to Knox, Aug. 20, 1781, CO 5/230, ff 176–7. And see the exchanges of views in Bull to Germain, July 2, 1781, and Germain to Bull, Sept. 1, 1781, CO 5/176, ff 144, 148–9; Andrew Elliot, Memo on governing conquered areas [Dec. 22, 1779], Cornwallis Papers, I, 20–1, PRO; James Simpson, "Observations on Elliot's Plan" [1780], *ibid.*, IV, 218.

36. Galloway to Germain, March 18, 1779, Germain MSS; Smith to William Tryon, June 3, 1781, *ibid.* Also, Smith's "Opinion on Restoring Civil Government," 1781, Clinton MSS; Upton, ed., *Smith Diary*, I, 24; and [Joseph Galloway], *Fabricius . . .* (London, 1782), 26–9. Smith, *Loyalists*

and Redcoats, 129–33, agrees with the loyalists that Clinton's failure to restore civil government in South Carolina was a serious mistake.

37. Irving to General Leslie, Dec. 4, 1781, Bull to Leslie, Feb. 18, 1782, both in T 1/571. Also, Treasury minutes, July 12, 1780, T 29/49; and Irving to Charles Steuart, Dec. 20, 1781, Steuart MSS, 5040, f 223. On the payment of these salaries, see the documents in Shelburne MSS, LXVIII, 115–74; and Treasury minutes, June 3, 1782, T 29/52.

38. See, e.g., Treasury minutes, Aug. 4, 1779, T 29/48 (esp. Mary Rothery); Nov. 10, 1779, T 29/49 (William Carson); Dec. 7, 1780, *ibid.* (James Wormeley); and Wormeley to Lords of Treasury, Oct. 20, 1780, T 1/563. The change in policy is apparent from the composite figures for each year: In 1778 the Lords awarded 69 pensions and 13 grants; in 1779, 38 pensions and 26 grants; in 1780, 30 pensions and 38 grants. Moreover, the pensions were divided as follows: 1778, 21 of less than £100, 26 of £100, 22 of more than £100; 1779, 10 less, 14 of £100, 14 more; 1780, 19 less, 9 of £100, 2 more. (Tabulated from T 29/46–50.)

39. E.g., Treasury minutes, March 23, 1780, T 29/49 (Seth Williams, Edmund Fielde); July 20, 1779, T 29/48 (Cain O'Hara); and O'Hara to Lords of Treasury, with an affidavit, Oct. 21, 1780, T 1/594.

40. Treasury minutes, March 25, 1779, T 29/48; July 12, 1780, T 29/49; July 13, 1781, T 29/50.

41. Treasury minutes, Nov. 23, 1782, T 29/52 (James Moody); Robert Auchmuty to Lord Hardwicke, March 17, 1783, Add. MSS 35620, f 181. See also Auchmuty's other letters to Hardwicke: *ibid.,* ff 135, 160, 185; and Add. MSS 35621, f 61. Also, Auchmuty to Lords of Treasury, June 23, 1783, T 1/589; and Treasury minutes, Aug. 21, 1783, T 29/54. John Tabor Kempe of New York became involved in a similar argument with the Treasury over his salary (Kempe to Lords of Treasury, July 8, 1783, T 1/591, with additional material in T 1/602 and 605; Treasury minutes, July 10, 1783, T 29/54; and May 14, July 29, 1784, T 29/55).

42. Smith to Lord Sydney, Jan. 26, 1784, FO 4/1, ff 93–4; Smith's documents, T 1/626; Upton, ed., *Smith Diary,* II, 135, 142. Smith recorded his struggle with the ministry in great detail in his diary (see esp. *ibid.,* I, 141–3, 230, 259, 274–7, 294–5; II, 140).

43. Treasury minutes, Aug. 29, 1782, T 29/52; John Eardley-Wilmot, *Historical View of the Commission for Enquiring into the Losses, Services, and Claims, of the American Loyalists* (London, 1815), 17–9. See Thomas Hutchinson, Jr., to Elisha Hutchinson, June 17, 25, 1782, Eg. MSS 2659, ff 368, 369. Eventually the allowances were paid at the old rate to October 10, 1782 (Treasury minutes, July 15, Oct. 29, 1782, T 29/52).

44. "List of American Sufferers, who now receive Annual Allowances from the Treasury," June 3, 1782, Shelburne MSS, LXVII, 372–93; Treasury minutes, Oct. 3, 1782, T 29/52; Elizabeth Shaw to Lords of Treasury, Dec. 3, 1784, T 1/600. For accounts of appearances before Wilmot and Coke: Thomas Hutchinson, Jr., to Elisha Hutchinson, Oct. 25, Nov. 19, 1782, Eg. MSS 2659, ff 386, 390; and Ward, ed., *Curwen Journal,* 355–6.

45. John Wilmot and Daniel Coke, Report to Lords of Treasury, Jan. 29, 1783, Shelburne MSS, LXVII, 466–7.

46. *Ibid.*, 471–2; Wilmot, *Historical View*, 20–1.
47. Wilmot and Coke, Report, Jan. 29, 1783, Shelburne MSS, LXVII, 471.
48. See, e.g., cases of Samuel Skingle (AO 12/103, f 116), James Hoare (AO 12/106, f 93), and Benjamin Pickman (AO 12/105, f 80).
49. Cases of Enoch Story (AO 12/106, f 84), John Inman (AO 12/105, f 71), Thomas Knight and Thomas Mitchell (*ibid.*, ff 1, 2), and John Lawless (*ibid.*, ff 13, 25); *The Parliamentary Register, or History of the Proceedings and Debates of the House of Commons*, X (1783), 211.
50. Wilmot and Coke, Report, Jan. 29, 1783, Shelburne MSS, LXVII, 471; cases of John Malcolm (AO 12/105, f 141) and Samuel Hake (AO 12/103, f 79). Also, cases of James Cotton (*ibid.*, f 1), Robert Nelson (*ibid.*, f 21), Timothy Hurst (*ibid.*, ff 56, 61), and John Patterson (AO 12/106, f 71).
51. Case of George Wilmot, AO 12/105, f 149. Similar comments are recorded in the cases of John Clapham (AO 12/104, f 76), Thomas Moffat (*ibid.*, f 44), and Elihu Hall (*ibid.*, f 52). The importance of the need factor is shown most succinctly by the contrast between the decisions in the cases of Bennet Allen and Jonathan Boucher, both of whom were Maryland clergymen (AO 12/103, ff 110, 111).
52. Cases of Louisa Oliver (AO 12/105, f 16) and Alexander Corbett (AO 12/106, f 58). And see case of Richard Corbin, *ibid.*, f 24.
53. Henry Hulton, Charles Paxton, John Robinson, and Benjamin Hallowell to Lords of Treasury, Dec. 5, 1776, T 1/520; Treasury minutes, Dec. 20, 1776, T 29/45; June 1, 1779, T 29/48.
54. See Charles Steuart to Elliot, Sept. 1, 1779 (draft), Steuart MSS, 5031, f 213; Elliot to Grey Cooper, July 3, 1780, Feb. 18, 1781, T 1/559, 566; Treasury minutes, April 2, 1779, T 29/48; Nov. 2, 1780, T 29/49; Aug. 2, 1781, T 29/50; and Elliot to James Robertson, Jan. 19, 1781, *Pennsylvania Magazine of History and Biography*, XXXVII (1913), 483–90.
55. There are a number of relevant documents in T 1/566; also Treasury minutes, Aug. 24, 1781, T 29/50; April 6, June 5, 1782, T 29/52.
56. Wilmot and Coke, Report, Jan. 29, 1783, Shelburne MSS, LXVII, 467–9; Treasury minutes, March 21, 1783, T 29/53. For modifications: various petitions from customs officers in T 1/583, 585, 594, and 620; Treasury minutes, July 24, 1783, T 29/54; Aug. 21, 1784, July 6, 1785, T 29/56; Dec. 22, 1786, T 29/58.
57. Wilmot and Coke, Report, Jan. 29, 1783, Shelburne MSS, LXVII, 472; Thomas Swan to Lords of Treasury, Feb. 20, 1783, John Randolph to Lords of Treasury, Feb. 14, 1783, both in T 1/586; Treasury minutes, Feb. 24, 25, 1783, T 29/53. Shelburne's opinion on the report is given in his letter to the king, April 6, 1783, in Sir John Fortesque, ed., *The Correspondence of King George III* (London, 1967), VI, 337.
58. Allen to Shelburne, Feb. 16, 1783, Shelburne MSS, LXXXVII, 278–9; Oliver to Germain, Feb. 25, 1783, Germain MSS.
59. Joseph Galloway to Lord [Germain?], n.d., Galloway Papers, LCMD. For an extreme example of such thinking, see John Saltmarsh to Lords of Treasury, May 29, 1783, T 1/586; July 1, 1784, T 1/605. Also, Saltmarsh to William Pitt, Aug. 29, 1790, Chatham Papers, CLXXV, 95, PRO.

60. Ward, ed., *Curwen Journal*, 58. Also, Peter Oliver to Byfield Lyde, June 24, 1776, MHS (photostat); Henry Barnes to James Murray, Feb. 21, 1777, Misc. MSS, MHS; and Samuel Quincy, "Diary, Oct. 9, 1776 — March 30, 1777," *MHS Procs.*, XIX (1881–1882), 211–23.

61. Isaac Low to Peter Van Schaack, June 5, 1787, Van Schaack Papers, CL; William Browne to Peter Oliver, Oct. 1779, Browne Letterbook, I, 38. Also, Ward, ed., *Curwen Journal*, 345.

62. Ward, ed., *Curwen Journal*, 231. For a fuller explication of this theme: Mary Beth Norton, "The Loyalists' Image of England: Ideal and Reality," *Albion*, III (Summer 1971), 62–71.

63. Hutchinson to Mr. Grant, June 2, 1775, Eg. MSS 2661, f 155. Hutchinson continually reiterated his love for America; see, e.g., Hutchinson to Mr. Sewall, Dec. 30, 1774, *ibid.*, f 97; to Israel Williams, Sept. 29, 1774, Williams Papers, MHS; and Hutchinson, *Diary and Letters*, I, 281, 356, 398.

64. Pepperrell to Isaac Winslow, July 18, 1778, Winslow MSS; Sewall to David Sewall, April 14, 1777, Misc. MSS, MHS. Also, Peter Oliver, *Origin & Progress of the American Rebellion*, ed. Douglass Adair and John A. Schultz (San Marino, Calif., 1961), 162.

65. Sewall to Thomas Robie, Jan. 29, 1779, Robie-Sewall MSS, ff 54–5; Thomas Hutchinson to ———, Aug. 8, 1779, Eg. MSS 2661, f 187.

66. Alexander Wallace to Nicholas Low, June 3, 1784, Nicholas Low Papers, box 60, LCMD; Pepperrell to Isaac Winslow, July 18, 1778, Winslow MSS; "Journal of Rev. Joshua Wingate Weeks, Loyalist Rector of St. Michael's Church, Marblehead, 1778–1779," *Essex Institute Historical Collections*, LII (1916), 346; Ward, ed., *Curwen Journal*, 208.

67. Ward, ed., *Curwen Journal*, 96; Hannah Winslow to a sister-in-law, June 27, 1779, Winslow MSS. For others with second thoughts: "Some Letters of 1775," *MHS Procs.*, LIX (1925–1926), 131 (Isaac Smith); Henry Barnes to James Murray, Aug. 14, 1776, Misc. MSS, MHS. A few loyalists even decided to try to return home in 1778. One of these was Sampson Salter Blowers, who was jailed in Boston upon his arrival and was deported almost immediately to Halifax. His account of the affair is in Blowers to [Jonathan] Bliss, Nov. 24, 1778, AO 13/43, f 532–3.

68. Pickman, *Diary*, 124–5; Browne to Thomas Hutchinson, Feb. 6, 1779, Browne Letterbook, I, 16, 18. Also, Samuel Quincy to his wife, July 24, 1775, S. Quincy MSS.

69. Pickman, *Diary*, 97; Randolph to Thomas Jefferson, Oct. 25, 1779, MHS (photostat). Samuel Curwen, though recognizing the advantages of hardship, observed wryly that he would "willingly dispense with some degree of honorable exaltation hereafter for a more favorable state of trial here." (Ward, ed., *Curwen Journal*, 96).

70. Caner to Silvester Gardiner, Aug. 28, 1779, Gardiner to Col. Browne, [1780?], Gardiner-Whipple-Allen Papers, MHS; Munro to his son Peter, June 9, 1789, Munro Papers, MCNY.

71. Ward, ed., *Curwen Journal*, 44; Elizabeth Duché to Nancy Coale, Jan. 29, 1782, Redwood MSS.

72. Samuel Peters to [Jonathan Peters], July 20, 1783, Peters-Mann Papers,

CSL (photostats) ; Peters to John Tyler, Aug. 4, 1782, Peters-Tyler Papers, CSL (photostats).

73. Harrison Gray to John Hancock, July 31, 1789, Otis Papers, MHS.

74. Pickman, *Diary*, 129; Stokes to Evan Nepean, Feb. 7, 1785, FO 4/1, f 230; Van Schaack to William Laight, Jan. 26 [1779], Van Schaack MSS.

75. Pepperrell to Isaac Winslow, July 18, 1778, Winslow MSS; Duché to Mary Morgan, Aug. 1, 1783, Redwood MSS; Low to Nicholas Low, March 8, 1788, Low MSS, box 67. Also, Andrew Allen to James Hamilton, Feb. 3, 1783, Dreer Collection, HSP; William Franklin to Benjamin Franklin, July 22, 1784, Benjamin Franklin Papers, APSL; and John Peters, Narrative, c. 1785, J. Peters Papers, NYHS.

76. Robert Auchmuty to Caty ———, March 13, 1779, Naval Historical Society Collection, NYHS; Robert Temple to William Tudor, Jan. 30, 1781, bMS am 1197 (138), HL; William Pepperrell to Isaac Winslow, July 18, 1778, Winslow MSS. And, S. S. Blowers to [Jonathan] Bliss, Nov. 24, 1778, AO 13/43, f 532; Gilbert Deblois to Elizabeth Inman, Sept. 30, 1776, J. M. Robbins Papers, MHS.

77. Henry C. Van Schaack, *The Life of Peter Van Schaack* (New York, 1842), 304.

78. Hutchinson, *Diary and Letters*, I, 231.

5: THE SEEDS OF SEDITION

1. John Adams and Jonathan Sewall (i.e., Daniel Leonard), *Novanglus and Massachusettensis* (New York, 1968: 1st ed., 1819), 159.

2. Thomas Jones, *History of New York during the Revolutionary War*, ed. Edward F. DeLancey (New York, 1879), I, 1–2; Myles Cooper, *National Humiliation and Repentance Recommended, and the Causes of the Present Rebellion in America Assigned* (Oxford, 1777), 12; Alexander Hewatt, *An Historical Account of the Rise and Progress of the Colonies of South Carolina and Georgia* (Spartanburg, 1962), II, 147. Also, *ibid.*, II, 127–8, 186–90. Cooper seems to have patterned his phraseology after [Thomas B. Chandler], *A Friendly Address to All Reasonable Americans* . . . (New York, 1774), 3.

3. Jonathan Boucher, *A View of the Causes and Consequences of the American Revolution* (London, 1797), 475, xxxiv; [Joseph Galloway], *Historical and Political Reflections on the Rise and Progress of the American Rebellion* (London, 1780), 4 (hereafter cited as *Rise and Progress*); Silvester Gardiner to ———, May 9, 1776, Gardiner-Whipple-Allen Papers, MHS.

4. Galloway, *Rise and Progress*, 3–4; Boucher, *View*, i. And see [Charles Inglis], *The Letters of Papinian* (New York, 1779), 73–4.

5. Cooper, *National Humiliation*, 12–3. Also, Peter Oliver, *Origin & Progress of the American Rebellion*, ed. Douglass Adair and John A. Schutz (San Marino, Calif., 1961), 145.

6. Hewatt, *Historical Account*, II, 307; Anthony Stokes, *A View of the Constitution of the British Colonies, in North-America and the West Indies* (London, 1783), 148; Oliver, *Origin & Progress*, 145.

7. Cooper, *National Humiliation,* 12; Inglis, *Papinian,* 74; Adams and Leonard, *Novanglus and Massachusettensis,* 196.
8. Galloway, *Rise and Progress,* 5–23, esp. 12, 23.
9. James Simpson to Lord Shelburne, Jan. 15, 1783, Shelburne Papers, LXXII, 435–6, WLC; George Chalmers, *An Introduction to the History of the Revolt of the American Colonies* (New York, 1971), II, 92; Galloway, *Rise and Progress,* 23.
10. Isaac Hunt, *Sermons on Public Occasions* (London, 1781), 39; John Vardill, "Thoughts on the State of the Colonies," 1774, Dartmouth Papers, I, 2, no. 1219, WSL.
11. Jonathan Boucher to [Germain], Nov. 27, 1775, Germain Papers, WLC; George Chalmers, *Political Annals of the Present United Colonies* (New York, 1968), I, 19; Boucher, *View,* xliii; J[ohn] Fisher to Germain, Feb. 2, 1778, Germain MSS; [Joseph Galloway], *Plain Truth . . .* (London, 1780), 41.
12. Boucher to [Germain], Nov. 27, 1775, Germain MSS; Stokes, *View,* 138. Also, Boucher, *View,* xliii–xliv.
13. Boucher, *View,* xxxvii; Oliver, *Origin & Progress,* 30; [Joseph Galloway], *Political Reflections on the late Colonial Governments* (London, 1783), 52 (hereafter cited as *Colonial Governments*); Galloway to Richard Jackson, March 20, 1777, in Benjamin F. Stevens, ed., *Facsimiles of Manuscripts in European Archives Relating to America, 1773–1783* (London, 1889–1895), 2051. See also Stokes, *View,* 137–8; and [Samuel Peters], *A General History of Connecticut,* 2nd ed. (London, 1782), 369–70.
14. Boucher, *View,* xxxviii, lxiv; Chalmers, *Political Annals,* I, 388, 295.
15. William Allen, *The American Crisis* (London, 1774), 53; Galloway, *Rise and Progress,* 106. And see Inglis, *Papinian,* 108; [John Mein], *Sagittarius' Letters and Political Speculations* (Boston, 1775), 71.
16. Chalmers, *Introduction,* II, 119.
17. *Ibid.,* I, 220; Boucher, *View,* 468; Jonathan Sewall to David Sewall, April 14, 1777, Miscellaneous Manuscripts, MHS; Oliver, *Origin & Progress,* 65.
18. Boucher, *View,* 416; George Chalmers, "A review of the conduct of the minority, as connected with the american rebellion," Sparks Papers, LIII, 18–9, HL; James Simpson to Lord Shelburne, April 27, 1782, Shelburne MSS, LXXII, 277. See *The Examination of Joseph Galloway, Esq; . . . Before the House of Commons* (London, 1779), 9n; and Boucher, *View,* xxvi–xxvii.
19. Adams and Leonard, *Novanglus and Massachusettensis,* 152, 153; Boucher, *View,* li–lii, 353–6.
20. "Letters of Rev. Jonathan Boucher, 1759–1777," *Maryland Historical Magazine,* VIII (1913), 340–1.
21. [Harrison Gray], *The Two Congresses Cut Up* (New York [1775]), 14; Thomas Hutchinson to ———, July 28, 1775, Eg. MSS 2661, f 161; Boucher, *View,* 144n; Myles Cooper to Samuel Clossy, Feb. 6, 1781, AO 13/79, f 112.
22. Adams and Leonard, *Novanglus and Massachusettensis,* 167; Oliver, *Origin & Progress,* 145–6. And, Jonathan Sewall to David Sewall, April 14, 1777, Misc. MSS, MHS; Chandler, *Friendly Address,* 48n.

23. Oliver, *Origin & Progress*, 145. Also [Joseph Galloway], *A Candid Examination of the Mutual Claims of Great-Britain, and the Colonies . . .* (London, repr., 1780), 85.

24. Edward H. Tatum, ed., *The American Journal of Ambrose Serle, 1776–1778* (San Marino, Calif., 1940), 149; Cooper, *National Humiliation*, 13; Gray, *Two Congresses*, 5.

25. James Moody, *Narrative of the Exertions and Sufferings of Lieut. James Moody*, ed. Charles Bushnell (New York, 1865), 13; Inglis, *Papinian*, 107; Tatum, ed., *Serle Journal*, 149; Hugh Wallace to Frederick Haldimand, Feb. 8, 1778, Add. MSS 21679, f 156. Also, Boucher, *View*, xlii; Oliver, *Origin & Progress*, 46–8, 163.

26. Boucher, *View*, xliv, 111–2; Inglis, *Papinian*, 76; Henry Caner to the Archbishop of London, July 22, 1775, Caner Letterbook, UBL. See Galloway, *Colonial Governments*, 78, and *Rise and Progress*, 54–5.

27. S.P.G. Journal, XXI, 127, S.P.G. MSS; Samuel Seabury, Address to Archbishop of York, Nov. 24, 1783, Seabury Papers, GTS; Henry Caner to Archbishop of London, July 22, 1775, Caner Letterbook. Also, Tatum, ed., *Serle Journal*, 115; Chalmers, *Political Annals*, I, 515–6.

28. Jones, *History*, I, 2–7. Others who blamed the Triumvirate were Samuel Seabury (claims memorial, Oct. 20, 1783, AO 12/19, ff 355–6), Jonathan Boucher (*View*, xxvn–xxviin), and Thomas Bradbury Chandler (*What Think ye of the Congress Now?* [New York, 1775], 37–9).

29. Oliver, *Origin & Progress*, 9; Boucher, *View*, xxix; Chandler, *Friendly Address*, 29n–30n. And see Mein, *Sagittarius' Letters*, 22, 32–4.

30. Chalmers, *Introduction*, I, 92; Galloway, *Rise and Progress*, 24, 32. In general, Oliver, *Origin & Progress*, 10–23; Galloway, *Rise and Progress*, 24–49, and *Colonial Governments*, 206–58, esp. 255–6.

31. Chalmers, *Introduction*, II, 69; Galloway, *Rise and Progress*, 46; Chandler, *Congress*, 36.

32. Cooper, *National Humiliation*, 13; Boucher, *View*, xxxiii–liv.

33. Chalmers, *Introduction*, II, 113; Samuel Seabury, Address to Archbishop of York, Nov. 24, 1783, Seabury MSS; Galloway, *Rise and Progress*, 54, and *Colonial Governments*, 251. For less formal statements of the same ideas, see William McCormick, claims memorial, March 13, 1785, AO 12/34, f 102; and Paul Hamilton, claims memorial, n.d., AO 12/51, f 3.

34. George Chalmers, "Review of the conduct of the minority," Sparks MSS, LIII, 20; [Joseph Galloway], *Letters from Cicero to Catiline the Second* (London, 1781), 81–2. Also, Oliver, *Origin & Progress*, 149; Boucher, *View*, xxxiin–xxxiiin; Inglis, *Papinian*, iv.

35. Chalmers, "Review of conduct of minority," Sparks MSS, LIII, 26, 31–3, 23; Jonathan Boucher to John James, Dec. 23, 1777, Boucher Papers, ESRO ("Cabalinarian Combination"). And, Galloway, *Rise and Progress*, 60–1; Oliver, *Origin & Progress*, 55, 58, 76–7; [John Vardill], *Unity and Public Spirit, Recommended* (London, 1780), 8.

36. [Thomas Hutchinson], *Strictures upon the Declaration of the Congress at Philadelphia* (London, 1776), 3–4. Also, Inglis, *Papinian*, 76; and *A Letter from His Excellency William Franklin, Esquire* (Bdse, 1776).

37. Galloway, *Colonial Governments*, 250; Hutchinson, *Strictures*, 4.

38. Galloway, *Rise and Progress*, 47; Oliver, *Origin & Progress*, 148, 147; Hutchinson, *Strictures*, 4–5. And, Galloway, *Colonial Governments*, 249; Peters, *General History*, 335.

39. Adams and Leonard, *Novanglus and Massachusettensis*, 208; Hutchinson, *Strictures*, 22; Jones, *History*, I, 18. In 1765 the loyalist authors had divided in their reaction to the act. Hutchinson opposed it, as may be seen in Peter O. Hutchinson, ed., *The Diary and Letters of Thomas Hutchinson* (Boston, 1884), II, 58. Oliver, on the other hand, thought it justified (*Origin & Progress*, 50), as did Hewatt (*Historical Account*, II, 316). Boucher changed his mind on the subject; see *View*, 590–2.

40. Hewatt, *Historical Account*, II, 313–8, esp. 314, 318; Oliver, *Origin & Progress*, 51.

41. [Joseph Galloway], *Letters to a Nobleman, on the Conduct of the War in the Middle Colonies* (London, 1779), 11; Hewatt, *Historical Account*, II, 317–8.

42. Hewatt, *Historical Account*, II, 326. There was unanimous agreement on the results of the Stamp Act repeal: see, e.g., John Vardill, "Thoughts," 1774, Dartmouth MSS, I, 2, no. 1219; Galloway, *Rise and Progress*, 12; Samuel Peters to Richard Hind, Jan. 11, 1774 (i.e., 1775), Miscellaneous Manuscripts, Connecticut, S.P.G. MSS.

43. Oliver, *Origin & Progress*, 56–7; Galloway, *Rise and Progress*, 15.

44. Adams and Leonard, *Novanglus and Massachusettensis*, 148–50.

45. Oliver, *Origin & Progress*, 65, 148, 41–3; Adams and Leonard, *Novanglus and Massachusettensis*, 151.

46. Oliver, *Origin & Progress*, 88, 93, 97.

47. Samuel Seabury, *Letters of a Westchester Farmer*, ed. Clarence Vance (White Plains, 1930), 75–6. Also, on the tea party, Gray, *Two Congresses*, 3–4.

48. Adams and Leonard, *Novanglus and Massachusettensis*, 194–5, 168–9. See *ibid.*, 193–4; and Oliver, *Origin & Progress*, 113.

49. Seabury, *Letters*, 77, 81; Galloway, *Colonial Government*, 59. And see Chandler, *Congress*, 11, 40; Jones, *History*, I, 35–6.

50. Galloway, *Rise and Progress*, 67, 66; Inglis, *Papinian*, 56, 65; Oliver, *Origin & Progress*, 121.

51. On the problem of the legitimacy of revolution, see the discussion in Pauline Maier, *From Resistance to Revolution* (New York, 1972), chapter 2.

6: *STRANGE AND UNACCOUNTABLE CONDUCT*

1. Silvester Gardiner to Henry Caner [1779], Gardiner-Whipple-Allen Papers, MHS (hereafter Gardiner MSS).

2. Peter O. Hutchinson, ed., *The Diary and Letters of Thomas Hutchinson* (Boston, 1884), II, 193, 189; Chandler to Samuel Seabury, June 2, 1778, Seabury Papers, GTS. Also, George A. Ward, ed., *Journal and Letters of the late Samuel Curwen*, 3rd ed. (New York, 1845), 175–6.

3. Barnes to Gilbert Deblois, May 18, 1778, Miscellaneous Manuscripts,

MHS; Oxnard, Diary, March 17, 1778, MeHS; Caner to Mr. Jones, April 22, 1778, Caner Letterbook, UBL.

4. Isaac Ogden to Joseph Galloway, Nov. 22, 1778, Balch Collection, NYPL; Myles Cooper to George Panton, July 31, 1778, Knollenberg Collection, YL; Silvester Gardiner, "Information," [1778], Clinton Papers, WLC.

5. James Simpson, "Reasons humbly suggested to show . . . that the Kings Forces should take possession of . . . Charles Town," Sept. 1, 1778, Germain Papers, WLC; Sir James Wright and John Graham to Germain, July 17, 1778, CO 5/116, ff 165–8; James Chalmers to Clinton, Sept. 12, 1778, Clinton MSS; Robert Alexander, "General Account of the Isthmus between Chesapeake and Delaware Bays" and related documents, Chalmers Papers, Maryland, II, 3–10, NYPL; Gardiner, "Information," [1778], Clinton MSS.

6. Germain to [William Knox], Oct. 19, 1776, Knox Papers, WLC. He was referring to a proposal of Sir James Wright's.

7. William Franklin to Philip Skene, Dec. 1, 1778, S.P.G. MSS, series B, III, 344; Boucher to [Germain], Nov. 27, 1775, Germain MSS. Also, William Franklin to Germain, Nov. 12, 1778, CO 5/993, f 259.

8. Hutchinson, *Diary and Letters*, II, 226; Elizabeth Galloway to her mother, July 17, 1779, Galloway Papers, LCMD. One of Galloway's proposals and the British reactions to it are printed in Sir John Fortescue, ed., *The Correspondence of King George III* (New York, 1967), IV, 245–53. And see Hutchinson, *Diary and Letters*, II, 233–4, 247, 259–60, for accounts of conversations with Galloway, and II, 187, 230, 239, for Hutchinson's timidity. Also, Hutchinson to Lord Hardwicke, Aug. 23, 1779, Add. MSS 35427, ff 193–4.

9. *A View of the Evidence relative to the Conduct of the American War* (London, 1779), *passim*, esp. 64; *The Examination of Joseph Galloway, Esq; . . . Before the House of Commons* (London, 1779), *passim*.

10. [Joseph Galloway], *Letters to a Nobleman, on the Conduct of the War in the Middle Colonies* (London, 1779), 9–10, v.

11. *Ibid.*, 34–5, 47, 50, 68, 92.

12. Sir William Howe, *The Narrative of Lieut. Gen. Sir William Howe* (London, 1780), 41–59.

13. [Joseph Galloway], *A Reply to the Observations of Lieut. Gen. Sir William Howe* (London, 1780), 113, 119–20. A year later Galloway was accusing the Howes of treason in *A Letter from Cicero to the Right Hon. Lord Viscount H———e* (London, 1781), 26–33.

14. Silvester Gardiner to Col. Browne, [1780], Gardiner MSS. For direct comments on Galloway's writings, see James Chalmers to ———, Aug. 20, 1780, Chalmers MSS, New York, IV, 81; Gardiner to [Robert] Hallowell, Dec. 6, 1780, and Hallowell to Gardiner, Dec. 18, 1780, Gardiner MSS. Concurring opinions are offered in Henry White to William Knox, Aug, 17, 1778, Knox MSS; and Henry C. Van Schaack, *The Life of Peter Van Schaack* (New York, 1842), 169–84.

15. B[enjamin] T[hompson] to Galloway, March 1, 1779, Balch MSS. For general English attitudes: Hutchinson, *Diary and Letters*, II, 183–5, 311;

and the reviews of Galloway's pamphlets in *The Gentleman's Magazine*, XLIX (Oct. 1779), 504–5, and L (Dec. 1780), 576–7.

16. George Rome to Charles Dudley, June 2, 1779, Rome-Dudley Papers, NHS. Also, on Grey's testimony: Hutchinson, *Diary and Letters*, II, 258; and Paul Smith, *Loyalists and Redcoats* (Chapel Hill, 1964), 118–9.

17. John Jeffries, Diary, May 21, 1779, MHS; George Chalmers, minutes of meeting, May 21, 1779, Sparks Papers, LIII, 76, HL.

18. Chalmers, minutes, May 26, 1779, Sparks MSS, LIII, 76. And, Jeffries diary, May 25, 1779.

19. George Rome to Charles Dudley, July 26, 1779, Rome-Dudley MSS; Elisha Hutchinson, Diary, July 2, 1779, Eg. MSS 2669, f 59; Chalmers, minutes, July 6, 1779, Sparks MSS, LIII, 77.

20. Address to the king, July 6, 1779, Sparks MSS, LIII, 77–8. The address was printed (without signatures) in *The Gentleman's Magazine*, XLIX (July 1779), 369.

21. Elisha Hutchinson diary, July 5, 8, 1779, Eg. MSS 2669, f 60; Rome to Charles Dudley, July 26, 1779, Rome-Dudley MSS.

22. Address to the king, July 6, 1779, Sparks MSS, LIII, 79–80.

23. Chalmers, minutes, July 1, 6, 1779, *ibid.*, 81.

24. Chalmers, minutes Aug. 2, 7, 1779, *ibid.*, 84, 86, 87. There is a possibility that some of the material in the Chalmers Papers, NYPL, may have been collected in response to the questions posed by the committee.

25. Chalmers, minutes, Aug. 2, 17, 1779, Sparks MSS, LIII, 84, 90–2; Anthony Stewart to Chalmers, Dec. 8, 1779, Chalmers MSS, New York, IV, 79; petition of loyal refugees in New York to the king, Dec. 23, 1779, CO 5/80, ff 567–70. The only other activity of the Loyalist Association was the organizing of a group of forty-nine refugees who offered their services to the king in preparation for a possible French invasion; see their petition to Germain, [Autumn 1779], CO 5/80, ff 1–3. Although this petition has traditionally been dated 1778 (*WMQ*, 2nd ser., I [1921], 70–1), Fortesque, ed., *Corres. George III*, IV, 430, would indicate a 1779 date. Moreover, some of the signers of the petition did not arrive in England until early 1779, so they could not have signed a London petition in the fall of 1778.

26. William Franklin to Germain, Nov. 12, 1778, CO 5/993, f 259. And see Germain's reply, *ibid.*, f 265. For concurring advice from other loyalists: William Bayard to [Germain], [Sept. 1778?], CO 5/155, f 123; Henry White to William Knox, Aug. 17, 1778, Knox MSS; John Lovell to Lord Hillsborough, Jan. 2, 1782, CO 5/1089; Joshua Upham to Guy Carleton, Nov. 12, 1782, Shelburne Papers, LXIX, 101–7, WLC.

27. For example, Piers Mackesy, *The War for America, 1775–1783* (Cambridge, Mass., 1964), 32, 36; Smith, *Loyalists and Redcoats*, ix–x, 46–59 (esp. 57), 173; George Guttridge, "Lord George Germain in Office, 1774–1782," *American Historical Review*, XXXIII (1927–1928), 34–5.

28. Smith, *Loyalists and Redcoats*, 79–99, 113–25, discusses the change in strategy. Mackesy, *War for America*, 251–6, overestimates Galloway's personal influence on the decision. Both authors recognize the importance of the petition of southern governors and lieutenant governors to Germain,

Aug. 29, 1777, CO 5/116, ff 161–2 (Smith, *Loyalists and Redcoats*, 89–90; and Mackesy, *War for America*, 157).

29. Isaac Ogden to Joseph Galloway, Feb. 6, 1779, Balch MSS; Charles Inglis to William Morrice, May 20, 1780, S.P.G. MSS, series B, II, 241; William Browne to John Sargent, June 19, 1780, Browne Letterbook, II, 17, MHS (microfilm).

30. Benedict Arnold, *To the Inhabitants of America* (Bdse, 1780); Benedict Arnold, *The Present State of the American Rebel Army, Navy and Finances*, ed. Paul L. Ford (Brooklyn, 1891), 12–4; Jonathan Sewall to Elisha Hutchinson, Nov. 25, 1780, Hutchinson-Watson Papers, MHS; Germain to Arnold, Dec. 7, 1780, CO 5/183, ff 179–80.

31. Isaac Ogden to Joseph Galloway, Nov. 22, 1778, Balch MSS; Bartholomew Sullivan to Silvester Gardiner, Feb. 26, 1779, Gardiner MSS; Jonathan Sewall to Isaac Smith, May 9, 1778, Smith-Carter Papers, MHS; Thomas Hutchinson to Lord Hardwicke, Aug. 3, 1778, Add. MSS 35427, ff 136–7. The Balch Collection, NYPL, is filled with such letters to Galloway.

32. The quotation is from *The Political Magazine*, II (Feb. 1781), 74 (see 73–80 in general). Also, "Accurate Copies of original Letters found in a Rebel Mail," *ibid.*, I (Dec. 1780), 758–64. For the loyalists' sending of information to ministers, see Charles Jenkinson to Galloway, Nov. 12, 1781, Add. MSS 38309, f 1b; Benjamin Thompson to Charles Steuart, Feb. 22, 1781, Steuart Papers, 5032, f 102, NLS; and CO 5/1110, *passim* (a volume of "intelligence" collected by William Smith).

33. Hallowell to Gardiner, Aug. 24, 1780, Gardiner Papers, MeHS. In much the same vein is the "Extract of a Letter from an American Gentl[ema]n now at Bristol dated the 7th of Feby 1780," Germain MSS.

34. For example, Daniel Batwell to George Panton, Feb. 6, 1781, Knollenberg MSS; William Browne to William Wanton, April 13, 1781, Browne Letterbook, III, 14; Gilbert Deblois to James Murray, May 11, 1781, J. M. Robbins Papers, MHS.

35. Hutchinson to Samuel Mather, Jr., Sept. 21, 1781, S. Mather Papers, MHS; Ward, ed., *Curwen Journal*, 283; Boucher to John James, March 15, 1781, Boucher Papers, ESRO; Oliver to Elisha Hutchinson, Feb. 14, 1781, Eg. MSS 2659, f 322.

36. Galloway, *Letters to Nobleman*, 31; Galloway to Elisha Hutchinson, Aug. 29, 1781, Eg. MSS 2659, f 336; Myles Cooper to George Panton, Dec. 30, 1780, Knollenberg MSS; *The Political Magazine*, II (May 1781), 291.

37. Galloway to Lord Hardwicke, [1781], Add. MSS 35617, f 189; to same, Sept. 12, 1781, Add. MS 35618, f 154.

38. Galloway to Hardwicke, [June 1781], July 20, 1781, Add. MSS 35618, ff 188–9, 48; to Elisha Hutchinson, Aug. 29, 1781, Eg. MSS 2659, f 336.

39. Hutchinson, *Diary and Letters*, II, 373; William Franklin to Germain, Nov. 6, 1781, CO 5/1002, f 56.

40. Sir William Pepperell to Isaac Winslow, Dec. 3, 1781, Winslow Papers, MHS; Franklin to Germain, Nov. 6, 1781, CO 5/1002, f 53; Hutchinson, *Diary and Letters*, II, 372–3. The government's reaction to the loyalists' complaints is in Fortesque, ed., *Corres. George III*, V, 315, 321.

41. Daniel Batwell to George Panton, Dec. 3, 1781, Thomas B. Chandler to same, Nov. 3, 1781 (additional section dated Dec. 3), April 1, 1782, all in Knollenberg MSS; Galloway to Lord Hardwicke, Oct. 1, 1782, Add. MSS 35620, f 2.

42. [Joseph Galloway], *Fabricius . . .* (London, 1782), esp. 4–6; Silvester Gardiner to Lord Shelburne, Nov. 2, 1782, Shelburne MSS, CLII, 31; John Calef, "Plan to Conquer America," Jan. 15, 1782, Calef Papers, WLC; Benedict Arnold, "Plan of Operation," Feb. 3, 1782, Shelburne MMS, LXVII, 211–8; Dunmore to Thomas Townshend, Aug. 24, 1782, *ibid.*, 411–6; John Cruden to Dunmore, Jan. 5, 1782, Chalmers MSS, Carolinas, II, 97–101.

43. Hutchinson to Elisha Hutchinson, Sept. 12, 1782, Eg. MSS 2659, f 378, referring to letters printed in *The Political Magazine*, III (Sept. 1782), 508–10. On the same letters, see Ward, ed., *Curwen Journal*, 353. Other similar publications are in *Political Magazine*, III (1782), 378, 468–74. The circumstances surrounding the New York petition are described in "Extract of a Letter from a Loyalist of Distinction at New York, Aug. 14," *The Gentleman's Magazine*, LII (Oct. 1782), 496. For Galloway's last-minute efforts to avert disaster: Galloway to Evan Nepean, July 13, 1782, CO 5/8, f 273; and Fortesque, ed., *Corres. George III*, VI, 64.

44. The following account of the peace negotiations will concentrate solely on the loyalist clauses. For a more detailed examination of the entire treaty-making process (and a different interpretation), see Richard B. Morris, *The Peacemakers* (New York, 1965), or Samuel F. Bemis, ed., *The American Secretaries of State and their Diplomacy* (New York, 1958), I, 47–111.

45. Instructions to Richard Oswald, July 31, 1782, FO 97/157, ff 47–52. The ministry may well have adopted this strong stance as a result of Andrew Allen's treatise on the subject of the loyalists, May 13, 1782, which was presented to Shelburne (FO 97/157, ff 2–7).

46. Francis Wharton, ed., *The Revolutionary Diplomatic Correspondence of the United States* (Washington, 1889), V, 93.

47. Oswald, minutes of conversation with Franklin, Aug. 11, 1782, FO 97/157, f 80; Thomas Townshend to Oswald, Sept. 1, 1782, *ibid.*, ff 161–2; preliminary draft of treaty, Oct. 7, 1782, *ibid.*, ff 152–4. Also Wharton, ed., *Rev. Diplo. Corres.*, V, 571, 811.

48. Shelburne to Oswald, Oct. 23, 1782, FO 97/157, ff 167–8. And see, on the ministry's reaction to the draft, Morris, *Peacemakers*, 349–50.

49. L. H. Butterfield, ed., *Diary and Autobiography of John Adams* (Cambridge, 1961), III, 46. On Oswald's character, see Morris, *Peacemakers*, 343; and Oswald to Townshend, Oct. 11, 1782, FO 97/157, ff 158–60.

50. Butterfield, ed., *Adams Diary*, III, 43–4, 46. Also Wharton, ed., *Rev. Diplo. Corres.*, V, 856.

51. Strachey to Townshend, with draft treaty, Nov. 8, 1782, FO 97/157, ff 183, 185–6; to American commissioners, Nov. 5, 1782, *ibid.*, f 192; American commissioners to Oswald, Nov. 7, 1782, *ibid.*, f 181. Also, Oswald to American commissioners, Nov. 4, 1782, *ibid.*, ff 179–80.

52. Henry P. Johnston, ed., *The Correspondence and Public Papers of John Jay* (New York, 1891), III, 44. Also ibid., III, 344. On Franklin, "the

most violent of the three for not admitting the Tories": Herbert E. Klingelhofer, ed., "Matthew Ridley's Diary during the Peace Negotiations of 1782," *WMQ*, 3rd ser., XX (1963), 132; and Albert A. Smyth, ed., *The Writings of Benjamin Franklin* (New York, 1906), VIII, 650–1. On Adams: Butterfield, ed., *Adams Diary*, III, 56.

53. Oswald to Townshend, Nov. 6 and 7, 1782, FO 97/157, ff 172–3.

54. Same to same, Nov. 15, 1782, *ibid.*, f 198.

55. Townshend to Strachey, Nov. 19, 1782, *ibid.*, ff 203–6, 210–2. Also, Fortesque, ed., *Corres. George III*, VI, 155–6.

56. Butterfield, ed., *Adams Diary*, III, 75; Strachey to Townshend, Nov. 29, 1782, FO 97/157, ff 221–2. For accounts of the final sessions, see Butterfield, ed., *Adams Diary*, III, 79–81; and "Ridley Diary," *WMQ*, 3rd ser., XX, 133. The precise text of the treaty may be conveniently consulted in Wharton, ed., *Rev. Diplo. Corres.*, VI, 96–9.

57. Wharton, ed., *Rev. Diplo. Corres.*, VI, 569, 132. On the ambiguity of the clause, *ibid.*, 338.

58. *Ibid.*, 284; "Letters of Benjamin Vaughan to the Earl of Shelburne, 1782 and 1783," *MHS Procs.*, 2nd ser., XVII (1903), 424; Wharton, ed., *Rev. Diplo. Corres.*, VI, 690, 574. Also, *ibid.*, VI, 106–7; and Smyth, ed., *Franklin Writings*, IX, 25–6.

59. Wharton, ed., *Rev. Diplo. Corres.*, VI, 287, 338; Strachey to Townshend, Nov. 29, 1782, FO 97/157, f 221. Italics mine.

60. Elizabeth Johnston, *Recollections of a Georgia Loyalist* (New York, 1901), 211; John Watts to Frederick Haldimand, March 28, 1783, Add. MSS 21735, f 52. And see Ward, ed., *Curwen Journal*, 368; Van Schaack, *Life*, 331; and Van Schaack, "Observations on the Peace," 1783, Sparks MSS, LX, 325–35.

61. Galloway to Lord Hardwicke, May 26, 1783, Add. MSS 35620, f 222. Also, Thomas B. Chandler to Samuel Seabury, March 15, 1783, Seabury MSS; James Ingram to Charles Steuart, May 31, 1783, Steuart MSS, 5032, f 69.

62. Strachey to Oswald, Dec. 10, 1782, FO 97/157, f 229; Henry E. McCulloh to William Johnson, March 28, 1783, Fanning-McCulloh Papers, North Carolina Department of Archives and History. This reference was supplied by Professor Robert Calhoon.

63. [William Cobbett], *The Parliamentary History of England from the Earliest Period to the Year 1803* (London, 1806–1820), XXIII, 412–3. For other similar predictions, *ibid.*, 389, 434, 437–8.

64. *Ibid.*, 564–9. Of course there were dissenters, most notably Germain (now Viscount Sackville) and North: *ibid.*, 404–5, 452–5. The loyalists also figured in the debates on Lord John Cavendish's "no confidence" resolutions of Feb. 21, 1783: *ibid.*, 503ff.

7: A DEBT OF THE HIGHEST AND MOST INVIOLABLE NATURE

1. [Joseph Galloway], *The Claim of the American Loyalists Reviewed and Maintained . . .* (London, 1788), 114.

2. Thomas Hutchinson, Jr., to Elisha Hutchinson, Jan. 31, 1783, Eg. MSS 2659, f 397; *The Gentleman's Magazine*, LIII (Feb. 1783), 174; George A. Ward, ed., *Journal and Letters of the late Samuel Curwen*, 3rd ed. (New York, 1845), 363–6, 373. The Hutchinson letter, which also mentions a New Hampshire meeting, is printed in part in Peter O. Hutchinson, ed., *The Diary and Letters of Thomas Hutchinson* (Boston, 1884), II, 389–90.

3. Samuel Peters to Benedict Arnold, Feb. 3, 1783, Peters Papers, I, 76, NYHS (film).

4. Ward, ed., *Curwen Journal*, 366, on Galloway's "sinister designs." There is no comprehensive list of the agents for 1783, and the one in the text was compiled from a number of sources. By autumn 1783, George Rome had joined the board as the representative of Rhode Island and George Chalmers had replaced Eden as the Maryland agent. In later years there were numerous other changes in the membership of the board. Only Pepperrell (who became chairman after Wright's death in 1785), Rome, and Galloway were not replaced. The new members were as follows, with the dates in parentheses indicating the first year they can be identified as agents. New Hampshire: Paul Wentworth (1785), Benning Wentworth (1787), John Wentworth, Jr. (1788). New York: Guy Johnson (1785), James DeLancey (1787). New Jersey: Daniel Coxe (1787), David Ogden (1788). Maryland: Robert Alexander (1787). Virginia: James Parker (1787), John R. Grymes (1788). North Carolina: Henry E. McCulloh (1788). South Carolina: Charles Ogilvie (1787), James Simpson (1788). Georgia: James Hume (1787), John Graham (1788).

5. Wright, Franklin, Wentworth, and Eden to Shelburne, Feb. 6, 1783, and "Petition intended to be presented to Parliament by the late American Governors, in Behalf of the American Loyalists," Feb. 8, 1783, both in Shelburne Papers, LXVII, 495–502, WLC; Ward, ed., *Curwen Journal*, 365; *The Gentleman's Magazine*, LIII (April 1783), 286–7.

6. Ward, ed., *Curwen Journal*, 365; Wright, Franklin, Wentworth, and Eden to Shelburne, Feb. 12, 1783, Shelburne MSS, LXVII, 1–4; loyalist agents, memorial to House of Commons, [Feb. 1783], FO 4/1, ff 87–8.

7. *The Case and Claim of the American Loyalists Impartially Stated and Considered* [London, 1783], *passim*, esp. 33–7; *Collections with regard to the Case of the American Loyalists* [London, 1783]. That these pamphlets were published in February is apparent from *The Particular Case of the Georgia Loyalists*, which is dated February 1783, and which refers to *The Case and Claim*. The Georgia publication and "Case of the Loyalists in North Carolina," which appeared in *The Political Magazine*, IV (April 1783), 265–7, called attention to the especially difficult plight of loyalists from those colonies.

8. [William Cobbett], *The Parliamentary History of England from the Earliest Period to the Year 1803* (London, 1806–1820), XXIII, 503ff. Also, *The Political Magazine*, IV (Feb. 1783), 118n–119n, and (April 1783), 264.

9. William Franklin, "Information communicated to the Commissioners," Sept. 17, 1783, AO 12/107, f 33; "General Account of the Claims of the

Loyalists of Georgia . . . ," Oct. 30, 1783, *ibid.*, f 49; Report of North Carolina Committee, July 30, 1783, *ibid.*, ff 126–40.

10. Dunmore to Thomas Dundas, Oct. 7, 1783, AO 12/107, f 56. On the South Carolina committee: Matthew Rugeley to William Rugeley, Feb. 18, 1783, Rugeley Papers, BRO. On the Virginia committee: AO 12/99, f 315; AO 12/54, ff 68, 330; AO 12/56, ff 424–5.

11. Report of South Carolina Committee, May 24, 1783, AO 12/107, ff 178–94; esp. 178–9, 181.

12. *The Gentleman's Magazine*, LIII (1783), 704, 615–6, 518–9; *The Political Magazine*, IV (May 1783), 331; V (Aug. 1783), 134. And, in general, *ibid.*, IV, 330–8, 343; V, 121–5, 130–3, 173–4, 225–6. On newspapers: Solomon Lutnick, *The American Revolution and the British Press 1775–1783* (Columbia, Mo., 1967), 217–8.

13. *The Political Magazine*, V (Oct. 1783), 272–3; *Parliamentary History*, XXIII, 1041–2. The debate on Cavendish's proposal emphasized the general nature of the inquiry (*ibid.*, 1043–5).

14. "General State . . . of the Property belonging to the American Loyalists, . . . prepared by the Agents for the American Loyalists and presented to Mr. Secretary Fox, in July 1783," CO 5/43, ff 502–3; Joseph Galloway to Lord Hardwicke, [July 1783], Add. MSS 35620, f 267; [Joseph Galloway], *Observations on the Fifth Article of the Treaty with America* (London, 1783), 8–9, 11–9.

15. John Eardley-Wilmot, *Historical View of the Commission for Enquiring into the Losses, Services, and Claims, of the American Loyalists* (London, 1815), 40–5, 101–8; claims commissioners, minutes, Aug. 30, 1783, AO 13/139, f 1.

16. Wilmot, *Historical View*, 45.

17. See AO 12/107, *passim*, esp. 27–40, 54, 59–75.

18. Chalmers, comments on compensation act, c. 1785, Sparks Papers V, II, 31, HL; "Information communicated to the Commissioners by James Simpson," Sept. 17, 1783, AO 12/107, f 13; James Stuart, "Further Intelligence communicated to the Commissioners," [Oct. 1783?], *ibid.*, ff 41–2.

19. Stuart, "Further Intelligence," AO 12/107, f 45; "Information communicated by . . . James Simpson," Sept. 17, 1783, *ibid.*, ff 5, 9. Also, Lord Dunmore to Thomas Dundas, Oct. 7, 1783, *ibid.*, ff 56–7.

20. [Board of agents], "State of Facts respecting the property of the Loyalists, with the Queries attending it," [Sept. 1783], *ibid.*, ff 17–20. For other lists of questions, *ibid.*, ff 46–7; and AO 13/93, ff 121–4.

21. "Information received from Sr James Wright," [Sept. 1783?], AO 12/107, f 4; Franklin, "Information communicated," Sept. 17, 1783, *ibid.*, f 33; George D. Ludlow, "Unconnected Hints," [Sept. 1783?], *ibid.*, ff 14–5; Zachariah Hood to commissioners, Aug. 7, 1783, AO 13/102, pt. 2, ff 814–5.

22. *Directions to the American Loyalists, in order to enable them to State their Cases* (London, 1783), *passim*, esp. 8, 17–9, 22–52. William Smith, for one, was criticized by the commissioners' clerk for submitting a memorial that did not follow the *Directions*: L. S. F. Upton, ed., *The Diary and Selected Papers of Chief Justice William Smith 1784–1793*

(Toronto, 1963) , I, 34–5. His very informal memorial is in AO 12/22, ff 333–6.

23. "Answers by the Board of Agents for the American Loyalists to the Queries proposed by the Commissioners," [Sept. 1783?], AO 12/107, ff 21–2.

24. See, e.g., Margaret Murray to Charles Steuart, Sept. 10, 1783, Steuart Papers, 5033, f 113, NLS; Richard A. Harrison to George Chalmers, Sept. 10, 1783, Sparks MSS V, II, f 1; William MacTier, testimony, [1789?], AO 12/37, f 155.

25. Polly Hutchinson to her father, [c. Aug. 1783] (draft) , Hutchinson-Watson Papers, MHS; Phineas Bond to Mrs. John Cadwalader, Feb. 11, 1784, Cadwalader Collection, HSP; Alexander Wallace to Nicholas Low, June 27, 1784, Nicholas Low Papers, box 60, LCMD. Also, Upton, ed., *Smith Diary*, I, 18.

26. Low to Nicholas Low, Feb. 3, 1784, Low MSS, box 67.

27. See William Fortune, testimony, AO 12/46, f 112; Samuel Shoemaker, Diary, March 15–8, 1784, HSP; and George Rome to Charles Dudley, April 28, 1784, Rome-Dudley Papers, NHS. Some loyalists had their memorials printed so that they could avoid the copying problem (e.g., Joseph Galloway's, AO 13/102, pt. 1, ff 371–6) .

28. The quotation is from George Chalmers, claims memorial, Oct. 14, 1783, AO 12/6, f 9. For examples of the arguments cited in the text: the claims memorials of Henry Stevenson, AO 12/6, ff 278–84; William McGillivray, AO 12/4, f 18; John Cumming, AO 12/20, ff 28–9; Henry Addison, AO 12/8, f 334.

29. Chalmers, memorial, AO 12/6, f 9; Daniel Dulany, Jr., claims memorial, [1784], AO 12/6, f 196; Daniel Coxe, claims memorial, March 13, 1784, AO 12/13, f 188.

30. Robert Leake to John Leake, March 13, Aug. 8, 1786, and John Leake to Robert Leake, May 17, 1786, all in Leake Family Papers, II, 40–2, NYHS.

31. For example, the loss schedules of Christopher Billopp, AO 12/19, f 37; Bennet Allen, AO 12/6, f 302; Thomas Lynch, AO 12/30, ff 313–4; and the testimony of Alexander Murray, AO 12/42, ff 14–5.

32. Robert Williams, Jr., claims memorial, March 17, 1784, AO 12/50, f 301; comments on the claim of George Rome, T 79/125, f 4; Alan Cameron, Narrative, Feb. 27, 1784, AO 12/56, ff 31–2.

33. Isaac Low to Nicholas Low, Feb. 28, 1786, Low MSS, box 67; Philip K. Skinner to Andrew Bell, Feb. 18, 1784, Miscellaneous Collection, WLC. Also, Alexander Wallace to Nicholas Low, April 4, 1784, Low MSS, box 60.

34. The agents' attitude is exemplified by George Rome's almost entirely inadmissible claim (described in T 79/125, f 4) and James Wright's informal memorials (Sept. 1783, AO 12/4, ff 34–7) .

35. "Resolution September 25, 1783," AO 13/93, f 106; Wilmot, *Historical View*, 113–7. By the time of their second report, December 23, 1784, they had also excluded claims for travel expenses, loss of the services of indentured servants, and demands on provincial assemblies. The report is in the Loyalist Commissioners' Papers, LCMD.

36. Wilmot, *Historical View*, 63; John Forster to William Fraser, Aug. 10, 1784, FO 4/3, f 173.

37. Wilmot, *Historical View*, 49–52. The categories were these: loyalists who rendered services, those who bore arms, "zealous and uniform" loyalists, British subjects not resident in America, those who took a state oath but later joined the British, and those who bore arms for the Americans but later joined the British (*ibid.*, 70–1).

38. Upton, ed., *Smith Diary*, I, 18; Alexander Thompson to commissioners, June 28, 1784, AO 13/137, f 301; Sarah Troutbeck to commissioners, June 5, 1787, AO 13/49, f 565. Also, Henry E. McCulloh, "An Explanatory Declaration," July 4, 1785, AO 13/94, f 195; and John Vardill to commissioners, Nov. 9, 10, 1784, AO 13/105, ff 309, 316–7.

39. For certificates, see e.g., those gathered by Harry Munro in the Munro Papers, MCNY. On problems of evidence collection: the claims memorials of William Franklin, AO 12/17, f 34; Roger Morris, AO 12/21, f 186; Ebenezer Jessup, AO 12/22, f 182; and Samuel Marshall, AO 12/34, f 298.

40. Wilmot, *Historical View*, 46, 49.

41. These cases are in AO 12/46, ff 4–300.

42. Thomas Hood, testimony re: Samuel Hake, July 26, 1784, AO 12/19, f 264. For instances of consultation between claimants and witnesses: Daniel Oliver to John Murray, Oct. 28, 1783 (draft), Hutchinson-Oliver Papers, MHS; Daniel Coxe to Sir Henry Clinton, Aug. 21, 1786, and [Sept. 1786?], Clinton Papers, WLC; Coxe, testimony re: Brereton Poynton, Dec. 13, 1784, AO 12/13, f 313.

43. Shoemaker diary, Sept. 2, 1785; Chalmers, testimony re: Anthony Stewart, AO 12/6, f 344; Robert Dee, testimony re: Robert Fisher, Dec. 14, 1785, AO 12/48, f 132; Donald Shaw, testimony re: Angus McDonald, Oct. 28, 1785, AO 12/34, f 283.

44. For typical examples, the testimony of William Demont (AO 12/42, f 256) and John Harrison (AO 12/48, f 335), and the memorials of Anthony Mosengeil (AO 12/14, f 346) and William Mackenzie (AO 12/36, f 110).

45. Report of committee of board of agents, 1784, Sparks MSS V, II, 33–7, esp. 35; agents to Pitt, Dec. 1784, Chatham Papers, CCXX, 39, PRO. Some of the information on state confiscation laws and policies collected by the agents may be consulted in AO 12/107, ff 158–65, 195–210; FO 4/3, ff 213–6; and *The Political Magazine*, VI (1784), 246–8, 507–8, 523–4. The committee probably consisted of Chalmers, Dunmore, Franklin, Galloway, and Wright (Wright to Marquis of Carmarthen, May 25, 1784, FO 4/3, f 149).

46. Sir James Wright to Lord Sydney, March 9, 1785, FO 4/1, f 240; *The Summary Case of the American Loyalists* [London, 1785]; Upton, ed., *Smith Diary*, I, 229, 219. The "unfunded debts" argument was first suggested by Chalmers in the fall of 1784; see Sparks MSS V, I, 93; and FO 4/3, ff 209–12.

47. Early manifestations of the agents' concern with debts appear in Wright to Marquis of Carmarthen, May 27, July 6, 1784, FO 4/3, ff 111, 163–4. Among the loyalists harassed by such suits were Edward Jessup of New

York (Jessup to Evan Nepean, June 3, 1786, FO 4/4, ff 401–2) and David Ogden of New Jersey (Ogden, petition to Parliament, c. 1787, T 1/652).

48. *Antill v. Kempe*, judgment Feb. 4, 1785, court of King's Bench Westminster, KB 122/505, membrane 1032, and *Kempe v. Antill*, court of Chancery, C 12/1687, membrane 4, both in PRO. William Smith heard Kempe's argument in chancery court (Upton, ed., *Smith Diary*, II, 20).

49. The original draft, June 10, 1785, in Chalmers' hand, is in Sparks MSS V, II, 22. The New York loyalists were especially concerned about debts; there are accounts of their activities in FO 4/3, ff 515–33.

50. Resolution of merchants trading to North America, April 13, 1787, Add. MSS 38221, f 334; Galloway to Pitt, April 24, 1786, April 14, 1787, with enclosures, Chatham MSS, CXXXVIII, 46, 48–50; "A Brief State of the Case of the American Loyalists, with Observations," *The Political Magazine*, XII (April 1787), 302–4.

51. Wright to John Forster, Feb. 21, 1785, AO 13/85, f 562; board of agents to Lords of Treasury, Sept. 1785, T 1/611; Thomas Boone to Pitt, March 6, 1786, T 1/628; "The case of the American Loyalists in regard to their confiscated Debts briefly stated, and considered," Chatham MSS, CCCXLIV, 289–92. Also, Wilmot, *Historical View*, 111, 131–2.

52. *The Parliamentary Register* (London, 1783–1789), XVIII, 517–8; Wilmot, *Historical View*, 57–8; *The Political Magazine*, IX (Dec. 1785), 413–4, 419; commissioners, minutes, Aug. 1785, AO 12/96, ff 17–20. There were similar distributions in 1786 and 1787; see Treasury minutes, July 27, 1786, T 29/57, and July 21, 1787, T 29/58.

53. John Watts to his son Robert, Sept. 10, 1785, Robert Watts Papers, NYHS; Upton, ed., *Smith Diary*, I, 284n.

54. Low to commissioners, Nov. 15, Aug. 21, 1786, AO 13/86, ff 161, 159; DeLancey to [John Forster], Jan. 28, 1786 (draft), DeLancey Papers, NYHS; John Graham to commissioners, May 28, 1788, AO 12/4, ff 122. Also, Joseph Galloway to [Charles Monro?], March 3, 1786, AO 13/102, pt. 1, f 361; and Daniel Coxe to John Forster, Feb. 27, March 10, 1786, AO 13/93, ff 277–8, 287.

55. Wilmot, *Historical View*, 55–6; claims commissioners, minutes, Aug. 22, 1785, AO 12/96, ff 15–6. Loyalists who had settled in the West Indies still had to come to England for claims hearings, though; on this point, see Henry Rugeley to Matthew Rugeley, July 6, 1784, Rugeley MSS. Other acts passed in 1787 and 1788 allowed the submission of further claims previously excluded, but some loyalists were left out of all the laws (two petitions from such men, c. 1788, are in the Clinton MSS).

56. Commissioners, minutes, Nov. 28, 1785, Jan. 27, 1786, AO 12/96, ff 71, 119–23. The journal of Anstey's clerk, Robert Woodruff, may be consulted in the APSL. The loyalists feared the results of his research, but 73 percent of the revisions based on his work favored the claimants in question (AO 12/109). See Pepperrell (for the agents) to [John Forster], Feb. 13, 1787, AO 13/137, ff 756–8; and William Bayard to William Bayard, Jr., Jan. 12, 1785 (i.e., 1786), Bayard Papers, NYPL.

57. "Desires of the Agents for the Amercian Loyalists," March 15, 1786,

Sparks MSS V, II, 8; Wilmot, *Historical View*, 154–60; House of Commons debate, June 26, 1786, Loyalist Commissioners' MSS, Misc., III, 46. Coke, though, thought the interest should be granted *(ibid., 47)*. See the agents' petition to the king on this issue, c. 1787, FO 4/1, ff 331–3; and also the memorial of professional men excluded from the 1785 distribution, March 3, 1786, T 1/629.

58. Pepperrell (for the agents) to Marquis of Carmarthen, March 6, 1788, FO 4/6, ff 183–4; agents to the king, [March 1788], *ibid.*, ff 777–80; agents to Parliament, [March 1788], T 1/518.

59. Galloway, *Claim of Loyalists*, 14, 103, 130, 129.

60. *Reasons why No Deductions ought to be Made from the Amount of Sums due to the American Loyalists* [London, 1788], *passim*, esp. 10; Wilmot, *Historical View*, 147–9, 161–6.

61. *Parliamentary Register*, XXIII, 538–9; *Parliamentary History*, XXVII, 610–7; Wilmot, *Historical View*, 69–72.

62. *Parliamentary History*, XXVII, 614–5, 618; *Parliamentary Register*, XXIV, 60.

63. Wilmot, *Historical View*, 79–82.

64. *Ibid.*, 90.

65. See, e.g., the claims of Thomas Phepoe (AO 12/47, ff 1–17), Isaac Ogden (AO 12/14, ff 147–78), and Isaac Low (AO 12/21, ff 90–130).

66. For the table from which these observations are drawn, see Mary B. Norton, "The British-Americans: The Loyalist Exiles in England, 1774–1789," (Ph.D. diss. Harvard University, 1969), p. 447 (hereafter cited as dissertation copy). The South Carolina committee tried to defend its vacillating constituents in its report to the claims commission, Feb. 21, 1785, AO 13/85, ff 288–91.

67. The fraudulent claims were (in the order mentioned in the text): Neil Maclean (AO 12/21, ff 292–301), John Potts (AO 12/38, ff 108–24), George Boyd (T 79/65, ff 1–31), Samuel Hake (AO 12/19, ff 237–87), John McAlpine (AO 12/20, ff 96–112), Thomas Skelton (AO 12/13, ff 1–13), William Haywood (AO 12/47, ff 123–40), Andrew Moore (AO 12/50, ff 94–9), Thomas Stringer (AO 12/4, ff 417–27), and J. F. D. Smyth (AO 12/6, ff 72–126).

68. Smyth, AO 12/6, ff 72–126, esp. f 119; commissioners to Lords of Treasury, June 24, 1784, T 1/605; Treasury minutes, June 25, 1784, T 29/55.

69. For examples of disallowals because of lies: reports on David White (T 79/124a, f 46), Samuel Greatrex *(ibid.*, f 47), and Bernard Cary *(ibid.)*. The report on William Franklin is in T 79/135, f 8.

70. For the table on which these comments are based: dissertation copy, p. 453.

71. *Ibid.*, pp. 454–61. The exact figures: small landowners, average return of 46.5 percent; tradesmen, artisans, and the like, 40 percent; professionals, 37 percent.

72. George Erving to William Erving, Sept. 28, 1785, David Greenough Papers, MHS. On Erving's claim: AO 13/44, ff 29–34; and T 79/126, f 3.

73. Cumberland Wilson and Robert Gilmour (for the merchants' committee) to Pitt, c. 1790, Chatham MSS, CCCXLIV, 202; merchants' committee to Joseph Smith, c. 1789, *ibid.*, 256. And, John Hopton *et al.* to claims com-

missioners, Feb. 2, 1789, AO 13/100, ff 401, 415; thirty-five American merchants to Lords of Treasury, Dec. 14, 1789, American Loyalist Material, APSL. On the later (post-1800) efforts on debts, see T 50/53. Also of interest is a pamphlet probably prepared by either the agents or the merchants, *Abstract of the Laws of the American States, now in Force, relative to Debts due to Loyalists, Subjects of Great Britain* (London, 1789).

74. Major Swiney to Pitt, Dec. 30, 1791, Chatham MSS, CLXXXI, 246; James DeLancey to Pitt, April 17, 1789, *ibid.*, CL, 44. Also, agents to Parliament, June 1789, *ibid.*, 46–7.

75. DeLancey to Pitt, Aug. 2, Dec. 1, 1788, Dec. 15, 1789, *ibid.*, 36–8, 40, 48–9; agents to Pitt, May 5, 1789, Chatham MSS, CCCXLIV, 280.

8: FINISHING THEIR DAYS AMONG STRANGERS

1. John Watts to his son Robert, Oct. 5, 1785, Robert Watts Papers, NYHS.

2. Florida claims records, AO 12/3; Florida claims commissioners, Report to Marquis of Carmarthen, Dec. 22, 1788, FO 4/6, ff 741–57. Also, various inhabitants of Florida to Lord Sydney, n.d., FO 4/3, ff 251–4.

3. Army and navy commissioners, Report, 1790, FO 4/8, ff 419–20. Records of the hearings are in AO 12, vols. 71–7, 115, 121–2, and AO 13, vols. 1–10, 86–8. The New York proceedings are summarized in AO 12, vols. 110–1, 117–8, and 138; the London inquiry (conducted by Charles Stedman), in AO 12/146. And see the petitions of loyalists with this kind of loss in T 1/604 and T 1/648, and Chatham Papers, CCCXLIV, 276–9, PRO.

4. John Eardley-Wilmot, *Historical View of the Commission for Enquiring into the Losses, Services, and Claims, of the American Loyalists* (London, 1815), 53–4; cases of Hugh Fraser, AO 12/100, f 13; James McCullough, Jr., *ibid.*, f 120; William Prowes, AO 12/99, f 236; and Robert Miller, *ibid.*, f 235.

5. Cases of James Rice, AO 12/100, f 356; Thomas Hier, *ibid.*, f 247; Jonathan Jackson, AO 12/99, f 82; and John Provey, AO 12/101, f 155.

6. Cases of Elias Ball, AO 12/101, f 149; Jeremiah Savage, *ibid.*, f 30; Joel Holmes, AO 12/100, f 88.

7. Cases of James Gowdy, AO 12/100, f 298; William Graham, *ibid.*, f 281; William Goodgion, *ibid.*, f 25; and Alexander Chevas, AO 12/101, f 87.

8. Tally for 1784 on unnumbered page in the back of T 50/8; "Totals of . . . Pensions payable to the American Loyalists," [1786], AO 13/70B, pt. 1, ff 24–5. On reductions: Treasury minutes, Nov. 2, Dec. 23, 1785, T 29/57; commissioners to Lords of Treasury, Dec. 21, 1785, T 1/619.

9. "Mr. Willmots Corrections 11 July 1786," Loyalist Commissioners' Papers, Miscellaneous, III, 50, LCMD; Account of American Allowances, March 6, 1787, DeLancey Papers, NYHS. And see the decisions in the following cases: Jonathan Edwards (AO 12/99, f 159), Farquhard Malcolm (AO 12/101, f 107), and Mrs. Robert Cargey (AO 12/102, f 73).

10. Claims commissioners, Report, March 31, 1790, FO 4/8, f 417; pension lists, T 50/11ff. And, Wilmot, *Historical View*, 86–7.

11. Wilmot, *Historical View*, 73–4, 95; Treasury minutes, Oct. 30, 1788, T

29/59; pension lists, T 50/31ff. Also, board of agents to Pitt, Aug. 4, 1786, T 1/634.

12. Thomas Hutchinson, Jr., to Elisha Hutchinson, April 1, 1789, Eg. MSS 2660, f 77; Charles Dudley to his wife, Aug. 6, Nov. 5, 1788, Dudley Papers, NHS.

13. Merchants' committee to Pitt, May 22, 1789, and c. 1790, same to Parliament, July 21, 1789, all in Chatham MSS, CCCXLIV, 33-4, 201-3, 252-3. Also, committee to Lord Hawkesbury, May 21, 1789, Add. MSS 38224, f 138; same to same, Jan. 1790, Add. MSS 38225, f 27. By contrast, Anglican clergymen, who were included on the professional income list, would have preferred to receive property compensation instead. Their petitions are in Chatham MSS, CCXX, 109-12; and AO 13/137, ff 63-4.

14. Germain to William Tryon, June 11, 1776, CO 5/1107, f 365; to Clinton, Jan. 23, 1779, and North to Carleton, June 15, 1783, both in T 1/608; Thompson to North, June 8, 1783, HO 42/2. And, *The Political Magazine,* IV (June 1783), 478-9.

15. [William Cobbett], *The Parliamentary History of England from the Earliest Period to the Year 1803* (London, 1806-1820), XXIII, 1050-7; *The Gentleman's Magazine,* LIII (Dec. 1783), 999. Also, *ibid.,* 478-9, 564-6.

16. Yonge to Thomas Steele, Aug. 11, 1784, and "List of Applications for Provincial Half Pay that have not been admitted," both in T 1/608.

17. Treasury minutes, March 24, 1785, T 29/56, and Oct. 20, 1785, T 29/57; Fawcett and Roy to George Rose, Oct. 13, 1785, T 1/613, transmitting notebooks now in T 1/608 and T 1/613.

18. Treasury minutes, Oct. 20, 1785, T 29/57; and Fawcett and Roy's reports in T 1/608 and T 1/613, which include the generals' comments. A successful reapplication may be traced in Yonge to Thomas Steele, Dec. 4, 1786, T 1/638; and Fawcett and Roy to Steele, March 24, 1787, T 1/643.

19. Militia officers: cf. Treasury minutes, April 8, 1786, T 29/57; and Faithful Graham to Treasury, Jan. 26, 1787, T 1/642 (see also note 18 above). The other categories: comments on Christopher Sower, William Rankin, James Moody, and Bartlet Goodrich in the lists in T 1/608 and T 1/613; also, on Thomas Crowell in T 1/628 and T 1/662; on Cornelius Hatfield and Joel Stone in T 1/634; and on Hamilton U. St. George in T 1/626 and Treasury minutes, Feb. 3, 1786, T 29/57.

20. John Collett to Clinton, July 1, 1786, Clinton Papers, WLC; Macknight, memorial to king, May 22, 1787, and comments on Macknight by Oliver DeLancey and Fawcett and Roy, all in T 1/647; "Estimate of the charge of Half Pay . . . for the year 1785," T 1/625; *Parliamentary History,* XXIII, 1050-3. Even Galloway applied for half pay; see Treasury minutes, Feb. 6, 1789, T 29/60.

21. Treasury minutes, Feb. 14, 1788, T 29/59; Nov. 15, 1788, Jan. 3, 14, 1789, T 29/60.

22. Mrs. Henry Barnes to [Miss Murray], Feb. 28, 1784, Barnes Papers, LCMD; Elizabeth Duché to Nancy Coale, May 29, 1784, Redwood Papers, HSP.

23. Elias Ball to Elias Ball, Nov. 1, 1787, Ball Papers, SCL; Low to Nicholas Low, Oct. 16, 1787, Nicholas Low Papers, box 67, LCMD. For accounts of marriages: Peter O. Hutchinson, ed., *The Diary and Letters of Thomas*

Hutchinson (Boston, 1884), II, 404; Mrs. Henry Barnes to [Mrs. Robbins], March 19, 1784, Barnes MSS.

24. Doctors: William L. Perkins to Isaac Perkins, May 14, 1787, Perkins Papers, WLC; Joseph Skinner to Col. Dundas, Dec. 17, 1788, AO 13/48, f 633. Merchants: in general, Parker Family Papers, LRO; Vincent P. Ashfield to Nicholas Low, Dec. 13, 1783, Low MSS, box 59; Alexander Wallace to same, Feb. 2, 1785, *ibid.*, box 60. Well-to-do: John Watts to Robert Watts, Aug. 5, 1789, Watts MSS. Ordinary loyalists: case of James Deas, AO 12/102, f 118; Samuel Shoemaker, Diary, Feb. 17, Sept. 19, 1784, HSP.

25. Helena Wells to Charles Steuart, Feb. 10, 1789, Steuart Papers, 5041, f 119, NLS; Mather Brown to the Misses Byles, Sept. 16, 1784, Byles-Brown Papers, MHS; Shoemaker diary, Dec. 29, 1784, and Feb. 8, 1785.

26. Thompson to North, June 25, 1783, HO 42/2; Thompson to Sir Robert Keith, Feb. 6, 1784, Add. MSS 35531, f 70; W. O. Raymond, ed., *Winslow Papers 1776–1826* (St. John, N.B., 1901), 169–70. On Stokes: Bahamas committee to Stokes, Dec. 22, 1785, AO 13/36, pt. 2, ff 1385–90. On Chalmers: Grace Cockcroft, *The Public Life of George Chalmers* (New York, 1939).

27. Among the Georgians employed in the West Indies were James E. Powell, lieutenant governor, Bahamas; James Robertson, chief justice, Virgin Islands; and Josiah Tatnall, surveyor general, Bahamas.

28. Jonathan Sewall to Thomas Robie, Feb. 7, 1785, Robie-Sewall Papers, f 67, MHS; account of loyalists evacuated from New York, Oct. 1783, CO 5/111, ff 235–6; Evan Nepean to George Rose, May 8, 1786, T 1/630. The Treasury's arrangements for loyalists leaving England for Nova Scotia may be traced in Treasury minutes, April 19, 30, May 7, 20, June 1, 8, 1784, T 29/55.

29. "Salem Loyalists—Unpublished Letters," *New England Historical and Genealogical Register*, XXVI (1872), 247; Robert Leake to John Leake, June 30, 1784, Leake Family Papers, II, 30, NYHS; L. S. F. Upton, ed., *The Diary and Selected Papers of Chief Justice William Smith 1784–1793* (Toronto, 1963), I, 115.

30. Upton, ed., *Smith Diary*, I and II, *passim*, esp. II, 87ff; Peter Livius to [Lord Sydney], April 19, 1786, CO 42/18, ff 112, 118; John Parr to Lord Sydney, Jan. 3, 1785, CO 217/57, f 22. For further on Livius and Smith: A. L. Burt, "The Tragedy of Chief Justice Livius," *Canadian Historical Review*, V (1924), 196–212; and Evan Nepean to Henry Hope, Sept. 3, 1785, CO 42/17, ff 246–7.

31. Parr to Evan Nepean, Aug. 13, 1784, CO 217/59, ff 196–7; Upton, ed., *Smith Diary*, I, 54, 72; Raymond, ed., *Winslow Papers*, 175. It is intriguing to note that the loyalists who settled in the Bahamas had the same types of problems with the incumbent governor. See Michael Craton, *A History of the Bahamas* (London, 1962), 162–86.

32. Parr to Evan Nepean, July 12, 1786, CO 217/58, f 177; Upton, ed., *Smith Diary*, I, 290; James Hume to Lord Sydney, Nov. 27, 1786, CO 217/36, ff 30–1.

33. Mathews to Evan Nepean, Nov. 13, 1784, CO 217/35, f 142; Mathews to

Thomas Dundas, June 12, 1790, Loyalist Commissioners' MSS, Misc., III, 88–9. Also, Mathews to Nepean, Aug. 11, 1784, FO 4/1, f 157.

34. [North] to Guy Carleton, Dec. 4, 1783, CO 5/111, f 187; Seabury to Evan Nepean, Dec. 5, 1783, CO 217/35, ff 242–3; Cooper to Peters, Feb. 2, 1784, Samuel Peters Papers, II, 4, NYHS (film) ; Peters to Cooper, Nov. 24, 1783, *ibid.*, I, 94. There is an account of the struggle for the appointment in Judith Fingard, "The Establishment of the First Colonial English Episcopate," *The Dalhousie Review*, XLVII (1967–1968) , 475–89.

35. Chandler to Thomas Hutchinson, Jr., March 30, 1785, Hutchinson-Oliver Papers, MHS; Chandler to Seabury, July 28, 1785, Seabury Papers, GTS; Boucher to Seabury, June 12, 1786, *ibid.*; Peters to Nathaniel Mann, Aug. 17, 1785, Peters-Mann Papers, CSL (photostats) .

36. Upton, ed., *Smith Diary*, II, 112; Peters to Nathaniel Mann, Sept. 4, 1787, Peters-Mann MSS. And see Peters' tirade against Inglis in Peters MSS, III, 1ff.

37. The creation of New Brunswick is discussed in Marion Gilroy, "The Partition of Nova Scotia, 1784," *Canadian Historical Review*, XIV (1933) , 375–91.

38. Charles Dudley to George Rome, May 17, 1784 (draft) , Rome-Dudley Papers, NHS.

39. Upham to Evan Nepean, April 6, 1784, CO 217/35, ff 199–200; Upham to Lord Sydney, April 15, 1784, FO 4/1, ff 124–5; Thomas Carleton to Sydney, Nov. 25, 1784, CO 188/3, f 23; Raymond, ed., *Winslow Papers*, 153, 175, 208–9, 214. On the appointments in general: W. S. MacNutt, *New Brunswick. A History: 1784–1867* (Toronto, 1963) , 42–53.

40. Case of Isaac Low, AO 12/100, f 150, and AO 12/101, f 9; case of Edward Winslow, AO 12/100, f 231; Shoemaker diary, Feb. 12–March 18, 1784, *passim;* case of Samuel Shoemaker, AO 12/100, f 182; Thomas A. Coffin *et al.* to Watson, July 7, 1783, and Watson to Guy Carleton, July 8, 1783, both in T 1/593. Both Smith and Shoemaker saw Watson frequently; see, e.g., Shoemaker diary, Sept. 12, Dec. 19, 1784. Copley's painting is, of course, *Watson and the Shark.*

41. Watson's councilor friends were Edward Winslow (see note 40 above) and Abijah Willard (AO 12/100, f 207) . On Sower: Shoemaker diary, Aug. 10, 1784, March 8, April 8, 1785; Clarence Ward, "The Story of Brook Watson," *New Brunswick Magazine*, I, no. 2 (Aug. 1898) , 101.

42. Accounts of attempts to return to Massachusetts during the war are in Sampson Blowers to [Jonathan] Bliss, Nov. 24, 1778, AO 13/43, ff 532–3; and John Amory, memorial to Massachusetts General Court, [1783], LCMD.

43. John Patterson to James Duane, May 18, 1783, Duane Papers, NYHS; Silvester Gardiner to Oliver Whipple, July 30, 1784, Gardiner-Whipple-Allen Papers, MHS (hereafter Gardiner MSS) ; Isaac Low to Nicholas Low, June 28, 1790, Low MSS, box 67; Polly Hutchinson to her father, c. 1783, Hutchinson-Watson Papers, MHS. Also, Edward Chandler to Samuel Thorne, Feb. 10, 1785, Chandler Papers, NYPL; and Andrew Allen to James Hamilton, Feb. 3, 1783, Dreer Collection, HSP.

44. John Gardiner to Silvester Gardiner, July 19, 1783, Gardiner MSS; Robert Auchmuty to Lord Hardwicke, Aug. 11, 1783, Add. MSS 35621, f 38;

Alexander Diack to James Parker, Nov. 23, 1783, Parker Family Papers, pt. 5, no. 11, LRO.

45. Francis Wharton, ed., *The Revolutionary Diplomatic Correspondence of the United States* (Washington, 1889), VI, 459; Edmund C. Burnett, ed., *Letters of Members of the Continental Congress* (Washington, 1934), VII, 167, 88, 440, 79.

46. Henry P. Johnston, ed., *The Correspondence and Public Papers of John Jay* (New York, 1891), III, 46–7; sundry citizens of Norwalk, petition to Connecticut General Assembly, Jan. 15, 1783, Connecticut Archives, Revolutionary War, 1st ser., XXVI, 247ab, CSL; *The Political Magazine*, V (Sept. 1783), 173–4. Also, *ibid.*, IV (May 1783), 330–2; and records of town meetings in Danbury (May 6, 1783) and Wallingford (April 28, 1783), Connecticut, CSL.

47. For example, Richard Walsh, *Charleston's Sons of Liberty: A Study of the Artisans, 1763–1789* (Columbia, 1959), 111–8; Richard Upton, *Revolutionary New Hampshire* (Hanover, 1936), 127, 203; Oscar Zeichner, "The Loyalist Problem in New York after the Revolution," *New York History*, XXI (1940), 290–5; and Zeichner, "The Rehabilitation of the Loyalists in Connecticut," *New England Quarterly*, XI (1938), 311–28.

48. George Rome to Charles Dudley, Sept. 13, 1783, Gratz Collection, HSP; Alexander Diack to James Parker, Oct. 24, 1783, Parker MSS, pt. 16, no. 12; John Wardell, claims memorial, Feb. 10, 1786, AO 12/14, f 130; Faithful Graham to William Roy, March 8, 1787, T 1/642.

49. "Stephen Mazyck to Philip Porcher," *South Carolina Historical and Genealogical Magazine*, XXXVIII (1937), 13; James Nixon, claims memorial, March 13, 1784, AO 13/68, pt. 2, f 285. Also, James Bowdoin to George Erving, May 8, 1783, James Bowdoin Letterbook, f 244, Bowdoin-Temple Papers, MHS; *The Political Magazine*, IV (May 1783), 343; V (Sept. 1783), 225–6; Samuel Knowles to Marquis of Carmarthen, Dec. 26, 1786, FO 4/5, ff 5–13; and a number of similar stories recorded in claims memorials: AO 12/48, f 205; AO 12/51, f 208; AO 12/54, f 344; AO 13/50, f 13.

50. Johnston, ed., *Jay Corres.*, III, 90; Wharton, ed., *Rev. Diplo. Corres.*, VI, 689; Burnett, ed., *Letters of Members of Cont. Cong.*, VII, 183; Elizabeth Smith to Isaac Smith, May 6, 1783, Smith-Carter Papers, MHS.

51. Harold Syrett, ed., *The Papers of Alexander Hamilton* (New York and London, 1961–), III, 367, 371; Wharton, ed., *Rev. Diplo. Corres.*, VI, 369; Burnett, ed., *Letters of Members of Cont. Cong.*, VII, 277.

52. John Tyler to Samuel Peters, Dec. 1, 1784, Peters-Tyler Papers, CSL; Albert A. Smyth, ed., *The Writings of Benjamin Franklin* (New York, 1906), IX, 313.

53. Wharton, ed., *Rev. Diplo. Corres.*, VI, 756–7; *The Political Magazine*, VI (June 1784), 507–8, 523–4. Also, Zeichner, "Loyalist Problem," *N.Y. Hist.*, XXI, 297–9; Walsh, *Charleston*, 118–24; Richard P. McCormick, *Experiment in Independence: New Jersey in the Critical Period 1781–1789* (New Brunswick, 1950), 28–39; and Merrill Jensen, *The New Nation* (New York, 1965), 268–81.

54. *The Political Magazine,* XI (Sept. 1786), 228; Samuel Sewell to Daniel P. Coke, Sept. 24, 1785, AO 13/48, f 531; William Greenwood to Lord Sydney, Sept. 4, 1786, FO 4/1, f 327; Henry Rugeley to Matthew Rugeley, Nov. 8, 1784, Rugeley Papers, BRO.

55. P[eter] A[llaire] to [Evan Nepean?], Dec. 6, 1786, FO 4/4, f 775. On the appointments: Twenty-six mercantile companies to Marquis of Carmarthen, Sept. 10, 1785, FO 4/3, ff 591–4; merchants of London and Liverpool to ———, April 12, 1787, FO 4/5, ff 211–3; John Hamilton to Carmarthen, Aug. 4, 1788, FO 4/6, ff 457–9; Hamilton to Lords of Treasury, Aug. 5, 1790, FO 4/1, f 414.

56. Amory, petition to Massachusetts General Court, [1783], LCMD; Smith to Atkinson, June 19, July 2, 1784, Atkinson Papers, WLC. Smith was apprehensive before he left London; see his letters to his father (Feb. 7, 1783) and his brother William (Jan. 4, 1784) in Smith-Carter MSS. Also, James Bowdoin to Silvester Gardiner, Aug. 10, 1783, Gardiner MSS.

57. "Letter from William Vans, Esq., to Judge Samuel Corwin [*sic*], Loyalist," *Essex Institute Historical Collections,* LVIII (1922), 288; Taylor to Atkinson, Oct. 8, 1784, Atkinson to Francis Atkinson, Nov. 28, 1785, both in Atkinson MSS. Also Isaac Winslow to Benjamin Davis, Sept. 14, 1784, Winslow Papers, MHS; John Jeffries, Diary, Nov. 10–1, 1789, MHS.

58. Henry C. Van Schaack, *The Life of Peter Van Schaack* (New York, 1842), 356; Chandler to William Morrice, Oct. 3, 1785, S.P.G. MSS, Miscellaneous, New Jersey; Jacob Ellegood to Charles Steuart, July 3, 1786, Steuart MSS, 5034, f 199. On Pennsylvania: Wilbur Siebert, *The Loyalists of Pennsylvania* (Columbus, O., 1920), 83–7.

EPILOGUE: A BRITISH-AMERICAN EMPIRE

1. [John Cruden], "An Address to the Sons of Abraham," c. 1785, Cornwallis Papers, Bundle 7, no. 65, PRO.

2. George A. Ward, ed., *Journal and Letters of the late Samuel Curwen,* 3rd ed. (New York, 1845), 178; William Pepperrell to Isaac Winslow, Feb. 23, 1778, Winslow Papers, MHS; [Charles Inglis], *The Letters of Papinian* (New York, 1779), 123–4; Hugh Wallace to Frederick Haldimand, Feb. 8, 1778, Add. MSS 21679, f 156.

3. Ward, ed., *Curwen Journal,* 387; William L. Perkins to Isaac Perkins, Jan. 2, 1787, Perkins Papers, WLC; Sewall to Mrs. Higginson, Sept. 10, 1783, Robie-Sewall Papers, f 65, MHS.

4. See, e.g., Peter Oliver's 1784 letters to Elisha Hutchinson, Eg. MSS 2660, ff 3, 5, 22, 29, 33.

5. Erving to William Erving, March 18, July 1, 1786, June 3, 1790, all in David Greenough Papers, MHS.

6. Coffin to his mother, Sept. 16, 1784, Coffin Family Papers, MHS; Elias Ball to [Elias Ball, Jr.], Feb. 26, 1786, Ball Papers, SCL. The refugees' opinions on American–West Indian commerce are in Add. MSS 38388, which is the record of a hearing on the subject before the Board of Trade in 1784.

7. Smith to Evan Nepean, Aug. 17, 1785, FO 4/3, f 571; *The Political Maga-*

zine, XI (Dec. 1786), 403–4; Jonathan Mallet to Robert Watts, April 20, 1787, Robert Watts Papers, NYHS.

8. William L. Perkins to Isaac Perkins, July 3, 1788, Perkins MSS; Ball to Elias Ball, Oct. 20, 1788, Ball MSS; Jonathan Boucher, *A View of the Causes and Consequences of the American Revolution* (London, 1797), lxix–lxx.

9. Boucher, *View,* dedication (unpaginated), lxxiii, 368n, lxxiv.

10. John Cruden, *An Address to the Loyal Part of the British Empire* [London, 1784], 10; L. S. F. Upton, ed., *The Diary and Selected Papers of Chief Justice William Smith 1784–1793* (Toronto, 1963), I, 94, 232; Peters to Samuel Huntington, Dec. 6, 1784, Peters Papers, II, 24, NYHS (film); William L. Perkins to Isaac Perkins, May 14, 1787, Perkins MSS.

11. Upton, ed., *Smith Diary,* I, 94–5; Chandler to William Morrice, Oct. 3, 1785, S.P.G. MSS, Miscellaneous, New Jersey. Also, Samuel Peters to Lord Rodney, Feb. 15, 1788, Peters MSS, III, 71.

12. Charles Stedman, *The History of the Origin, Progress and Termination of the American War* (Dublin, 1794), I, 2. For various plans: Julian Boyd, *Anglo-American Union: Joseph Galloway's Plans to Preserve the British Empire, 1774–1788* (Philadelphia, 1941); Mary Beth Norton, "John Randolph's 'Plan of Accommodations,' " *WMQ,* 3rd ser., XXVIII (1971), 103–20; Robert G. Mitchell, ed., "Sir James Wright Looks at the American Revolution," *Georgia Historical Quarterly,* LIII (1969), 509–18; William Nelson, "The Last Hopes of the American Loyalists," *Canadian Historical Review,* XXXII (1951), 22–42.

13. John Eardley-Wilmot, *Historical View of the Commission for Enquiring into the Losses, Services, and Claims, of American Loyalists* (London, 1815), 14.

14. Robert Alexander, claims testimony, Jan. 17, 1787, AO 12/8, f 105. Also, ff 106–7, 117.

15. Peter O. Hutchinson, ed., *The Diary and Letters of Thomas Hutchinson* (Boston, 1884), II, 216.

16. Thomas Jones, *History of New York during the Revolutionary War,* ed. Edward F. DeLancey (New York, 1879), I, 61.

Index

A NEW and Complete PLAN of LONDON WESTMI